FIREPLACES

FIREPLACES

ADDING IMPROVING
HEAT SAVING SYSTEMS
WOOD STOVES

ROBERT JONES
MONTE BURCH

CREATIVE HOMEOWNER PRESS®

A DIVISION OF FEDERAL MARKETING CORPORATION,
24 PARK WAY, UPPER SADDLE RIVER, NEW JERSEY 07458

COPYRIGHT © 1980 CREATIVE
HOMEOWNER PRESS®
A DIVISION OF FEDERAL MARKETING CORP.,
UPPER SADDLE RIVER, NJ

Manufactured in United States of America

Current Printing (last digit)
10   9

Editor: Shirley M. Horowitz
Assistant Editor: Marilyn M. Auer
Art Director: Léone Lewensohn
Jacket design and cover photo: Jerry Demoney
Technical Consultation and Review: Theodore J. Brevik, Professor, College of Agricultural and Life Sciences, University of Wisconsin—Madison; Kent Keegan, Associate Professor, School of Architecture and Urban Planning, University of Wisconsin—Milwaukee; Pamela Keegan, Architectural Designer

We wish to extend our thanks to the many designers, companies, and other contributors who allowed us to use their materials and gave us advice. Their names, addresses, and individual indentifications of their contributions can be found on page 122

LC: 80-67153
ISBN: 0-932944-26-4 (paper)
ISBN: 0-932944-25-6 (hardcover)

CREATIVE HOMEOWNER PRESS®
BOOK SERIES

A DIVISION OF FEDERAL
MARKETING CORPORATION
24 PARK WAY,
UPPER SADDLE RIVER, NJ 07458

Foreword

The information in this book has been carefully compiled and researched by authors and editors who share a strong affection for the subject matter and a sincere concern for the consumer. We want the homeowner to be able to enjoy an existing fireplace with a minimum of danger, difficulty or heat loss. We hope those considering adding a fireplace will discover money-saving, time-saving facts that will teach how to build (or hire out) a fireplace, or to install a prefabricated unit.

Fireplaces is a direct result of consumer demand. Interviews with many new or prospective homeowners during the last decade included the question: ''What features are (were) desired and sought

after when looking for a home?'' More than 90 percent of those responding included fireplaces in their lists of options wanted. If the positive answers had been confined to areas with colder climates, the responses would not have been surprising. However, the desire for a fireplace in the home was not confined to states such as Alaska, Minnesota, Kansas or Vermont. People in Florida, Hawaii, California and in the South also indicated a strong preference for this architectural feature.

This information is supported by increased sales in the last decade for prefabricated fireplaces and all types of fireplace accessories. In addition, sales of products that increase the efficiency of the

fireplace have skyrocketed. These devices—whether simple metal pans placed behind the fire to better radiate the heat, or more complex fireplace inserts that help recirculate heat, or scientifically designed grates—enable the homeowner to use the fireplace as an additional heat source rather than operate it as a heat-losing instrument.

This book also covers wood stoves, cutting wood, maintenance and renovation of existing fireplaces, as well as troubleshooting and safety. The authors and editors have tried their best to foresee and answer all questions dealing with fireplaces, from how they add to the appearance to your home to how they add, or should add, heat to your home.

CONTENTS

1
TYPES OF FIREPLACES

A fireplace is a desirable feature in most homes today. The reason for its popularity is quite clear. In addition to the cozy atmosphere that a fireplace adds to a home, the fireplace can provide unusual decorative effects, increase overall heat efficiency, or fulfill specialized personal tastes.

There are many fireplace designs, styles and options available to the homeowner. In addition to the traditional masonry fireplace, prefabricated zero-clearance and free-standing models are available. While each type and style of fireplace has its own merits, the choice is most often determined by price or the installation requirements.

THE TRADITIONAL FIREPLACE

The popular masonry fireplace, a fireplace constructed of either brick or stone, is still preferred by many despite the inroads of modern alternatives, which have made it easier, faster and less expensive to install a prefabricated metal fireplace than to build a masonry fireplace. However, if you choose a masonry fireplace, keep in mind some of the many variations, some of which are not widely known.

Variant Styles

The basic single-face fireplace found in most homes is popular, but the variations possible can provide unusual visual effects, increase heat efficiency, or fulfill specialized needs.

The standard masonry fireplace, as a rule, is symmetrical and is built into a wall of the dwelling with chimney construction hidden inside or with a typical outside chase.

Two-face adjacent. One interesting

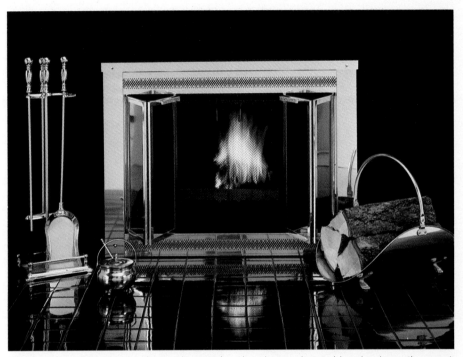

The fireplace, a sought-after feature in most American homes, is considered a decorating asset. With heat-efficient options, it also becomes an energy-saving feature.

variation on the basic configuration is the two-face fireplace—with two adjacent hearth openings. Not only is the hearth open on the front, as in a conventional fireplace, but also on one of the adjacent sides. While the fire can be seen more easily, its efficiency is reduced due to the decreased firebox surface. This reduces the directional quality of the radiated heat.

Opposite-faces opening. Along this same line is a masonry fireplace with two opposite faces or openings. In this design the back of the fireplace—as well as the front—is open. This permits a common fire for two adjacent rooms, or allows the fireplace to jut out from a common wall, forming a peninsula in the room and dividing it into separate living areas.

Another option that is available using the opposite faced opening fireplace is the "island" design. This unit "floats" between the living spaces, acting as a divider. There could be a living room on one side and a dining room or den on the

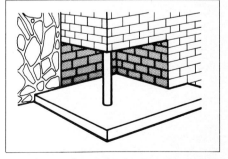

A two-faces-adjacent fireplace may be a corner fireplace or one that can be viewed easily from two areas of the same room.

other. This type of design uses only one flue and chimney since, even though it is open on both sides, it is only one fireplace. Each side may have its own separate hearth and hearth design. The opposite face fireplace does have a major drawback. Since the firebox is open on opposing sides, it requires a larger amount of draft in order to sustain an evenly burning fire. The fire does not radiate as effectively as the single face fireplace does. However, the visual quality of the fire seen from opposing sides is quite pleasing.

Three-face adjacent. A third version of the traditional fireplace is the three-

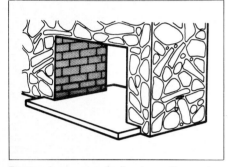

The two-faces-opposite fireplace will serve two rooms with different uses and may have different surround treatments on each side.

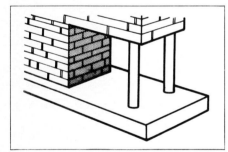

A three-faces-adjacent is a peninsula fireplace and is often used as a partial divider or in areas with different adjacent levels.

RECOMMENDED PROPORTIONS FOR MULTI-OPENING FIREPLACES

Two sides adjacent

Opening	Firebox depth	Flue size
30x34"	20"	12x16"
30x36	30	16x16
42x42	24	16x20

Two faces opposite

30x42	24	16x20
30x34	28	16x16
36x38	28	16x20

Three faces

24x34	24	16x16
30x38	28	16x20
36x38	28	20x24

face adjacent fireplace. This style is a combination of the first two, since it uses the peninsula technique of the opposite-face fireplace and adds the open side of the two-face adjacent style. It is built out from a wall, preferably near the center of a room.

Limitations of the multi-faced fireplace. Because of the size and number of openings in multi-faced fireplaces, caution should be exercised in their selection. The openings create a need for a continuous draft. This draft can be provided mechanically through the installation of a chimney fan. However, if the chimney fan is not switched on when the fire is

A multi-faced fireplace can dominate a room and will usually be the center of attention.

The two-faces-opposite fireplace serves two rooms and provides an attractive partition.

This fireplace, scaled to fit a small area, is open on three sides to offer views of the fire from many areas of the room.

started, it could result in a very smoky room. The multi-faced fireplaces are quite good-looking, and they can be highly visible in the room. This somewhat compensates for the lessened radiation of heat. Multi-faced fireplaces are often considered more decorative than functional. Their installation also is more complicated than a single-face unit.

Rumford fireplace. Because of high fuel costs, many homeowners want the pleasure of a fireplace but also want a unit that will heat the home efficiently. One such unit is the Rumford fireplace, developed by Count Rumford about two hundred years ago.

At first glance, the Rumford looks like any other ordinary single-face masonry fireplace. Although the outward appearance is the same as a standard masonry fireplace, the firebox—the area in which the fire burns—is built differently. The flat back wall is a small square, narrower than the wall in a traditional fireplace, and the side walls are not vertical. They slant in toward the back and lean toward the

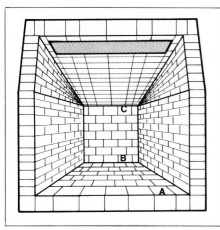

A Rumford fireplace is small and shallow. The distance from A to B is the same as from B to C. The flat, back wall is one-half as wide and one-half as high as the front opening.

center, creating a pair of wedge-shaped walls. The Rumford fireplace has always been and probably always will be one of the most successful designs for a heat-efficient fireplace. Its design helps to direct much of the heat into the dwelling rather than letting most of it go up the flue.

Russian brick "Grubka". One other variation of the fireplace is the Russian Brick Fireplace, known as a "grubka." This will suit those who may want the beauty of a masonry fireplace but are concerned about retaining large amounts of heat. The grubka is actually a combination of a fireplace and an oven, and has been in use even longer than the Rumford. It has been built for hundreds of years on the European continent; the design has been handed down through generations of masonry workers. A small grubka will consist of roughly 500 bricks and 40 or 50 firebricks.

In some ways, the grubka is a predecessor of the circulating fireplace currently manufactured out of steel. The grubka is built so that the brick walls receive, retain and radiate the heat of the fire into the home for many hours, even after the fire has gone out.

The grubka works by circulating wood gasses and smoke through a series of switchback flues instead of letting these valuable heat gasses fly straight up the chimney with the smoke, as happens in the conventional brick fireplace. The temperature of the fire rises, burning the gasses and keeping the chimney clean. The heat then saturates the brick walls of the firebox and the chimney. This works well because the interior is a brickwork

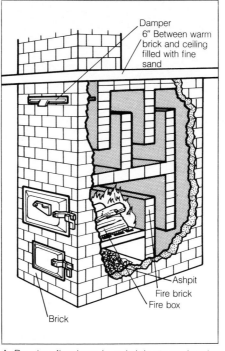

A Russian fireplace is a brick stove. Interior baffles increase burning efficiency and heat production with little energy waste.

maze through which gasses, smoke and heat pass slowly before passing out the chimney top. Because of the flue's labyrinth design, the logs in the grubka will burn over several hours generating up to 1200° of heat and burning all gasses. A grubka is nearly 90 percent heat efficient.

The grubka does have a few disadvantages. It may be difficult to add to a house, since large portions of the dwelling's foundation and upper structure may have to be removed and reconstructed before building the grubka. If you plan to remodel or build a house, and wish to use an alternate heat source instead of a utility-based one, a grubka may be a good choice. The grubka has an old world charm, giving a rustic, country effect to Early American or country decor in a home.

The cost of this type of fireplace, even a small version, may vary widely. It will have to be built by a professional mason, preferably by one who has built this type of fireplace before. In the northeast United States there are masons who specialize in grubkas. Be sure to check on previous jobs when hiring a contractor to build a grubka. This fireplace requires a thick, solid foundation, since it weighs a great deal and needs adequate room between the warm brick and the combustible ceiling and flooring. There should be ten inches of insulation between the firebox

The zero-clearance fireplace can be built in anywhere in a home. The finished installation may be styled for any period.

The knotty-pine mantelshelf gives a casual look to this fireplace. A formal mantelshelf would create a totally different impression.

and a combustible floor and six inches of insulation are needed between the chimney and the ceiling. It will take patience to build correctly.

ZERO-CLEARANCE FIREPLACE
The zero-clearance fireplace is for those who require a particular answer to a set of conditions or who wish to add a fireplace without disrupting the household for any great length of time. The zero-clearance can be placed to look like a traditional fireplace. It is available from several manufacturers, including such brand names as Superior, Malm, Prangway and Heatilator. The major advantage of the zero-clearance fireplace is that when installed in existing construction the construction requirements are minimal. In new construction, the cost is lower and the labor saved to install the unit is quite an advantage over that of a masonry fireplace.

A zero-clearance fireplace is so called because it can be placed right next to an existing wall, needing no (thus "zero") clearance from combustible materials. The unit comes ready to install, shaped like a traditional masonry fireplace, complete with the ductwork and chimney pieces. Elaborate instructions are provided. Because it already is in standard fireplace form when purchased, it can be installed by surrounding it with a wood-work framing that reaches from the floor to the ceiling. (For installation instructions, see Chapter 8).

Zero-clearance fireplaces can be finished with any design you wish, and can be faced with simulated brick or stone.

THE FREE-STANDING FIREPLACE

The free-standing fireplace unit is the easiest type to install, and is usually the least expensive. Like the zero-clearance unit, a free-standing fireplace can be installed with a minimum of carpentry knowledge, a few simple tools, and anywhere from a weekend to a week's worth of work time. The chimney is installed in the same manner as the zero-clearance, although it is usually exposed, similar to that of a wood-burning stove chimney.

A free-standing fireplace, as its name implies, stands on its own base rather than resting against a wall. It can be placed in the center of the room for even heat distribution. Some models are open on all sides, with glass enclosures to keep the flame visible, but holding in any sparks. The shapes available include round, square, rectangular or octagonal, in a variety of colors and bright metallic finishes such as copper, brass, stainless steel or even chrome. Constructed of cast iron or formed metal, they absorb heat and radiate it evenly to all areas of a room.

The primary advantage of the free-standing fireplace is its ease of installation and cost. It needs no framework construction or additional finish, but it must be placed on a fire-resistant pad that is large enough to extend beyond the edges of the firebox. The installation requirements for the chimney flue are similar to those of the zero-clearance fireplace.

THE CIRCULATING FIREPLACE

The circulating fireplace is the answer for those who want both a simple to install fireplace unit and a heat producer to supplement the furnace. This type of fireplace is much the same as a zero-clearance unit, manufactured of sheet metal and lined with fire brick. It comes ready to be installed, similar to the

A standard fireplace can be turned into a heat-circulating fireplace with the addition of an insert unit with an exchanger/blower.

zero-clearance unit. However, it has an added provision for drawing in air from an outside source, circulating it about an inner shell, and blowing it out into the dwelling. Therefore, it never uses any preheated air from the home. These units are very fuel-efficient, and may come with thermostatical controls to let the owner adjust the amount of heat generated. There are also versions that connect to the dwelling's existing furnace ductwork. These take workload off the furnace and let wood fuel heat the entire house until the fire dies, whereupon the furnace will automatically cut back into service. These units, however, should be installed by a licensed contractor who can handle thermostatic control systems and duct-work. They also cost more than the zero-clearance unit, yet the savings in gas or electric bills each winter will be quite substantial, and eventually can pay for the cost of the product and its installation.

WHICH TYPE IS BEST FOR YOU?

Consideration must be given to several areas when picking out the right type of fireplace for the home. How much of the house do you intend to heat? How large is the house? Where in the house do you intend to install the fireplace? If you have a house of average size but you are not looking for a unit to heat the entire house (as with a circulating fireplace), then a free-standing unit could be the most suitable. A small zero-clearance unit may also serve as well. If you have a large house or are building a house, and if you intend to let the fireplace handle a large percentage of the heating duties, then it would be advisable to obtain a circulating fireplace. This would permit you to install the correct ductwork at the outset, instead

A modern, combined firescreen and glass door unit often includes options of heat exchangers and circulating fans. These features increase the energy efficiency of a fireplace.

Even masonry fireplaces can have unexpected variety. Although more difficult to do, a round opening can be built with brick.

of cutting open walls—as you must if you are adding such a unit to an existing home.

There is one added option available to any of these styles of fireplaces, except the circulating type, and that is the use of gas. Either the masonry, zero-clearance or free-standing units can all be adapted to operate on gas, should wood be at too high a cost in your part of the country. Some local and state building codes prohibit the use of gas-burning fireplaces. You should consult with your local building inspector to determine what their requirements are. In the event that a gas-burning fireplace is permitted, you should be prepared for an increase in your gas bill. Some manufacturers supply very authentic looking fireplace logs and grating that, when lit, look very much like a natural wood fire.

The fireplace is the focal point of this very traditional room. The painted wood paneling and stenciled floor are uniquely American colonial.

Contemporary lines in this fireplace are created with the traditonal material—brick. A mantel is implied by the soldier course.

2
DECOR POSSIBILITIES

A fireplace is a room's most dramatic focal point. Its size, location, shape, and style will influence—often dictate—the major elements of room decor: texture and pattern, furniture placement and traffic flow; period style and scale of furniture and accessories.

LOCATION OF A NEW FIREPLACE

In new construction, you can control from the outset how domineering the fireplace will be. During the planning stages, keep in mind how furniture will be placed in relation to the fireplace, as well as to doors, and windows. Consider how fireplace facing materials will look with your color scheme, and how well the fireplace will augment other strong features of the room. For example, if you have chosen to build on a particular lot because of its spectacular view, you will

A wall hanging above this fireplace softens the strong, vertical brick surface of the chimney breast, the wall space that is above the mantel.

want wide expanses of windows so you can enjoy the scenery. The fireplace, then, must be situated so it will not block important lines of vision. There are many types of fireplace furniture arrangements that can be adapted for such a situation: an in-wall fireplace surrounded by windows; a peninsular fireplace that juts out into the room; a free-standing fireplace; or, a fireplace built across a corner of the room.

Furniture Arrangements

When deciding where to situate a fireplace so that the view outdoors could be fully enjoyed, the scale and placement of furniture is crucial. In general, the furniture in these settings should be long and low, so the view out the windows is not blocked by high sofa or chair backs. Parallel arrangements (Figure 1) work well with all types of fireplaces. The conversation grouping is kept cozy, and

normal traffic flow through the room is not hampered.

Right-angle placement of the major seating pieces near the fireplace allows best view of the fire and the vista outside; it also assures a logical arrangement for conversation grouping.

Enclosed or U-shaped furniture arrangements work well in very large rooms. In small rooms, however, such groupings tend to block traffic flow and make fire tending unnecessarily cumbersome. These movable "conversation pits" are very popular, so you are likely to find some sectional units scaled down in bulk to accommodate smaller spaces.

Scatter-block arrangements (Figure 2) are dictated by traffic patterns in and throughout the room. Often there will be only enough room for two comfortable chairs flanking the fireplace. The sofa, sofa table, and chairs will be grouped together elsewhere in the room. Whatever

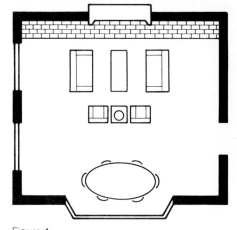

Figure 1

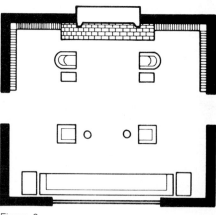

Figure 2

furniture arrangement you choose, it is always wise to have one or more fairly large tables conveniently located within the seating group around the fireplace.

EXISTING FIREPLACES

When the style of the house and its fireplace are both pure period—whether rustic log cabin, Victorian townhouse, or Georgian mansion—you would not want to restyle the fireplace. It would be simpler and more sensible to follow the decorative cues already there.

Although it is a focal point, this fireplace does not dominate this room with a view.

This cultured marble reproduction mantel is designed to work with a prefabricated fireplace or an existing unit.

Ranging between cabins and mansions, however, are countless homes with fireplaces offering little or no decorative clues. The majority of the post-war frame houses and pre-war bungalows appear to have been given fireplaces because people wanted them, but often without well-thought-out functional considerations. Consequently, they are ignored or eventually closed-off, or hidden behind wallboard or paneling.

Today, as fireplaces reassert themselves as an important heat source, homeowners may find they need help to make the fireplace attractive as well as useful.

Materials

The decorative materials used nearest the firebox—the hearth and margin (fireplace opening)—must always be nonflammable. Choose those that will best harmonize with your decorative scheme. Traditional preferences include brick, stone, marble, and slate. You may instead use ceramic tile, quarry tile, brass, steel, iron, or copper. Each one can be used in combination with two or three others to create an interesting fireplace. Another possibility is simulated brick or stone; many of these products are formulated for safe use in hearths and on margins.

Farther away from the strong source of heat, there are many materials you can use for mantels, facings, spaces on the wall above the mantel, and on the walls surrounding the fireplace. The combination of different materials, colors, and textures on the fireplace wall will determine the overall visual effect of your fireplace. The decorative functions of

The smooth surfaces of slate and marble combined with the sharp, stright lines of this fireplace facing to give a contemporary look.

hearth, margin, facings and trims are: (1) to give the fireplace greater emphasis inside the room, or (2) to render the fireplace less emphatic; and, (3) to bring the fireplace and room decor into harmonious balance.

Less Emphasis

If you want your fireplace to blend with the room in a quiet, unobtrusive manner, cover it with facing materials that match the surrounding walls. You can choose among paint, plaster, wallpaper, wood or prefinished paneling. The fireplace opening (margin) can be edged with brick, stone, marble, or metal. Often, nonemphatic fireplaces have very simple, understated mantels or no mantel at all. The expanse above the fireplace opening can be used to display a large painting or framed mirror. Massed collections of objects also look well and draw the eye away from the fireplace.

Greater Emphasis

If you want the fireplace to be a dominant focal point, consider facings of natural

This wood storage design gives the impression of a fireplace or wood stove, and all the desirable associations, without the construction work and worry of actually adding one.

A huge stone face and heavy mantel on this heat-circulating fireplace dominate the room.

The surfaces in this room are covered with different textures; the restful quality desired is maintained with a monochromatic decorating scheme.

The furniture arrangement before this fireplace allows a view of the painting above the opening while still providing a conversation grouping.

This small, Victorian fireplace appears to have a marble surround, but the marble was created with paint; the technique is called faux marbre.

materials. Few have more impact than fieldstone, creek or river stone or fine solid wood paneling. Used brick or ceramic tile are other excellent choices. Granite or marble used as a facing from floor to ceiling gives a fireplace great visual impact. Fireplace materials that have textures and colors in contrast with surrounding surfaces also help establish emphasis. In a room that will be filled with smooth fabrics and wallcoverings, plan a fireplace faced in rough plaster, wood planks, or rough stone. If colors in the room are pale, use dark colors for the fireplace.

Decor Changes

Paint. The number of fireplaces that have been desecrated by paint are beyond count. Many determined homeowners have spent seemingly endless hours stripping old paint from fine marble and fine carved wood. However, after the work has been done, they tend to agree that it was worth the effort to expose the treasure hidden underneath.

Although paint is a convenient, inexpensive way to quickly update a room with a tired-looking fireplace, ask yourself "Will this material be hard or impossible to replace or refinish another time? Antique ceramic tile, exquisite old wood, and marble, are all best left in their natural states, as are stone and slate. No new material is likely to match their real beauty, and you will have a difficult time getting the paint off later if you change your mind.

Paint over plaster, or smooth contemporary-style wood mantels give a fireplace a new look. Such surfaces are easy to paint over later, and not too expensive to replace or repair.

Whether or not to paint over brick is a hard question to answer. Your decision must be based upon personal preference and a clear understanding that, once applied, the paint is not easy to remove. Sandblasting is one way to remove paint from brick. Another method is thorough cleansing with paint stripper, which requires heavy scrubbing and a stiff wire brush.

In all probability, you would not want to paint used brick or very old brick, which have a rosy pink glow. Each of these has a soft, aged beauty that adapts to all decorative schemes, whether contemporary or period style. If you wish to paint existing brick, such as the cold, flat brick sometimes used by contractor, here are the basic techniques.

Nonglazed surface. Brush on a coat or two of masonry sealer before you apply paint. Brick is porous and will drink up more paint than you may care to use. After the sealer is dry, roll or brush on one or two coats of masonry paint. If you are using white, you may have to apply a third coat to conceal the dark brick underneath. In time, some paint may chip and crack off. Treat the spots locally, first working off all loose paint using the tip of a screwdriver or a paint scrapper. Then scrub with a stiff wire brush and reapply sealer and paint.

Glazed surface. If the brick is glazed, brush on a coat of flat primer or undercoat; let dry. Now cover with paint. You might prefer using one of the epoxy paints formulated for use over ceramic tile and porcelain.

Prefinished paneling. For a rustic effect, choose paneling with one of the barnsiding finishes. For more formal approaches, there are finishes of walnut, chestnut, teak, or rosewood finishes. You apply paneling to fireplaces just as you do on walls:

(1) attach furring strips to support the panels, using nails or wall anchor, carefully shimmed to level
(2) attach the paneling to the furring strips, using paneling nails and prefinished moldings.

Natural woods. One of the most interesting natural wood facings is a floor-to-ceiling facing of narrow planks of solid wood which are set on the diagonal or in a

The diagonal plank paneling on this fireplace surround leads the eye toward the center of the wall—and the fireplace. The arrangement of decorative objects reinforces this plan.

The plain paneling on the chimney breast of this fireplace makes the antique Persian tile surround and hearth the focus of this installation.

chevron pattern. Narrow planks set horizontally or vertically also are visually effective. This kind of facing tends to give the fireplace a clean, modern look, especially if the natural wood grain is allowed to show, protected only by clear varnish.

A facing of knotty pine tongue-and-groove paneling conveys a casual or Early American look. Solid wood panels with shaped inserts and raised moldings look best in Colonial and other period settings. These panels can be painted or stained, or left natural. Stained and natural woods should be given clear finishes of conventional or polyurethane varnishes.

Marble and mirror. Whether used as full-face coverings or merely as trim, marble and mirrors add dignity, glamour and richness. Marble and mirror are held in place by cements and adhesives that are applied to the back of each section, then pushed into place over a foundation of cement or plaster. These materials are heavy and difficult to cut. Unless you have experience in working with them, it will be wise to have professionals handle installations involving large areas.

Ceramic tile. Facings and trim of ceramic tile can brighten or completely change the look of a fireplace. There are many patterns, colors, and shapes with which you can work. If the budget is a concern, mix a few expensive tiles with plainer ones; the effect of the prized tiles will carry into and disguise the more modest ones.

For ceramic tile work, you will have to prepare the face of your fireplace for tile application. If you are building a new home with a fireplace—or adding one to an existing home during a remodeling, you can give the surface around the opening a smooth coat of plaster. After this is dry, you may apply tile without difficulty.

If you are renovating an old fireplace, you probably will have to apply a smooth coat of some material, such epoxy plaster, to the brick or stone to create a surface that is level enough for tile application.

You may also want to create a new look to your fireplace by building a new surround and just edging the opening with tile. For the last, it is advisable to use wood that has been given a fire resistant treatment, such as Non-Com made by Koppers Company, Inc.

More readily available ceramic tiles were used here to give a small, imitation fireplace a dominant position in this room.

Installation. Determined the layout plan of the tile. If the spacing does not work out exactly as you wish, you can make adjustments with grout line spacing, or cut filler tiles to complete your pattern. Apply an epoxy mortar to the area where you will install the tile. Epoxy needs good ventilation but dries quickly, so do not apply more mortar than you can cover with tile in 30 minutes. Set each tile firmly in the mortar base with a slight twisting motion. If there are no spacer tabs on the tiles, use toothpicks or paper matchsticks to make proper size joints. If the mortar is soft and the tiles are heavy, you may have to hold the tiles in place with props or strong tape.

Choose a tile grout that will complement the color and pattern of the tiles. Mortar and joint compounds are made by L&M Surco Manufacturing Company, South River, NJ 08882. They are Tri-Poxy Mortar, for the basic mortar bed; Floor Grout; Flexible Grout Additive (helps prevent cracking and grout fallout); and Ceramo Cleaner, to remove grout from face of the tiles.

Plaster. Whether smooth, rough, or heavily textured, plaster offers interesting variations for fireplace facings and trim. The final finish can be tinted, left white, or painted. Semi-precious gemstone and other geological finds can be pressed into the surface before it dries, as can shells, unusual shapes of driftwood, bark, twigs; ceramic tiles, or shards of old pottery.

You can texture the surface of wet plaster using such tools as combs, the backs of spoons, the flat face of an old piece of wood, a damp sponge, a wisk broom, and, of course, trowels—either smooth or tooth-edged. Texturing en-

hances any fireplace facing that will serve as backdrop for woven wall hangings, unusual lighting fixtures and candle holders, wood carvings, or glass and pottery.

Moldings. A fireplace with a plain and undecorated face will be very attractive in and suitable for an extremely contemporary home. However, many architectural styles demand more elaborate treatment of the fireplace face. It is possible to create an elaborate—yet inexpensive—custom period fireplace with the application of appropriate moldings of either wood or plaster.

Some communities have plaster studios that specialize in reproducing various decorative period plaster leaves, garlands, capitals, rosettes, and moldings. They may have molds for just the type of fireplace face or decoration you want. However, many styles can be reproduced with combinations of wood moldings applied to the face of a fireplace. With the right combination of molding, you can create the impression of a unique and hand-carved fireplace and mantel.

Simulated materials. Artificial brick and stone offer convincing substitutes for the real materials, in terms of appearance, ease of handling, and cost. They are noncombustible—safe for use as fireplace facing and trim. They serve as thick but lightweight veneers that are held in place with mortars and cements. There are preformed shapes for use on inside corners, outside corners, and flat surfaces. If you plan to add fireplace facings and trimwork by yourself, and budget is a consideration, one of the simulated materials can be a good choice. Antique brick, used brick, modern brick, stone that closely resembles natural fieldstone, flagstone—these are the most popular choices.

Z-Brick Company (Woodinville, Washington 98072) is one company that makes a variety of styles that resemble used brick. Their Z-Ment, Z-Sealer, and Ruff-It compounds provide all you need for the installation. The Ruff-It compound can be used as a surfacing material by itself. It can be troweled on, then textured while still damp.

Wonder-brix. A new, decorative, fire-proof material is Wonder-brix. This material allows you to create many patterns and styles that will look like brick, slate, or stone. The application is simple and virtually foolproof.

First cover the face of the fireplace and/or the forehearth with the mortar base. This comes in several colors and combinations. Smooth on and let dry, then create a pattern with the narrow tape provided for application on the mortar. This tape creates your "mortar" joints. After the tape is in place and you are

A simple answer to fireplace resurfacing is provided with fireproof, imitation brick.

satisfied with the appearance of the pattern, apply the brick, stone or slate overcoat. As soon as this coat is applied and has set for a few minutes, remove the tape by pulling it up through the overcoat layer. The tape lifts the overcoat layer on it, and you will have an immediate result—brick and mortar, slate and mortar, or stone and mortar surface on your fireplace face.

PREFABRICATED FIREPLACES

Prebuilt free-standing fireplaces, which you can install in the middle or in a corner of a room, come complete with firebox, hood, flue and flue extensions. Some have built-in firescreens; others have ready-made hearths; a few show you how to build your own hearth. Just make sure that before you order one of these fireplaces, you check out local codes and regulations to be sure your installation, and the fireplace, are legal and safe. Another fireplace innovation is (as discussed in Chapter 1) the pre-engineered fireplace system acceptable for zero-clearance installation—which means you can install one against the wall, as opposed to the free-standing fireplace that can be placed certain distances away from combustible wall and floor material.

Choose the materials for any walls close to the free-standing unit not only for nonflammability, but as a suitable accent to the room.

Framework

Enclosing framework (which you have to build) for a prefabricated fireplace usually consists of 2x4s covered in ½ inch plywood, which is finished with stone, brick, plaster or whatever final covering you prefer.

Raised fireplace. For a raised fireplace, the fireplace unit and its framework can be built on a platform of 2x10s set on edge and braced like floor joists. The platform can be covered in two layers of plywood: ⅝ inch overlaid with a ½ inch sheet. This in turn is covered by a sheet of Wonder Board for hearth extension. Wonder Board, available at building supply dealers, is a non-combustible material composed of cement overlayed with fiberglass. It is installed with roofing nails and can be cut with a masonry saw blade, or scored and split to size.

BUILT-IN FIREPLACE SURROUNDS

Some existing fireplaces are so shallow that they appear weak and unimportant-looking in an otherwise well-shaped room. Then again, a fireplace can be so massive that it would look better if some of its bulk were disguised. In either instance, a built-in surround can help control shape and proportion of a fireplace, whatever its size. Bookcases or surrounding cabinets also create new style directions for both the fireplace and the room.

Decide what kind of built-in you want—open, closed or a combination of both. Bookcases over a row of base cabinets might give you the kind of open-closed storage space you need. If the fireplace is deep and bulky, the enclosing rows of shelves and cabinets will reduce its massiveness. A similar built-in surrounding a shallow fireplace will add dimension and weight to the fireplace wall.

Recessed Fireplace

To give a shallow fireplace even greater importance, consider a built-in surround that projects outward beyond the perimeter of the fireplace itself. Let the projecting built-in be enclosed across the top, also. This will create, in effect, a recessed fireplace alcove. Such a built-in could be a solid wall of paneled doors (with or without exposed hardware). Behind the doors could be a warren of large and small storage units—for everything from coats to stereo equipment to a hidden dry bar. The kind of facing material you use

on the built-in framework determines the atmosphere of the room—whether a sleek modern look, a rustic facade, or your favorite period style.

Framing The Built-in

Choose your framing material according to the weight it will support; 2x4s for uprights, ceiling floor plates if you intend to create closets and other storage spaces inside the built-in. Use 2x4s also if you plan to face the structure with heavy sections of marble, mirror or solid wood planks. Lightweight framing members such as 2x2s or 2x3s will be suitable for surrounds that carry only prefinished paneling.

HEARTHS

There are three kinds of hearths: raised, surface, or flush. Whatever style of hearth your fireplace has, or will have, the general principles of hearth-building are governed by two guidelines: (1) the material must be noncombustible, (2) the hearth must be wide enough and long enough to protect the adjacent floor from being burned by heat on flying sparks. Front-to-back depth usually equals the height of the fireplace opening. Length of the hearth (side to side) usually is twice the opening's width (measured from center line of opening).

Hearth materials include brick, stone, slate, marble, ceramic tile, quarry tile, concrete, and simulated materials formulated for hearth use. If you are lucky enough to find a single slab of stone, slate, or marble, the hearth can be installed without mortar. Otherwise, small sections of hearth materials should be joined by appropriate joint compounds such as cement, or the Tri-Poxy compounds produced by L&M Surco, mentioned above.

Flush hearths are inset (recessed) into the floor so that the top surface of the finished hearth is flush with that of the floor. These hearths fit especially well into small rooms, or where an interior design calls for smooth, uninterrupted visual flow.

A surface hearth is actually one that is laid directly on top of the floor. The floor is protected first by a sheet of metal or Wonder Board. Thick strips of beveled molding nailed to the floor form a shallow recess in which the finished hearth material is laid and mortared in place.

Recessed in a conversation pit and set on a raised hearth, this fireplace is open on two sides so the fire can be seen from more angles.

A very shallow raised hearth is just deep enough to support a unit containing a firescreen, glass doors and an electric-powered heat exchanger.

A combination wood storage and pass-through is built into this fireplace. The storage box door matches the paneling of the chimney breast.

A slightly raised hearth is attractive and allows a better view of the fire. A raised hearth may be a few inches high, but it may also be high enough to serve as seating.

A raised hearth is one that is 6 inches or more above floor level. The most attractive and useful are built up to comfortable seating height and are extended to serve as a log holder or display shelf. A raised hearth can make firetending a more pleasant task—no more stooping, bending, squatting. A raised hearth can be made entirely of brick or stone—as either a single row of the material, or as stacks if the floor can take the weight. A slate hearth looks especially attractive over a base of natural stone or white-painted brick.

FIREWOOD CUT AND WAITING

When you are planning new construction, try to have a pass-through wood storage box for your fireplace. Wood thus can be stacked and stored outside the house, but retrieved from inside. Imagine the steps saved, the the trips you will avoid making in sleet, rain, and storm of night, carrying in the firewood.

You might be able to construct a pass-through wood storage box in an existing house if there is room enough to cut an opening in an exterior wall. However, the inside door and storage cavity of the box should be well insulated to prevent heat loss from the house.

Outside, the storage box can be open at the top or on a side that is most protected from the prevailing wind. Fit the opening with a hinged flap. For appearance you can add shingles, brick, or stone to the box's exterior sheathing. Inside, the pass-through box can form part of a raised

A log basket, styled to match the other fireplace accessories, holds extra wood for a fire.

hearth, be hidden inside a built-in, or concealed by the doors of a base cabinet.

Less ambitious projects for making firewood boxes include building containers that look like wooden blanket chests, painted trunks or slant-topped cabinets, as well as tubs, barrels, cubes, and rectangles of redwood lumber.

You can buy strong brass or iron woodboxes and chests. Great baskets of strong willow make excellent wood holders, as do big black iron kettles. Let the kind of woodbox you choose be one that blends harmoniously with the room's decorative theme.

MANTELS

That protruding horizontal lip extending above the fireplace opening can be made of just about anything: a distressed beam from an old barn, a split log, a railroad tie, a built-out row of bricks or stones, a slab of concrete, a slice of marble, slate, or flagstone.

If you prefer to have a ready-made mantel, you can find one in a fireplace shop, better department store, home building center, decorator or home accessories shop, or through a mail-order catalog. Millwork houses keep a vast supply of mantels flowing into the marketplace. Most are made of wood, but some are marble. Others are combinations of natural and synthetic materials. (Some sources are listed in the Appendi-

The practical purpose of a mantelshelf is as a heat deflector; however, most people view it as a display shelf and part of their total design plan.

ces.) You will find unfinished mantels, as well as those already finished.

If you are a scavanger of demolition sites, or enjoy prowling through salvage yards, you may be fortunate enough to find truly old mantels of marble or wood. These are worth paying for and carting home if you anticipate ever having a fireplace in your home.

HOOD

Hoods can be tall, towering flared shapes or short and squat—but still flared. Either way, a fireplace with hood has enormous visual impact. If you want a shy fireplace to look important, build or buy a hood.

This fireplace is basically a hearth and a round hood. The hood catches the smoke and directs it up the chimney.

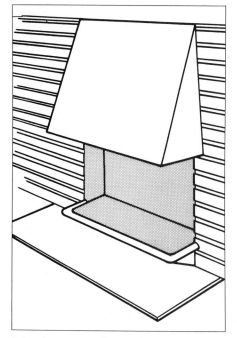

A hood may control a smoke problem and is required for an open fire box.

Hoods can be functional or purely decorative. Those used with free-standing island or peninsular fireplaces are designed to be both, since the fireplace is a central feature of the room. The flared hood and its matching flue act to shield and direct the flow of heat and smoke. They also give off extra heat through radiation and convection.

A hood for a wall fireplace can also be styled and constructed for both decorative and functional purposes—if you are building the fireplace from scratch. It is nearly impossible to outfit an existing fireplace with a functional hood because you would have to tear out and reconstruct the old firebox and flue. In this case it is better to settle for a decorative hood instead, fitted around the existing structure.

Decorative Plaster Hood

Although most fireplace hoods are made of metal—painted steelplate, glowing copper, satiny stainless steel or aluminum—you can build a nonfunctional decorative hood out of plaster. Here are the steps:

(1) construct a wooden framework of 1x2s or 2x2s;
(2) cover the frame with metal mesh;
(3) trowel on a thick coating of plaster;
(4) before the plaster dries, texture the surface with whisk broom, damp sponge, or trowel;
(5) trim the hood edges with simulated brick, strips of copper or iron or ceramic tile (optional).

Because plaster is very heavy, attach the wooden framework firmly to the walls and fireplace, using wood screws, masonry nails, or Molly bolts, depending upon the material into which you are fastening the framework. To build the 1x2 or 2x2 framework, judge height, width, and extent of hood flare according to the size of the fireplace, the size of the room and its ceiling height. Also, the hood should not be so low or so flared that it would interfere with fire-tending chores.

You may fabricate a purely decorative hood out of copper, steel, or aluminum, rather than plaster, if you have had experience working with sheet metal. In this case, you can fasten the metal to the wooden framework. If you have not had experience handling sheet metal, let an expert handle this for you.

ACCESSORIES

Decorative appearance is certainly important, but fireplace accessories are supposed to perform important jobs, most of them in the heavy-and-dirty category. A set of good-looking fire tongs are not worth paying for if they cannot grip anything more substantial than kindling. Size and proportion are more important than looks. If the fireplace is a deep one, make sure tongs, poker, log fork, brush and shovel have strong, long handles. If you have the type of fireplace that can accommodate long, heavy logs, a log fork will be more efficient than tongs.

Whether you burn coal or wood, you will need a hearth-side container that is generous in size, attractive to look at, and easy to handle and keep clean. Copper, brass, steel, leather and wrought iron buckets and holders come in many styles and shapes.

Andirons, as discussed in Chapter 9, are not as good a choice as a grate. They do serve as ornamentation in many homes. Serious fire-tenders rely on a sturdy, iron log rest, grate, or fire basket with open ends so that an extra-long length of wood can rest firmly within the firebox. Oversized logs and sticks of wood propped at an odd angle or braced against a side of the firebox can damage the interior of the fireplace, and are always in danger of toppling out.

Fireplace screens are both decorative and functional in equal measure. They protect human beings and their home from the hazards of flying sparks, and they give the fireplace a finished look.

There are many kinds and styles of firescreens; they are thoughtfully designed to complement all types of decor. A firescreen made of folding glass doors is a delightful way to view a cheery fire in

Decorative accessories for a fireplace may be anything from a decorative glass door unit to an art object placed nearby.

To create a truly effective environment, the home style, the fireplace style and the furniture style must coordinate.

Brass andirons are largely decorative. For more efficient burning, set logs in a basket grate. Brass fireplace tools, however, are both useful and decorative.

The hard symmetry of a brick surround may be softened with various decorative elements such as pillows and plants.

all its sparkling glory. They are safe, aid in the control of combustion air, and help reduce air loss from inside the room. Glass doors are supported on a metal frame that is fastened on the fireplace opening. (See Chapter 9 for detailed discussion.) Another kind that requires permanent installation are the metal mesh screens that hang like draw draperies and are operated by a pull-chain. Free-standing firescreens require no installation and come in folding or one-piece models. No fireplace should be without a screen.

DECORATING HINTS

Sometimes an existing fireplace needs to be changed or up-dated so it will conform with your possessions and the style of the room. In most cases, however, the fireplace is so pleasing and outstanding that you wish only to have materials and furnishings that work well with it. How you plan and furnish a room must be guided by personal preference, but there are some general tips you may find useful.

A good rule-of-thumb to follow is to aim for an interesting interplay of textures. For instance, if the fireplace is large

and rough textured (jagged stone, coarse brick), have smooth textures on the floor—bare wood or velvety rugs. On furniture use smooth materials such as polished leather, suede, velvet, cotton, or linen.

If the fireplace is done in one of the sleek formal materials like marble, mirror, polished metal, ceramic tile, choose furnishings having the same level of formality and use fabrics like nubby silk, crushed velvet, damask, textured floor-coverings.

Smooth-finished or textured plaster looks best with touches of copper or black iron, and surrounded by white and pale wheat-toned wood. Or, you can create a lively setting for a white plaster-finished fireplace by surrounding it with sharp vivid splashes of color and hefty textures—hand-loomed rugs and wall hangings, thick, richly-carved natural wood chests and tables. A hearth of slate or irregular quarry tile looks especially fine before fireplaces finished in plaster.

Free-standing fireplaces come in rich reds, blues, orange, yellow, white as well as deep brown, jet black, charcoal. Use their color to establish a key accent color

in the room. Since most of these fireplaces have smooth, shiny finishes, nubby textures, and dense fabrics like velvet, look well with them.

Ordinary brick which is unpainted and unglazed, seems to absorb light and deaden the colors used around it. You would do well to use plenty of shiny metals, glass, and mirror in the room. Polished woods and fabrics will lighten the effect still further.

Painted brick, on the other hand—either white or dense charcoal—looks delightful surrounded by strong color, dull wood finishes, and lots of live green plants.

3

COMPONENTS

HOW A FIREPLACE WORKS

If you are building or remodeling a home, you are likely to include a fireplace in your plans. While there are several types of fireplaces available, a masonry fireplace provides the solid quality and aesthetic that are so desirable. A masonry fireplace requires quite a lot of attention and detail in order for it to function properly.

Creation of an effective fireplace involves three steps: correct design, construction, and use of fuel.

Unless the homeowner has an engineering background, the fireplace usually receives consideration only in terms of its appearance. While everyone agrees that a fireplace gives a warm and welcoming look to a room, a fireplace is more than just a focus for a decorating scheme. It must, of course, be designed so the size, scale and shape complement the whole. Design in this sense also refers to function. The firebox must be large enough to contain a fire, draw sufficient air for combustion, have a smokeshelf to prevent downdrafts from pushing smoke back into the room, as well as a damper to close off outside air when the fireplace is not in use. The chimney must be smooth and relatively straight. The cap must rise above the roof a specific distance to avoid downdrafts. There should be no large trees or other buildings nearby to divert airflow.

The homeowner who is adding a fireplace to an existing home or building a new home with a fireplace has the advantage of being able to construct whatever style fireplace he desires. Although it is possible to create an energy-efficient fireplace without making major alterations to any basic fireplace design, the

The visual impact of a fireplace comes from the opening and the surround. These are the areas we enjoy in a fireplace.

homeowner may—if willing to forego the traditional large, open firebox—use the design of the Rumford fireplace for even greater heat effectiveness. The interior of a Rumford fireplace is a modification of the traditional firebox with a small, square, flat back wall, half the height of the front opening. The sides and the upper back wall angle sharply toward the front, creating a large reflecting surface, which sends heat back into the room. This is important because a fireplace produces radiant heat. Radiant heat is thrown in straight rays into the room and heats the bodies or objects that the rays come in contact with.

Another functional principle of a fireplace is that hot air rises and cold air falls. As a fire is started in the firebox, the smoke rises because it is lighter than the air around it. To prevent the smoke from circulating in the room, the opening at the top of the firebox narrows to form a throat that aids the smoke in continuing its journey upwards. At this point, the

smoke would stop moving vertically without the aid of the smoke chamber and smoke shelf. Cold air descends the back wall of the chimney flue, strikes the smoke shelf and is deflected forward and upward meeting the rising smoke. The cold air and smoke mix and move upwards on the inside surface of the smoke chamber. This action is the "draw" of a fireplace. The hot air and smoke from the fire are pulled on their vertical journey up the chimney flue. The flue extends through a cap at the top of the masonry wall. At this juncture, the smoke and hot air are traveling at a rapid pace and are dispersed into the atmosphere. A chimney pot, designed to control excessive downdrafts and further enhance the draw, or a spark arrester—to prevent sparks and hot ash from blowing on to adjacent combustible material—is placed over the end of the flue.

Overview

As this cycle is repeated over and over, the brick lining that forms the back and the sides of the firebox begin to retain the heat radiated in their direction. This further increases both the amount of heat generated by the fire and the updraft. Long after the fire has died out, the firebrick will continue to give off heat.

To clarify the respective roles of the components, a more detailed description is necessary. We will begin at the ground and work upwards in the same way that smoke rises up the chimney.

The foundation. The thickness and reinforcement of the foundation is determined by local and/or state building codes. Because code requirements will vary from one section of the country to another—depending upon weather patterns, subsoils, and ground faults—you must check with your municipal or county building inspector. Generally, however, the footing for a fireplace requires eight to twelve inches of reinforced concrete. It must be remembered that even a small fireplace and chimney will weigh between eight and twelve tons; such weight needs a sturdy, reinforced foundation. The house foundation may be adequate for chimney support, but there must be at least six inches clearance between the house framing and the masonry on all sides of the fireplace base. You will find that in a cold climate the foundation footings must be at least eight inches below the frost line and in a warm climate the foundation should sit at least a foot below the grade level.

In a house without a basement, the fireplace will rest right on a thickened cement slab. When installing a fireplace above a basement, you will have to build walls of cement, concrete block, or brick from the basement or slab foundation to the level of the hearth. This section of walls will also act as your ash pit, and—if you are designing an efficient fireplace—an access way for outside combustion air.

Ashpit. The ashpit is the hollow space created by the foundation walls. It is as large as the firebox and extends from your basement floor to the base of the hearth. The ashpit is the part of the fireplace that collects the ashes left over from a fire. Depending on the overall height of the pit, several years' worth of fire remains can be stored. The primary purpose of the ashpit is to eliminate the hauling of ashes through the living area and to simplify the cleaning of the fireplace. This operation, especially in a living room or family room, can be a very dirty chore. A cleanout door in the base of the ashpit provides access for final disposal of the ashes.

The hearth. The hearth is the flat surface on which the fire will be built. The complete hearth consists of two different parts, although usually both are made of noncombustible material. The section within the firebox or combustion chamber is the basic hearth, and the area in front is designated the forehearth. The hearth is usually finished with firebrick, a type of brick resistant to high temperatures, but it may be made of stone, concrete or almost any noncombustible material.

If the house is on a solid slab, without a basement or crawlspace, the hearth can be laid directly on the reinforced concrete slab. If there is to be an ashpit, the firebrick is laid on a reinforced concrete slab that covers the pit. The pit may be built with brick or concrete block. The front, interior wall of the ashpit is often

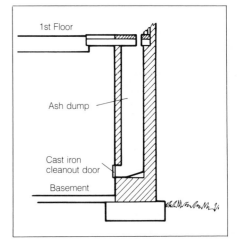

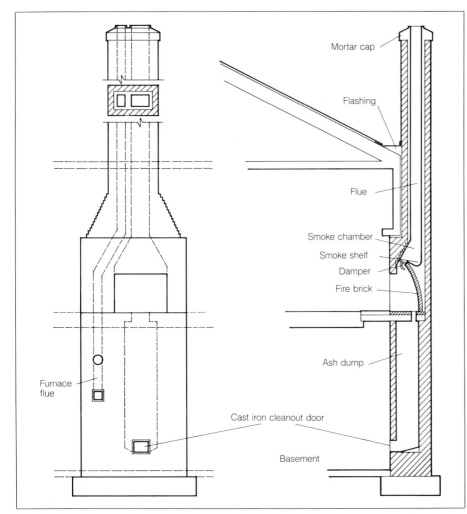

In a home with a basement, the fireplace reaches from the foundation footings to well above the roof line. Many hidden components are necessary for the efficient function of the firebox.

The foundation footing supports the fireplace. An ash pit is enclosed in the foundation wall space to permit cleanout access from the basement.

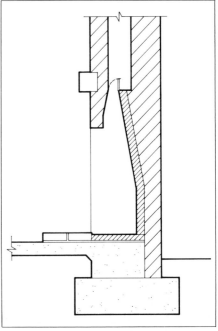

In areas of frost heave, a slab will have deep footings. The fireplace sits on the thick footings; the hearth support is part of the slab.

corbelled outward to serve as a partial support for the forehearth.

When the walls are within 8 inches of the desired level of the firebox and hearth, the ashpit is covered with a sheet of heavy gauge steel plate—with an opening cut out for the ash dump. The forehearth is often framed in and the bottom covered with a sheet of ¾ inch Exterior grade plywood. The ash dump opening is framed with a form and 4 inches of concrete poured for the base of the hearth and forehearth.

The forehearth support may be brick or stone, but the framing must be set into the floor so the forehearth will not rest on any joists. The support may be a set of brick arches that extend from the inside wall of the foundation to a ledger strip nailed to a double header that frames the floor opening parallel to the fireplace wall. The forehearth base can also be made of bricks supported on a series of long T-shaped steel strips extending from the foundation wall to the ledger strip. The forehearth may also be a concrete slab described above reinforced with steel rods from the foundation to the ledger strip. No matter which method is used to support the base, the forehearth is always surfaced with a non-combustible material such as brick, concrete, stone or even decorative ceramic tile. The forehearth must project 16 inches (minimum) in front of the firebox and eight inches beyond the opening on each side.

Hearth level. Another consideration is the level of hearth. Both the floor level and raised hearths function equally well. A floor-level hearth and firebox may appear elegant and formal; a raised hearth—and firebox—may be easier to fuel, view and clean. A raised hearth may seem to provide more warmth. If the raised hearth is large enough and high enough, it can offer extra seating in your room, a consideration if you entertain large groups.

The firebox. The area above the hearth is the firebox. Although it is termed "firebox", it is not usually box-like in shape. The firebox should never have right angle corners nor should the walls be absolutely vertical. The ideal firebox has a back wall that is vertical for the first 12 to 15 inches above the hearth, then the wall slants inward to direct heat into the room and to create a base for the smoke shelf. Firebox sides are usually straight up and down but are angled toward the back wall, which is narrower than the fireplace opening. All fireplaces should approximate this shape, although the size of the angles vary.

The inner wall, or lining, of the firebox consists of a two-to-four inch thick layer of firebrick, installed with a fireclay, heat-resistant form of mortar. The mortared joints between these bricks should be no more than a quarter inch thick. A fireplace can be built without a firebrick lining, but the wall thickness will have to be a minimum of 12 inches and it must be

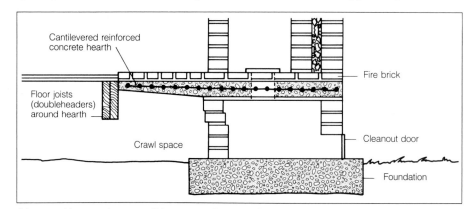

A house with a crawl space will have a small ash pit. Fireplace foundation walls are built on a thick footing. The interior wall is corbeled into the crawl space for hearth support.

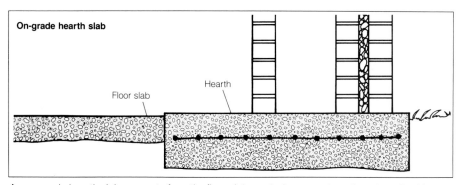

An on-grade hearth slab, separate from the floor slab, works in areas where there is no frost heave. Reinforcing rods increase slab support strength.

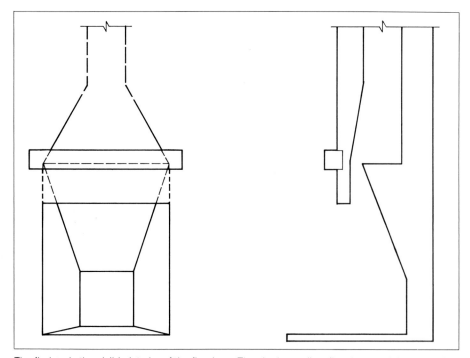

The firebox is the visible interior of the fireplace. The sloping walls reflect heat and the narrowing spaces direct the flow of smoke up and away from the opening.

remembered that any wood framing to surround such a fireplace must have an additional four inches of insulated clearance between the wood and the brick. If this is the way you wish to build the fireplace, without a lining, be sure you will have more than enough room to accommodate the required wall thickness.

The walls surrounding a lined firebox, in accordance with building codes, must be built of masonry or reinforced concrete, and be a minimum of eight inches thick. As you can see, building a fireplace with a lining will be somewhat less expensive since you will use less brick.

The face. The jambs of the fireplace, which are the exposed edges of the sides, and the area directly above the lintel, constitute the fireplace surround. This area can be left plain brick or faced with a non-combustible material of your choice. The width of the jambs may be greater than that of the sides of the firebox. For a fireplace with an opening three feet wide or less, the non-combustible jambs should be a foot wide. If you have only exposed masonry, the jambs should be a minimum of 16 inches wide. For most attractive proportion, the width of the jambs should be in proportion to the opening. The larger the opening, the wider the jambs.

If you would like to use woodwork on the jambs, such as the jambs of an Early American fireplace, the wood should be more than six inches away from the firebox opening. Above the opening, woodwork extending out as little as ½ inch requires a separation of at least a foot from the top of the opening.

The lintel is the support across the top of the fireplace opening on which the masonry above sits. It may be stone, precast concrete, iron or steel. The lintel can enhance the style of the fireplace as well as provide functional support. The easiest lintel to install is a wide, ⅜ to ½ inch thick, steel bar either flat or angled to 90 degrees. The lintel can support an expanse brick above it equal to the width of the opening. There are companies that manufacture a combination lintel and damper, which means you will have less work when you install the damper.

The throat. The throat helps control the draft that draws smoke into the flue and helps reflect heat into the dwelling. The throat is the open space above the lintel inside the fireplace. The formation

This fireplace has uneven jambs. The right jamb meets minimum code requirements. The left jamb is larger. The masonry projects in steps to protect the wood mantel from the heat.

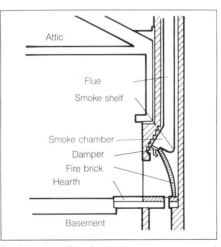

Each section of the fireplace has a purpose and function. You cannot leave out or change the proportions without creating problems.

of the throat should begin no less than six inches above the lintel. The masonry should be perfectly vertical from the lintel to the base of the throat then angle to an opening no smaller than the flue. The throat should be the same width as the width of the fireplace opening, but the masonry slants so that the throat opening becomes only a few inches deep from front to back.

The damper. The damper is a modern addition; years ago no fireplaces were built with dampers. Contemporary fireplaces have dampers that save energy and money. The damper keeps warm air in the home whenever the fireplace is not in use. A damper may also keep insects, birds, small rodents and dust out of the home.

A damper usually is made from iron or steel and consists of a framework with a pivoting metal door that swings open and closed. The door is usually controlled by a lever, a chain or a turnscrew device. The lever control is the most basic. The lever arm extends from the damper into the firebox. To operate the damper, you insert the end of a poker through the hole in the lever arm and either push the damper open or pull it closed. The turnscrew control extends through the masonry face of the fireplace, and you turn it to open and shut the damper. However, this mechanism is susceptible to dirt and soot that will clog the gears and make the damper difficult to operate in time.

Dampers range from a very simple bent iron plate design to a combination damper and lintel. Some of the latter are in a high, pyramid shape that help support the upper masonry work and form the smoke chamber of the fireplace. There are also twin-doored, single-frame dampers for use in back-to-back fireplaces with separate flues in the same chimney. Most dampers are manufactured in several sizes to fit nearly all standard fireboxes.

The smoke shelf. This lies directly behind the throat and under the flue. It may be either a flat or a concave shelf projecting from the back wall. In the traditional fireplace the concave design is usually better because it directs the flow of smoke and gases upward from the firebox more efficiently and will also deflect any downdraft that would force smoke into the interior of the house. However, the smoke shelf of a Rumford fireplace is flat. The smoke shelf is as wide as the throat, and it is usually from six to twelve inches deep. Of course, the depth of the smokeshelf is determined by the depth of the firebox.

The smoke chamber. The area which exists between the top of the throat to the bottom of the flue is the smoke chamber. This is a transitional point between the fireplace and the flue, and it is a point where the smoke and gases collect before being funneled through the flue to the outside. Because the flue is immediately above the firebox in a Rumford fireplace, this type of fireplace has no smoke chamber. When building the smoke chamber, make the inner sides as nearly perfectly smooth as possible. Any projection will catch and obstruct the upward flow of exhaust, so the surface must be a smooth layer of mortar, troweled out flat and even. However, the use of the high pyramid shaped damper, mentioned before, will also serve as the smoke chamber.

The flue. The flue extends above the smoke chamber, and, like the firebox and throat, must conform to specific size requirements to provide proper draw. The

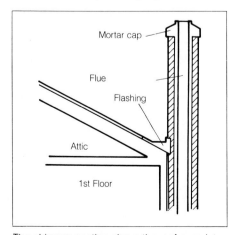

The chimney section above the roof completes the fireplace unit. It must be built and sealed to withstand wind, precipitation and heat.

Brick Institute of America suggests specific sizes (see the chart on page 36).

To mathematically determine the required flue area dimensions and the proper height of the chimney, you will have to apply a formula. The opening of a lined flue 22 or more feet high should have an area $\frac{1}{12}$th the size of the area of the firebox opening. A lined or unlined flue less than 22 feet high should have an opening $\frac{1}{10}$th the size of the firebox opening.

The flue should be made with a liner of smooth fireclay. The liner stock comes in two to three foot sections, and it should be not less than $\frac{5}{8}$ inch thick. The larger the flue opening the thicker the flue lining required. A 24x24 inch flue requires a liner $1\frac{5}{8}$ inch thick. Using these liners means that outside brick walls only need be four inches thick. However, a chimney built of stone around a liner should still be 12 inches thick.

The flue liner is very heavy and must be well supported at the base, set on solid masonry at the bottom of the flue. Otherwise the lining must be supported on at least three sides by brick courses which project even with the inside surface of the lining. As each section is put into place, the joints are made airtight with mortar and then struck smooth on the inside. After each section is in place, the brick chimney wall is built up around it. The process should proceed slowly to allow mortar joints to set well. Because each flue tile is very heavy, laying several quickly may force the mortar out of lower joints before each has set. It is important that no flue liner joints align with brick mortar joints. Since both are subject to possible cracking from heat, stress or strong winds, the chimney would be seriously weakened if it cracked along aligned joints. The brick walls should not touch the flue; there should be a space between the liner and the brick. This space should be filled with rubble.

Because of the way the flue and walls are constructed, the mixture of the mortar is important. Use fireclay mortar, a mixture of one part Portland cement, $\frac{1}{2}$ part hydrated lime, and three to four parts sand.

The top of the flue liner, which is also the top of the chimney, should protrude a minimum of eight inches above the surrounding masonry. This allows enough room for the cap piece.

The flue should be as straight as possible, but there are times when it must be angled on its way up. The bend must be no more than 30 degrees from the vertical, and the liner must be mitered so that there are no reductions and no uneven surfaces in the area of the flue at the bend.

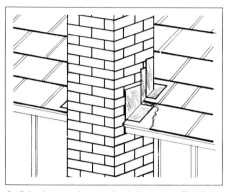

A 2-inch gap is required between fireplace framing and masonry. Flashing covers the roof gap to protect the house and chimney from rain.

Flashing. Flashing seals the opening between the brick chimney and the wood framed roof that surrounds it and provides a weathertight connection between the two materials. Clearance must be provided where the chimney passes through the roof, and the gap created will be covered with flashing. As with some other masonry work, this is a job often better left to a professional. Flashing is applied to seal the open area and to provide a path for quick run-off for snow or rain. Lead coated copper or galvanized sheet metal are common materials used for flashing. Different types of fiber reinforced materials are also satisfactory for this purpose. The flashing will often be further sealed with an asphalt base pitch or roofing cement where gaps occur between the materials.

There must be no wood or other combustible materials in contact with the chimney. A two inch minimum clearance should be left between the masonry and the surrounding wood framing.

Above the roof line. It is usually recommended that the upper section of the chimney be corbelled—angled via a series of steps in the brick. This will help strengthen the chimney and create a lip to keep rain from running straight down the masonry walls. A tall, narrow chimney is subject to sway in heavy winds and may crack at joints of both the flue and the chimney walls. This would interfere with the drawing of the fireplace and could create a fire hazard. In addition, a narrow chimney is not usually attractive on most houses, so corbelling helps enlarge a chimney to a proper aesthetic proportion.

For the chimney to draw correctly and to conform with building codes, the top must be at least three feet above the highest point of the roof where the chimney emerges, and it must also be two feet above the highest point in the dwelling or any part of any building within ten feet. (Details are shown in chapter 8 on installing prefabricated units.)

Cap. The cap is the "crown" or top of the chimney proper. It is normally used as the weathering part of the chimney. It can be as simple as a concrete wash that is spread over the top of the masonry. To insure proper drainage, the cap is pitched down to the outside edge. Some caps are made of granite, cast stone or cast concrete. No matter what material is used as a cap piece, it must be watertight and properly anchored to the brick masonry support. If a crack should occur between the flue which protrudes above the cap and the cap material, water penetration is inevitable. This will certainly shorten the life of the chimney.

Chimney Pot/Spark Arrester

The chimney should be finished with some form of spark arrester or chimney pot at the top of the flue and above the cap. The spark arrester serves two purposes. The first is to keep leaves and dust out and to keep sparks from emerging and starting a fire, the other is to improve the drawing abilities of the chimney. In fact, building codes may require a spark arrester if the chimney is on or near combustible roof material. The spark arrester should be made of a rust resistant material and should have screen opening no smaller than $5/16$th of an inch or larger than $5/8$ths of an inch. It should enclose the entire flue discharge area and be securely fastened to the flue or cap. The chimney pot protects the chimney from downdrafts. If you have two adjacent flues in one chimney that are in a line so that prevailing winds pass over one and then the other, the 2nd (leaward) chimney pot should be slightly higher or smoke, gas and ash may be drawn from one into the other. Most fireplace dealers will have a wide selection of spark arresters or chimney pots to choose from. Corrosion resistant metals such as copper, zinc,

terra cotta, or lead are usually used, or galvanized steel or tin sheeting which require occasional painting.

Hooded chimneys may be required if the slope of the adjacent terrain, nearby tall trees, or tall buildings create a strong down draft that forces gusty winds into the chimney and eventually the fireplace.

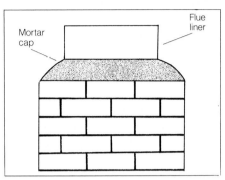

The tile flue liner extends above the masonry chimney. A mortar cap seals the top and slopes away from the tile for good drainage.

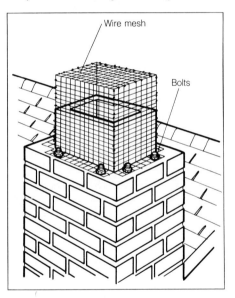

A box of wire mesh protects the roof and adjacent structures from sparks. It will also keep leaves and debris out of the chimney.

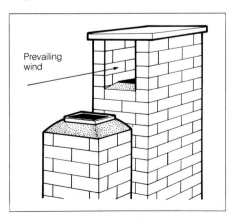

A hooded chimney controls the air flow for a good chimney updraft. A hood may be needed in areas subject to gusty winds.

A hooded chimney permits air to flow over the chimney opening in a controlled manner. A raised cover is placed over the chimney pot to allow the prevailing winds to pass over the opening but cutting down on the amount of air moving directly over the flue. It takes considerable skill, strength and experience to handle a large project such as the construction of a masonry fireplace. The instructions in this book will present the basic requirements for design, materials and construction in enough detail for you to understand the process and determine how much help will be needed in planning, designing and constructing your unit.

Planning

The first step in designing the fireplace is planning. You should do this even before contacting an architect or fireplace mason to build your unit. Before doing anything else, you must decide where the fireplace will be located because the location either on an outside wall or in the interior of the house will influence cost, design and difficulty of construction.

Location. If you are building a new home, the location for the fireplace is not as significant as it will be if you are remodeling to add the fireplace. If you choose an outside wall, you will save interior space and you will probably reduce the building costs because the framing and construction around the masonry is simpler. Exterior wall fireplaces are easier to flash, and because the masonry is open on three sides, it will be easier to repair any leakage and to perform general maintenance.

However, an outside chimney will have to be located so it appears integral with the design, or it may detract from the appearance of the dwelling. An outside chimney may be inappropriate to the style of your home, especially if it looks like an added feature rather than part of the original house. An inside chimney will take up considerable floor space because building codes usually specify a minimum of 2 inches clearance between the sides of the chimney and any adjacent combustible materials. This loss of space is compensated for by the fact that this fireplace and chimney will give considerably more heat to the house. Expense may be less because you can use one central chimney to house a number of flues for multiple fireplaces, the furnace and the

This small, prefabricated, heat-circulating fireplace is set in an imposing surround. The raised hearth holds air intake vents; warm air is blown through the brick grid above the opening.

water heater. Central chimneys are known to have better draft-pulling qualities because the central position is usually the highest point in a roof. You will also benefit because the brick will retain heat longer and give it off more evenly. However, if remodeling, an inside chimney is only economically reasonable if installed in a one story building. In a two or three story home extensive cutting and rebuilding of large sections of the upper walls and floor framing will be required for the chimney and the clearance space.

The fireplace face. The next consideration is whether the fireplace will be flush with the wall or project into the room. If your fireplace projects into the room, it will take up floor space. In a small room, this may prove awkward. You may also discover the spaces created on each side of the fireplace difficult to utilize. While it is possible to flank the fireplace with bookcases or cabinets, unless your room is is generously proportioned, what was to be a cozy fireplace may overwhelm your room. On the other hand, a flush fireplace may not have the impact you desire. If you have studied your room carefully and understand why you are adding the fireplace, you should see these problems and make your choice wisely.

Ventilation. Today, ventilation is central in planning a fireplace. Modern homes are built nearly airtight in order to conserve energy, with weather stripped windows and doors. Because a fire needs air for combustion, a fireplace in any well sealed house will draw off heated air in the home and waste energy. Therefore, when you plan a fireplace, include a ventilation system that draws air from outside. There are several ways to do this. The most direct method is to install an air intake pipe through the base of the back wall of the fireplace. In place of one brick, inside and out, install a louvered metal grill with a closing lever to shut the vent when the fireplace is not in use. Such a system may be hand-made or purchased from a manufacturer, such as KapCo.

If your house has no basement and is built on a solid concrete foundation, the ashpit is nothing more than a foot deep hole covered by a door in the bottom of the hearth. A small bucket fits in the hole. If you make this hole slightly larger than the bucket—or use a smaller bucket—and run a pipe or duct through the outside of the foundation, you will have a ventilated fireplace. When you combine this ventilation with a fireplace heat-exchanger grate, you may have an energy efficient heating unit in your home. (Also see the Chapter 9 on Minimizing Heat Loss.)

You may wonder whether it is feasible to install a new fireplace and have it share an existing flue or chimney in the house.

The answer is no. It is a general rule of construction, and the law in several states, that in a dwelling every unit with an exhaust system must have its own flue. Many older homes already have a multiple flue chimneys. These chimneys must be carefully inspected and well maintained. Multi-flue chimneys are potentially dangerous because any cracks in the flue liner or mortar joints may allow sparks and gases to pass from one flue to another, and a mixture of gases from a furnace with those from a stove or fireplace is potentially dangerous.

Other Considerations

Other ideas to consider when planning a fireplace are tool storage areas, either built into the masonry to keep the hearth tools visible or out of the way, wood storage—which can be incorporated into the hearth itself (or into an adjacent wall)—and bookshelves or cabinets built alongside the fireplace. Remember these necessities and accessories when working out your plans.

FIREPLACE DESIGNS
Traditional

The opening in a traditional fireplace may be a 24x24 inches (square) or a rectangle as large as 96 inches wide and 40 inches high. The size and proportion of the opening and the fireplace face is dictated to a large degree upon the size of the wall and the proportions of the room in which it is located. The depth of a traditional fireplace ranges from 16 inches to 24 inches. The exterior masonry is a minimum of 8 inches thick; the returns on the face are 4½ inches thick. This dimension is what determines the size of the air inlet, which sits parallel with the front face returns and is the same width and the thickness of the returns.

The general proportion of the firebox in a traditional fireplace is that the back wall is 12 inches narrower than the front opening. The back wall begins to slope forward (to create the throat and the smoke shelf) at a point approximately one third of the distance from the floor of the firebox to the top of the opening. The traditional fireplace has, therefore, a flat, rectangular back wall. The sides of the firebox angle toward the flat back wall from the backs of the front face returns.

The distance from the top of the opening (on the face of the fireplace) to

A fireplace surround of knotty-pine paneling is an attractive facing for an informal room. Storage built-ins are covered with the same paneling for a unified look.

A very formal room, particularly in a period house, requires a special mantel/hearth. This prefabricated unit of pressed, powdered marble is authentic in detail and period style.

the flat surface of the smoke shelf will have a vertical measurement of at least 8 inches. The horizontal measurement at the narrowest point of the throat usually will be 8¾ inches. Larger units with openings from 54 by 37 inches to 96 by 40 inches will have a throat opening 13 inches wide.

The interior chimney flue wall rises on a straight vertical line from the back of the smoke shelf. This wall extends from the 8-inch thick back wall that rises from the base of the fireplace. From a point even with the smoke shelf, the interior front face of the fireplace slopes back to create a flue space 8 inches deep. The sides of the throat also slope inward, toward each other, to create a flue width of 12 inches. This flue dimension is for a firebox with a width between 24 and 28 inches. The larger the opening and firebox, the greater the flue size required.

Rumford Fireplace

This fireplace is much shallower than the traditional fireplace and the flat back wall is much smaller—a perfect square. The size of the square is determined by the depth of the fireplace and the size of the opening. For a fireplace with a 24x24 inch opening, the back wall will be 12 inches square; the depth of the fireplace is one half the height of the opening. The side walls are angled to the back from behind the face returns as in the traditional fireplace. However, because the flat wall is shorter and narrower than on the traditional fireplace, the angle is greater. These sharply angled walls are designed to reflect the maximum amount of heat from the fire into the room. The interior appearance of the Rumford is very different from the traditional because of its extreme angles. This means that the visual impression will be different. Because it is unusual, it may not be as pleasing to the eye as the standard, traditional fireplace.

In the Rumford fireplace the throat is smaller than in the traditional. It is only 3 to 4 inches from front to back and the centerline of the throat is the same as the centerline of the firebox. The smokeshelf also is only 3 to 4 inches deep. The sides of the throat narrow in the same manner and proportion as in the traditional fireplace, but the size of the flue opening is always one-tenth the size of the fireplace opening.

CONVENTIONAL FIREPLACE DIMENSIONS

Opening		Firebox				Throat	Flue Sizes	Lintel bar
Width	Height	Depth	Width	Flat wall/Height	Sloping rise	Width		Length
24"	24"	16"	11"	14"	18"	8¾"	8x12"	36" (A)*
26	24	16	13	14	18	8¾	8x12	36 (A)
28	24	16	15	14	18	8¾	8x12	36 (A)
30	29	16	17	14	23	8¾	12x12	42 (A)
32	29	16	19	14	23	8¾	12x12	42 (A)
36	29	16	23	14	23	8¾	12x12	48 (A)
40	29	16	27	14	23	8¾	12x16	48 (A)
42	32	16	29	14	26	8¾	16x16	54 (B)*
48	32	18	33	14	26	8¾	16x16	60 (B)
54	37	20	37	16	29	13	16x16	72 (B)
60	37	22	42	16	29	13	16x20	72 (B)
60	40	22	42	16	31	13	16x20	72 (B)
72	40	22	54	16	31	13	20x20	84 (C)*
84	40	24	64	20	28	13	20x24	96 (C)
96	40	24	76	20	28	13	20x24	108 (C)

*A: 3x3 angle iron of ³⁄₁₆ inch metal; B: 3½x3½ x½ inch; C: 5x3½ x ⁵⁄₁₆ inch.
Information courtesy of Brick Institute of America

A fireplace should be a visual and a practical asset to a room. The addition of an attractive and warming fireplace may make a previously unused room area a new center of activity.

The Rumford does have advantages for those adding a fireplace to an existing home. The entire unit is shallower and the chimney is not offset. The fireplace could be added without taking up too much of the interior of the home or projecting too far on the outside. If your community building code requires considerable setbacks from lot lines, you may not have much area into which a new fireplace may project on the outside of your house.

The addition of glass screens to close off room air as the fire dies down will prevent the loss of heated air from the house or the introduction of unheated air into the house. Glass screens for a traditional fireplace may require vents for better combustion, but a completely sealed screen in required for a Rumford.

PREPARING THE DRAWINGS

The design may be done by you, a mason experienced in building fireplaces, or an architect. An architect will provide plans, materials lists and specifications for the fireplace and chimney and can design the adjacent wall, mantel, any desired cabinets, bookcases or windows. A mason is usually qualified to design and build fireplaces, and many have developed their own very efficient styles. You may do the designing yourself, but, unless you are an experienced masonry worker, it will take a professional to determine if your design is acceptable and within building code requirements and can be constructed from your plans. An experienced builder/ mason will also be able to tell you about such things as prevailing seasonal winds or other environmental factors that may affect the way your fireplace will function.

CONSTRUCTION

After the fireplace has been designed, it has to be built. As mentioned before, this is not something to be attempted by everyone. In fact, many architects and masons will not design a fireplace if they know the client intends to build it himself. It is a matter of safety and caution. The information in Chapters 6 and 7 will give you an idea of the steps involved in building a fireplace. Anyone may plan and design a fireplace, but not everyone has the strength, endurance and skill to build a fireplace.

4

HEARTHS AND MANTELS

Both the hearth and mantel play not only an important functional part in any fireplace, they also can be used to create the decorating scheme of the fireplace, or even the entire room. Through the years much has been written about the positive emotional and visual contributions of the family hearth, and many an old-timer has fond memories of warm, rough hearth stones on a cold winter morning. A hearth of natural stone or of brick can create the look and warmth of years gone by. On the other hand, ceramic tile can be used to create a fireplace hearth of traditional or modern elegance. In fact, without the hearth and mantel a fireplace often appears to be nothing more than a "hole in the wall." There are many different materials and designs you can choose for both the hearth and mantel, regardless of whether you are building a new fireplace or updating and renovating an old one.

THE HEARTH

The hearth is immediately in front of the firebox and its main purpose is to prevent sparks from burning holes in the surrounding combustible floor. The hearth is required by standard building code requirements "to be made of brick, concrete, stone, or other approved styles of noncombustible hearth slab. This slab should be a minimum of 4 inches thick and must be supported by noncombustible materials or reinforced to carry its own weight and all imposed loads. The hearth must extend at least 16 inches in front of, and not less than eight inches beyond each side of, the fireplace opening. Where the fireplace opening is six feet square or larger, the hearth shall

This small fireplace is unobtrusive and not very impressive. The simple, flat face makes no particular impact on this room.

The same fireplace now looks entirely different. The face was widened slightly and a simple, classic mantel and surround were added. The entire mantel unit is prefabricated.

This late-Victorian fireplace is perfectly scaled to the room. The firebox—which burns either coal or wood—is small, but surround surfaces enlarge the fireplace to room scale.

extend at least 20 inches in front of and at least 12 inches beyond each side of the fireplace opening.''

When constructing a new fireplace, these measurements must be taken into consideration when pouring the foundation, making sure the foundation extends out past the sides by 8 inches and the front by 16 inches. In addition, the foundation should be another 4 to 6 inches larger all around. This is fairly easy to accomplish when the hearth proper is a concrete slab poured on grade. When the hearth slab is to be above grade, then the hearth quite often is a cantilevered, reinforced concrete slab.

Many older fireplaces utilize the poured concrete slab as the finished surface of the hearth. This can provide a highly functional and easily cleaned hearth surface, but not often a particularly attractive one. Hearth slabs may be covered with a variety of surfacings including brick, stone, marble, ceramic tile, and simulated brick such as that offered by the Z-brick company. The latter material is available in many different designs, including standard brick, used brick, or fieldstone. There are many of these simulated brick and stone products on the market. Check that the one you choose is noncombustible before you buy it for use as a hearth covering.

A Victorian fireplace, found in an antique shop, was saved until a room was built onto the period house. The hearth is marble; the surround is ceramic tile and hand-carved wood.

The carved wood repeats motifs in the tile and enlarges the scale of the decoration.

Hearth Level

Flush hearth. A hearth may be flush with the surrounding flooring, or preferably just a little higher, such as ¼ to ½ inch.

Raised hearth. The height of a raised hearth can range from one brick high to two or three courses high for use as a seating bench in front of the fireplace, extending to either or both side(s).

Sunken hearth. Naturally, this type of hearth is a great deal easier to accomplish when planning and building a new fireplace rather than when updating an old one. In order to lower the hearth of an existing fireplace below the floor level, even just slightly, you will have to knock out the existing foundation and lay a new one. This is a pretty extensive and complicated job and should not be tackled unless you have a great deal of construction knowledge and background.

When constructing a new home, one fairly common method of achieving the look of a sunken hearth is to actually raise the rest of the surrounding floor. The fireplace becomes part of a sunken conversation pit, which can be a cozy, intimate corner of a large room and help provide a means of dividing use areas in a room. Again, this job is fairly complicated and professional help is often necessary for proper construction.

Extending the Hearth

Probably one of the most common problems plaguing an older hearth is that it is not large enough to prevent sparks from

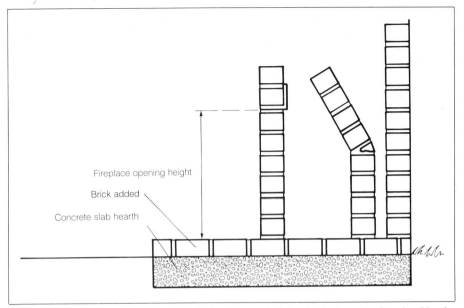

Fireplace opening height

Brick added

Concrete slab hearth

The hearth may be any convenient height, but frequently it is raised above the floor level by the thickness of brick or tile used to decoratively face the plain concrete hearth slab.

damaging the surrounding flooring materials. Let's take a simple floor-height hearth first, since that is the simplest to remedy. In most instances this will actually be about ¼ to ½ inch higher than the surrounding wood floor. The first step is to decide how much farther you want the hearth to extend into the room. In some cases you can even measure out past the burn marks left by sparks flung beyond the existing hearth.

Subfloor for hearth. Cut ¼ inch plywood (or thickness necessary to match

the height of the current hearth) to create a subfloor surrounding the existing hearth, extending out to fill the area you desire as a hearth. Cut the plywood pieces to size, smear their backs with latex glue and then nail them down using ring shank flooring nails. Make sure the extended hearth is square on all sides. Then "dimple" the nails (set them slightly under the wood surface with a hammer and a nail set). Fill all cracks with water putty or wood dough. Seal the joint (crack) between the old hearth and the

A fireplace may be given an authentic period mantel/surround with this prefabricated unit.

A raised hearth is often used to give greater visual impact to a fireplace. This unit is prefabricated and comes complete; both the brick work and the woodwork are ready to fit in place.

Install a plywood underlayment to a thickness equal to the height of the old hearth.

Seal nailheads and the spaces between plywood sheets and the hearth and underlayment.

Once the sealer has dried, sand the surface smooth with a belt sander.

Spread a cement-based adhesive with a square-notched trowel. For best results, hold the trowel at about a 45-degree angle.

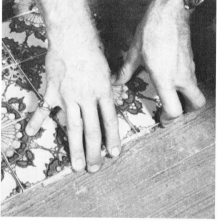

Lay the tile carefully to ensure straight courses and grout lines. Place any cut tiles at the joint between the hearth and fireplace.

The finished tile hearth will provide ample protection from sparks, need little maintenance, and last for many years.

new wood subfloor using latex concrete patching cement.

Use a coarse belt on a belt sander to smooth down the entire hearth area old and new. This leaves a smooth, level surface for installing the covering material. In the example shown the new hearth covering is of tile. Even if the old hearth were tile, in most cases you would not want to try to keep the old tile because matching it up exactly would be very unlikely. Both the old and the new hearth areas will be covered by the new hearth surfacing material. Regardless of what type of material is used to cover the hearth, the entire surface must be smooth and flat or the covering materials will rock and will not adhere properly—and may break or crack from the pressure of walking on them.

If the existing hearth is higher than $\frac{1}{4}$

inch, such as two inches, you can usually use a stack of plywood pieces to extend the hearth and build it flush with the existing hearth. Then finish off with the surfacing material such as synthetic brick to cover existing hearth with the new fireplace material.

In the case of a raised hearth you will have to extend it by first building a platform framing it with 2x4s, then cover it with $\frac{3}{4}$ inch plywood and finally the noncombustible covering material. Check the foundation underneath in case an extra joist, or bridging between joists, is needed for support.

Surfacing material. The wooden surface must be covered with a noncombustible material, as mentioned earlier. Most of these are merely cemented in place using a latex cement. The first step is to vacuum all sanding dust from the area.

Then make sure you use the proper mastic as suggested by the manufacturer of the material you are using—whether ceramic tile, synthetic stone, brick, and so on —and apply using the manufacturer's directions. Apply the adhesive with a knife or serrated trowel. The bed should be evenly applied and leveled out properly. Press the tile, brick or stone in place. It is a good idea to start at the front of the hearth with the full tiles (or brick or stone) and install the cut tiles or bricks at the back next to the existing hearth.

The easiest way to cut a straight line on tile is with a tile cutter. This can be purchased, or even rented, from the tile dealer. It is a good idea to practice by cutting several scrap pieces before you start the actual tiling job.

Straight cuts on tile also are easily made without the cutter by using an ordinary glass cutter and a straight edge, preferably a steel ruler or steel bar. First, scribe a line on the glazed side of the tile. Place the scribed line face up over a straight piece of wire approximately ⅛ inch in diameter (a wire coat hanger is an excellent choice). Put the wire on the floor; lay the tile over the wire and step on the tile, with one foot on each side of the scored line. The tile will snap.

Cuts for irregular spaces are made by nibbling off very small pieces of tile with either a ceramic tile nipper or an ordinary pair of slip-joint pliers. Holding the tile with the glazed side up, take small, ⅛ inch bites with the pliers and break off the tiny pieces to create the shape you wish. Take your time; don't try to take too large a bite or you will crack the tile. Safety glasses should be worn during the process. The nibbling method takes care of practically all irregular cuts that are required.

An abrasive stone or coarse file should be used to smooth sharp edges after cutting. However, don't bother to hone down tile when the edges are to be hidden under trim.

Cutting marble. Marble can be used as a hearth surfacing; however, it is a little hard to cut. Cut your marble with a carbide grit blade in a hacksaw, or with tile nippers. The easiest cutting method calls for use of power equipment and a masonry cut-off blade.

Grouting. Allow the materials to set up over night. Then apply the grout material. In the case of ceramic tile, use a latex tile grout in either a matching or complementary color to the tile. Darker grouts help hide dirt. This grout is a powder that mixes with a liquid latex material to the consistency of heavy cream. Spread it evenly over the surface, forcing down between all the tiles, using a putty knife. Allow it to set for a few minutes, according to the package directions. Remove the excess with a wet sponge. Allow the grout to dry thoroughly and polish the surface with a clean, soft, dry cloth.

To grout the brick or stone facing, substitute a thin paste of portland cement plus lime for grout. Apply it between the joints of bricks or stones, wiping off any excess, until you have created the effect of a masonry hearth. If the facing material manufacturer suggests a grout, you can utilize the type recommended.

Existing stone hearth. If the existing hearth is a stone hearth, you can lay flat stones that match in a bed of portland latex tile cement. In this case, do not sand the existing hearth. Allow the cement to set solidly in place. Mortar between the stones using a cement mortar mix.

Variation: matching hearth and floor. Another idea is to make the hearth and the flooring of one material; in other words, blending the floor and the hearth together. This makes the room appear larger. Achieving this requires basically the same principals explained previously in extending the hearth, only in this case you would extend it through the entire room. In other words, use the correct thickness of plywood to build the room up level with the existing hearth. Then cover the floor with fieldstone, flagstone, brick, tile, or any other noncombustible material. This results in a very startling, appealing effect.

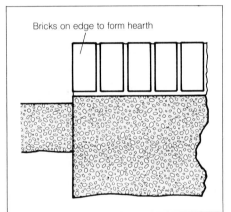

Bricks on edge to form hearth

To raise an existing hearth several inches without making any structural changes, set bricks on edge in a bed of mortar.

Raising the Hearth

The simplest way to raise the hearth is probably to use full-size brick, cementing them directly onto the existing hearth and, (if enlarging also, the extended subfloor). The raised portion outside the firebox must be matched by adding additional brick inside the firebox, so that both surfaces are the same heights. The course(s) added to the firebox must be of firebrick, using fireclay mortar.

You must be careful when raising the hearth because if it is made too high the fireplace will smoke. To test this, dry-lay the new courses inside the firebox, and outside on the hearth. Light a large piece of paper or a cigarette and stick it into the opening to see if the smoke goes up or comes out into the room. In most cases,

you will not be able to raise the hearth by more than two or three bricks without causing this undesirable condition.

Once you determine that the height of the new hearth and firebox interior will not create problems, lay the brick in a ⅜ to ½ inch bed of mortar. Outline the area to be bricked in, and then fill in. If laying a second course, offset the second course by half a brick to create a running bond pattern. Do not tool the mortar joints, or they will be difficult to keep clean.

You undoubtedly will need to cut or break the brick to get some of the sizes you need. For even, smooth edges, follow these steps:

(1) lay the brick on a smooth solid surface;
(2) score the brick where it is to be cut;
(3) using a wide brick chisel and a ball peen hammer, tap on the chisel—do not try to break the brick on the first blow;
(4) turn the brick over, tap on the opposite side in the same manner;
(5) the brick usually will snap in two.

MANTELS

As with the hearth, the design of the mantel can range from simple, classic lines to an ornate, overwhelming feature—anything from a very simple wooden beam to an elaborately carved and decorated showpiece that sets off a room of provincial decor.

The style and scale of a mantel should be appropriate to the style and scale of the room or the piece will look out of place.

In the early history of the fireplace, the mantel was used as a warming shelf upon which to place food and keep it warm while the rest of the meal was cooking. In those days, the fireplace was used both as the dwelling's central heating system and as the only means of cooking. This meant that the mantel also was a heat reflector, bouncing out into the room the heat that was rising from the firebox.

The mantel has also been one area of the fireplace that craftsmen have traditionally worked and elaborated upon, creating ornately columned and and sculptured pieces of art with which to surround the fireplace opening. Such mantels were and are a decorative focal point of a room. On the other hand, even a simple slab mantel applied to a fireplace can draw the eye, add personality to the room, and provide a shelf on which to display collectibles.

Adding a Mantel

Solid-surfaced front fireplace. The solid-surfaced front fireplace is straight up and down, without any position for a mantel. If you wish to add a mantel it can be done quite easily; the effect will completely change the appearance of the fireplace. Actually, all you are doing is adding a shelf.

The first step is to measure the width of the opening. The mantel should be about three to six inches longer than the opening on each side. Use of a 2x6 will result in a good-looking mantel, but for a larger fireplace you may need to work with a larger piece of lumber, such as a 4x6 (or even larger). This can be either a rough-sawn wood such as oak or white cedar or,

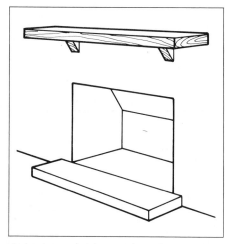

A simple wood slab mantel may be added to a solid-surfaced front fireplace to give display space and help deflect warmth into the room.

for a more traditional mantel, surfaced stock such as walnut. In either case, the mantel is supported on wooden brackets fastened to the masonry front of the fireplace. These brackets should be of 2x6 stock. The simplest way to create them is to cut diagonally across a square block of 2x6 to produce two brackets. A three-to-four foot mantel usually requires only two brackets, one supporting each end. Longer mantels need at least one bracket to support the middle; better support would be four brackets spaced equally under the mantel. The brackets can be cut into curved and elaborate shapes, as shown, using a sabre or band saw. They can be further decorated by shaping the outside edges, using a router or sander.

To fasten the brackets, drill counter-bored holes in the brackets to hold long lag screws. Then bore holes in the masonry front, using a carbide tipped masonry bit, and insert masonry anchors. Fasten the brackets in place, securing the long lag screws into the masonry anchors. The holes in the front of the brackets can be filled with pieces of wooden dowel tapped in flush and sanded smooth. For a more decorative look, use chair plugs. These tapered plugs fit in the holes and have rounded heads that protrude above the wood surface.

Place the mantel beam on the brackets, fasten in place with countersunk screws either inserted through the brackets or the mantel beam shelf, depending on the thickness of the brackets and beam.

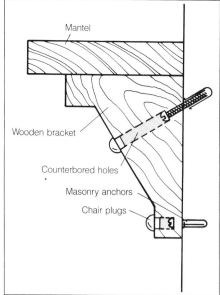

Support brackets for a slab mantel are held by bolts set in masonry anchors. The deep, counterbored holes are hidden by wooden plugs.

If the mantel is to be rough-sawn, stain it with a sealing stain and leave it as is for a rough-hewn look. A finished mantel, however, should be stained and finished with varnish as needed to suit other wood trim in the room.

Creating a Larger Mantel

Another method for creating a new mantel is to build a wooden box over an old mantel to enlarge it and change it entirely. Shown in the accompanying drawing is a basic fireplace which was changed by

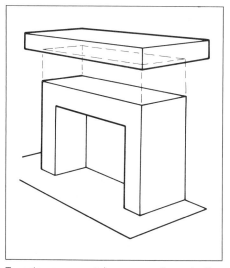

To enlarge a mantel on a small, projecting surround, build a box frame and top and nail the unit to the old mantel.

this method. The mantel shown is just a wooden box made of roughsawn 1x12s. It fits over the old mantel and up against the front and sides of the fireplace. The main thing is to make sure the mantel is tightly fitted to the fireplace so there are no open holes through which mice can crawl. When the author removed an old mantel on his fireplace, the hollow space in it literally was filled with mouse nests.

Construct the mantel box, placing it carefully in position on the fireplace to measure for an exact fit. Remove it; stain and finish the box to suit. Then install the box in place, screwing it firmly into the surrounding wooden frame members—or use screws in masonry anchors. Make sure it is level in all directions and that it follows the lines of the bricks or stone on the fireplace front. The mantel would look peculiar resting at an angle on the fireplace, even though it were sitting perfectly flat on the top brick. The design of this type of mantel can be changed by putting drawers, storage spaces or even a small book shelf into the box.

Prebuilt Mantels

If you do not have a mantel, but you do not want to build one from scratch, there are ready-made mantels available. Such mantels can be installed with simple household tools and come with instructions. These mantels can range from handsome wooden shelf systems offered by Holly Mills and Lyon Wood Supply to the ornate, carved, sculpted, Victorian, Early French or Roman style marble mantels offered by Gorman Inc. These are also easily installed with the brackets supplied with the mantelpiece. A list of manufacturers of these units (and their addresses) can be found at the back of this book.

Removing Mantel for Flush Face

Since a mantel is not a necessity today—few homeowners, if any, use it as a food warming shelf—you can often update a fireplace by removing an old mantel. This can give the room a more spacious feeling and can complement either a modern or formal decorative scheme.

If the fireplace has a flat front, removing the mantel involves gently pulling it out of the wallboard or plaster. Start with a pry bar or hammer claw. Once you have dislodged the mantel a little, you can hammer wedges between the mantel and the wall. This enables you to withdraw the mantel with less damage to the wall than just ripping out the mantel. If your fireplace is built into a wall with a floor-to-ceiling stone or brick face, then removal of the mantel would be difficult without damage to the existing material.

If the front has a recessed top for the mantel, fill in above the mantel using 2x4 framing covered with sheetrock or wallboard. You can cover the fireplace front with a suitable style of paneling (see Chapters 2 and 5) and then apply molding to surround the opening of the fireplace. Apply a matching molding design directly above the fireplace opening. This combination of molding and paneling offers a traditional touch, especially if your entire room is paneled and molding applied in the same style all around the room.

In conjunction with the molding, you might want to use a decorative ceramic tile to surround the fireplace opening. Apply it with mastic and grouting. Edge the outsides of the tile with thin molding and the fireplace will become a self-contained, compelling room feature. You might even consider combining materials such as ceramic tile and marble as shown to create the simple elegance of an ultra modern fireplace.

The Right Mantel Style

When adding or replacing a mantel, plan carefully so the fireplace will blend well with your style of interior decor. The wrong mantel over a fireplace will create an imbalance in a room. If your decor happens to be Early American, a rustic dark, wooden beam is the right mantel, and with the correct style of fireplace accessories and wrought iron cooking utensils, the fireplace will give the feeling of Early Americana. This same attention to stylistic consistency is also required with an elaborate Victorian style mantel. Make sure all your fireplace accessories match, because conflicting styles will not harmonize.

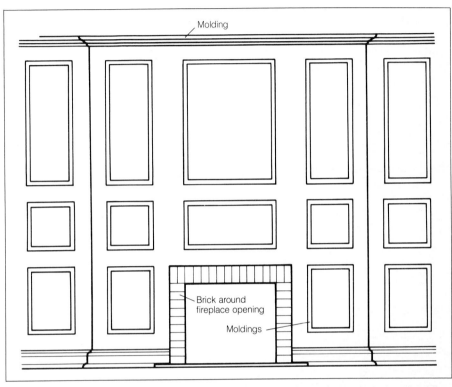

A plain, flat-faced surround may be turned into a more elegant wall with the application of molding. The brick around the opening has been left exposed as required by codes.

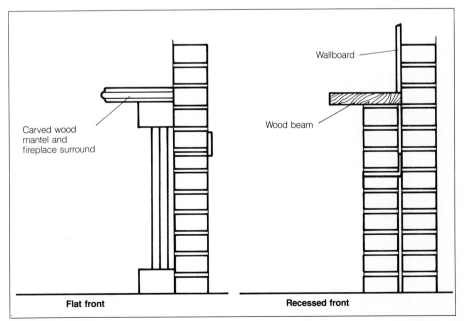

Changes to hearths and mantels are easier on a flat-faced fireplace, because adaptations to recessed-front fireplaces are limited by the thrust of the surround.

5

RENOVATING THE OLDER FIREPLACE

Not all fireplaces are beautiful. When you move into a new house, the fireplace may appear to have a certain charm. However, once the decorating has been completed, what started out as "one of the finest features of the home" has become a dull, off-color, eyesore. Over the years, with repeated use and additional decorations added, the mantel ends up beaten and chipped. The fireplace has fallen behind the rest of the house in renovation. You may need to replace a few bricks and some mortar, even if not the entire firebrick lining, the damper, or maybe just an old, worn-out grate.

CLEANUP TIME

If you have recently acquired a home with an existing fireplace, cleaning it up may be the first item on your fireplace fix-up list. Cleaning brick can be a simple operation, involving some hard scrubbing and removal of soot and dirt that has accumulated above the hearth. If the fireplace has been painted, you will be faced with a slightly more complicated job of stripping off the layers of paint and then additional hard scrubbing to bring the brick back to its original quality and appearance.

If you only want or need to clean the brick and masonry work of soot and dirt buildups, you will need some heavy steel wool, a wire brush, heavy detergent such as TSP (Tri-Sodium Phosphate) or Spic N' Span, and a strong arm. Mix a good quantity of detergent and water; take the steel wool and dip it into the solution. Scrub the brick, using a swirling motion. This helps clean out the little pores in the brick and whitens the cement joints. It also avoids scratching and chipping the brick, which might occur if a sand blaster were used. If the bricks are smooth, then probably you can clean them easily with only steel wool. However, if the bricks are rough (such as "used bricks" or other similar surfaces) you may have to use a wire bristle brush to get all the dirt from the cracks and crevices. A small brass bristle brush such as is sold for cleaning automobile tires is an excellent choice; it does not scratch the brick surface as does a steel bristle. Brass bristles also will not cause future rust stains, which can happen if tiny pieces of steel wool are left embedded in a roughened brick surface.

Stripping Paint

If the brickwork was at one time painted over, either to have matched the colors of the surrounding walls or to make it stand out in the room even more, removing the paint and restoring the natural brick face become nearly the same process, with only a few more steps added. In addition to the steel wool, you will need a bristle brush, detergent, paint stripper (a thick brand, not a thin mixture that will run down the brick and drop all over the hearth—probably the best choice is a stripper called BIX), a paint brush, paper towels and a pan. Wear neoprene gloves to protect your hands from the chemicals and detergents. Do not use a normal

A fireplace that gets consistent use will eventually get smoke-smudged. Regular care is needed to keep it attractive.

Routine cleaning includes scrubbing with a brass-bristled brush and TSP to remove smoke film. Cracks in mortar must be repaired, too, to keep the fireplace safe for use.

rubber glove; the paint stripper will dissolve the gloves after a short period of time.

The first step is to place a drop cloth on the floor around the fireplace. In addition, you should protect adjacent walls. Paint stripper is very strong, and can damage nearly everything with which it comes in contact. It is especially important to cover all surrounding painted wood surfaces. This can be done with newspaper and wide strips of masking tape.

Pour a sufficient amount of stripper in the pan, and use the paint brush to dab it onto the brick. Put a thick layer on, applying it in only one direction, and cover the entire masonry work. Let the stripper sit for fifteen to twenty minutes, but no longer than that. Test the stripper to see if it has started to loosen the paint from the fireplace. If it has not, apply more stripper to prevent the first coat from drying out; wait a little longer. Do not allow the stripper to dry out at any time, or you will have a real problem in removing it entirely. On the other hand, allow enough time to ensure that the stripper has loosened the paint. If there are several layers of paint, only try to remove one layer at a time. In many cases, paints of different composition— such as latex over oil—will stop the stripper, allowing it to work on only one coat. To handle this situation, remove the first coat of paint with the stripper and then repeat as necessary.

Once the stripper has soaked into the paint and brick, scrape the surface with either a scraper or brush, removing as much of the paint as possible. Now dip a pad of heavy steel wool into the stripper and scrub the brick briskly, in a steady, swirling motion. This will help loosen paint which has become set into the small pockmarks of the brick.

After waiting a short while longer to let the stripper soak in again, clean off the brick with fresh towels. Try to make each wipe with a fresh section of towel.

If there were many coats of paint, and it is still thick in spots, repeat the process with the steel wool and stripper, following up with several wipes with the paper towels. If the paint requires more work, then the brush may need to be applied once again. When the paint reaches a thin, filmy layer, dip the steel wool into the stripper and swirl it on. Let it sit. This time, do not wipe it off with the towels. Mix a half a cup of TSP to a gallon of water. Soak a fresh pad of steel wool in the solution. Scrub the brick thoroughly, following it with a rinse of fresh water. Do this as often as necessary until the brick has achieved a used, but natural, appearance. Check that all the stripper has been washed off the brick surface. Otherwise, it will continue to flake and can cause hard-to-remove stains.

BRICK AND MORTAR REPAIRS

After cleaning the brick, you may find other points of needed repair, both on the interior masonry work and on the exterior fireplace or chimney masonry work. It is important that these be repaired, especially if the brick and cement has been cracked, chipped, and otherwise damaged on the outside. In a colder climate, the intense cold of the winter and the heat of the summer will make the brick and cement swell and shrink, causing cracks and chipping. Without any repair, the fireplace will become damaged; it could even become inoperable or unsafe.

Interior Work

Start with the brick on the interior, beginning with the hearth, and check for loose mortar. If you find loose mortar, or if pieces of it are missing, clean out—or chip out—the cracked and loose portions. Brush off any remaining particles. Then moisten the exposed brick with water. This will cut down on moisture absorption from the fresh mortar by the dry brick.

Mix up a mortar mix consisting of 1 part portland cement, 3 parts sand and ¼ part hydrated lime. Add water until the mixture is pliable and thoroughly mixed, yet will stand up and hold its shape when pulled up into a pile with a mixing hoe. Incidentally, you can use mortar cement instead of mixing portland cement and lime. Apply this to the joint(s) that have been damaged, using a small pointing trowel to lay the mortar between the bricks. Pack it in tight, and then use a spoon or dowel—or better yet, a mason's jointer—to pack the cement in even tighter and to smooth out the material to a grooved, uniform appearance to match the rest of the mortar work.

Exterior Work

This method applies to the exterior brick-work also. If you discover bricks that have cracked in two, or with large chunks missing (or even an entirely missing brick), then you must remove what is left of that one brick. Clean the area out; moisten; then, on the bottom and sides of

The broad mortar joints in a stone fireplace may crack as the foundation naturally settles. The cracks should be widened slightly and then filled with fresh mortar to seal spaces.

Mortar for tuckpointing can be mixed in a small wheelbarrow. Joints and bricks (or stones) must be moist before applying mortar.

the space, apply the cement mixed according to the formula given above. Lay the brick on the cement and tap it down, settling the brick firmly onto the cement. With the trowel, scrape off the excess cement. Next, just as you would for the inside brickwork, lay down the top layer of cement, placing it in the joints. Use a spoon, dowel or jointer to smooth and groove the mortar joint.

Sometimes you will start on the outside repairs and find that you must completely rebuild the top portion of the chimney because of damage due to weather exposure. Check not only the visible chimney portion, but also sections that run through the attic. Loose and missing mortar in this area can be a fire hazard, especially if you are unlucky enough to have a chimney fire. Examine also the locations at

which the chimney goes through the ceiling and house roof. Thoroughly patch any loose mortar joints, and repair. Look for stains on a chimney in an attic; this could indicate an unsafe chimney.

Whether you are working on the interior fireplace facing, on the exterior, or the chimney, always wear protective goggles or a face shield when chipping mortar joints to prevent flying mortar chunks

Begin making harness by wrapping a length of sturdy rope, such as a braided nylon climbing or nautical lifeline rope, around the waist—twice.

Each end of the rope is looped twice around the double thickness at the waist, then drawn back through the beginning of the loop in a modified Tarbuck knot.

The ends are looped in front, drawn to the back and crossed, then brought down over the shoulders and pulled through the doubled rope at the waist.

Now loop the end of the rope around both shoulder and waist lines, pulling the ends through the first loop to complete the knot—a modified Tarbuck.

To secure all the knots and prevent any possible slippage, tie a square knot and pull it against the Tarbuck knot. Leave enough slack for comfort.

Attach safety line—a very strong, sturdy rope that will withstand friction from the eaves, shingles and ridge—with a Tarbuck knot as shown here.

A roof is a dangerous place to work. Even a slight slope may cause a person to feel insecure. A rope harness will distribute pressure on the back should you fall. Leave little slack in the safety line; adjust slack each time you change position on the roof. Use sturdy rope. Climbing rope will withstand friction. It is expensive but a life-saving investment.

Obvious water seepage indicates need for major repairs. All joints are cleaned and filled. An easier job in this attic space.

from injuring your eyes. When working up on the roof, wear shoes such as tennis shoes or other rubber-soled shoes. Use a chicken ladder, or other type of roofing ladder, and rig a safety harness for your body—fasten it securely to something solid. A simple but secure harness can be made with a rope and a length of 2x4. Take a 2x4 at least one foot longer than the width of a window on the opposite side of the house from the chimney. Lay the board across the inside of the opened window, flat side against the window frame. Tie a long, sturdy rope around the

center of the 2x4. Throw the other end of the rope over the roof to the chimney side. When you climb up on the roof, double wrap and knot the rope around your waist, then loop the end of the rope around the chimney twice. Keep other people in the household well away from the area below where you are working. Someone could be injured easily by falling debris or a dropped tool.

Although outside repairs will soon weather and blend in with the older work, the inside, once repaired, will not do so. If you have repaired the mortar on the fireplace inside the dwelling, you will clearly be able to distinguish between the new mortar and the old. To avoid this, and to give the fireplace a fresh look, mix a paste of portland cement and brush it on all the joints of the masonry work. It will dry and the fireplace will appear much newer. Any excess mortar that gets on the bricks can be cleaned off with a brass bristle brush, a little water and TSP.

Chimney cap. Once the brick or mortar has been repaired, check the top section of the chimney—especially the chimney cap. If the cap is slightly cracked or chipped, mix portland cement and water into a thin paste and brush the mixture evenly onto the cap. In the event that the cap is badly cracked or portions are missing, you might be better off chipping the remainder away with a masonry chisel and heavy hammer (again wearing safety glasses); then rebuild the cap as shown in the drawing, using a good mix of mortar. If the structure of the cap has been damaged, you probably will need a new one.

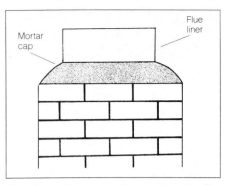

The ideal chimney cap is one where the flue liner rises above the masonry and the joint is sealed with a sloping mortar cap.

This chimney requires both tuckpointing and some reconstruction. Clearing joints for pointing reveals weak mortar.

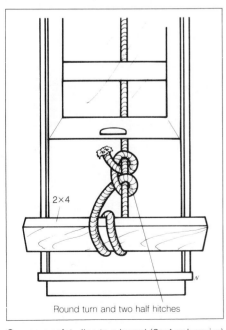

Round turn and two half hitches

Secure a safety line to a board (2×4 or heavier) overlapping inside window frame. Stress on knots will tighten them.

If mortar repairs are necessary, you should coat all joints of the fireplace so that repairs are not conspicuous.

The top courses of this chimney require total reconstruction. Lower courses, more protected from the elements, only need repair.

Moisten brick and mortar joints before repair or they will pull moisture from new mortar too quickly for good and firm curing.

If reusing old bricks, clean them of all old mortar. The claw end of a mason's hammer will chip the mortar free.

Rebuild the upper courses before beginning general tuckpointing repairs. Check level and plumb as you build.

Fill all mortar joints that have been cleaned out. Force as much mortar as possible into joints with a trowel.

Finish the joints by tooling them smooth. Scrape all excess mortar from the brick with the trowel. Get brick as clean as possible.

A reinstalled stone cap overhangs brickwork to protect it from rain. The cap needs a mortar wash coat; the crack must be filled.

The flashing around the chimney base and between the masonry and the roof must be sealed with roofing cement.

Finally, the masonry is cleaned of excess mortar and the whole chimney is brushed with a liquid masonry sealer.

Next, look at the flashing that covers the area where the chimney passes through the roof. Although the flashing is merely tacked and tarred down on the roof itself, it is embedded in the mortar joints of the chimney and, as a result, is actually very hard to replace. If it has separated from the roof, tack it back down and seal with roofing compound (asphalt cement). You also may have to tuckpoint the mortar joints at the flashing, or you may be able to seal the joints with caulk. To clean up the metal, wash the flashing and then rub vinegar on it to neutralize the galvanizing. Then rinse with clear water and paint the metal with a brand intended for use with galvanized metal. If the flashing has separated completely from the chimney, you might be faced with having to contact a contractor. The flashing itself might need to be replaced.

Sealing the brickwork. After making repairs, seal the exterior brickwork of the fireplace and chimney. Use a high-quality clear masonry waterproofing sealer (available from most home centers). The sealer may be brushed, rolled or sprayed on. The sealer should cover the entire brick structure, including the cap. This application should become a yearly ritual for anyone who lives in a cold climate. It is a good preventive measure that ensures less frequent repairs and a longer life for the fireplace.

Caulking. One very important maintenance job for older fireplaces is caulking and sealing around edges where the masonry joins the framing of the house. In many cases, the framing surrounding fireplaces of older homes will have shrunk. This can leave gaps and holes that allow a lot of heat to escape. These are best sealed using a latex caulking cartridge in a caulking gun. Cut about ¼ inch off the top of the cartridge; then, starting at the bottom joint between fireplace masonry and the house siding, apply the caulk with a gentle squeeze. At the same time, bring the gun up in a smooth, even, continuous motion. Fill all cracks and crevices.

Firebrick

If the firebrick lining in the firebox has broken or become cracked, do not use the fireplace until the firebrick area has been repaired or replaced completely. This can be done in the same method as for regular

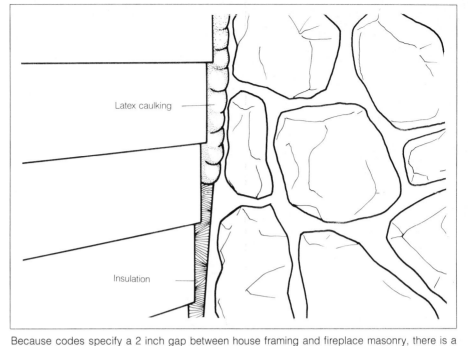

Because codes specify a 2 inch gap between house framing and fireplace masonry, there is a space to be filled and sealed. The gap should be filled with noncombustible insulation such as fiberglass. The joint should be filled with flexible (latex or other) caulk.

brick but using firebrick high-temperature cement instead of the regular mortar. You may even wish to replace the entire firebrick lining. Find the nearest fireplace dealer who distributes prefabricated firebrick linings and see if they have the right size to fit your fireplace. Although prefab liners do not come in every size, there may be one that will fit your fireplace. It is much easier and cheaper to use a prefab liner than to have a masonry contractor do the work by hand. Also, if you should happen to have a zero-clearance fireplace without any firebrick lining or with a damaged one, the prefab liner comes in a size for nearly every style of zero-clearance fireplace. Prefabs may soon be available in enough different sizes that the homeowner may replace the firebrick lining for a masonry fireplace of any size.

DAMPERS

Many older fireplaces were built without dampers. Some old dampers are so encrusted with mortar, creosote or debris that the plates need to be replaced.

If your fireplace has no damper, installation of one should be your next major fireplace concern. This actually is neither a large nor a difficult project. There are many firms that make dampers to fit any size fireplace; these dampers install easily without special tools or professional help—although a little expert assistance never hurts. However, one way to install

a damper cheaply, yet effectively, is to build a simple one yourself. For those of you with the necessary equipment and skills, this would be a feasible project.

Homemade Version

First, measure the flue opening or the throat of the firebox, both length and width. Weld together a damper by joining two pieces of ⅛ inch steel flat plate, so the pieces meet at right angles. The pieces should be ½ inch shorter than the throat from side to side. The width of the plate pieces should be just a bit more than the front-to-back opening of the throat. Drill a hole on one of the flat sides at the mid-point, drilling at a slight angle, Put a 2-to-3 inch long closed eyebolt in the hole, using a nut on each side of the angle iron to hold the eyebolt in place. Once it is cinched down tight, it should rest at a slight angle, not straight up and down. Then, with a light piece of steel rod (roughly a foot or so long, depending on just how high up in the flue the damper is going to be) fashion a large loop at one end to use as a handle, and a small loop at the other end to insert into the eyebolt. Insert through the eyebolt and close the small loop over the eyebolt. The angle iron can now be placed on the smokeshelf where the damper would sit, laying flat on the side without the eyebolt. With a light tug on the large loop, it will flip over and close off the flue, with the angled eyebolt

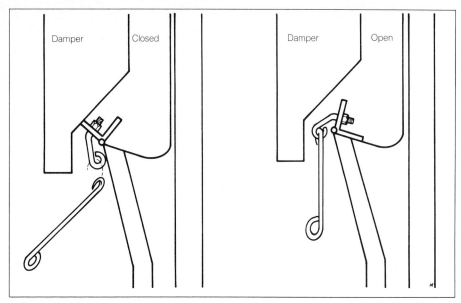

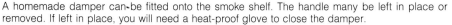

A homemade damper can be fitted onto the smoke shelf. The handle many be left in place or removed. If left in place, you will need a heat-proof glove to close the damper.

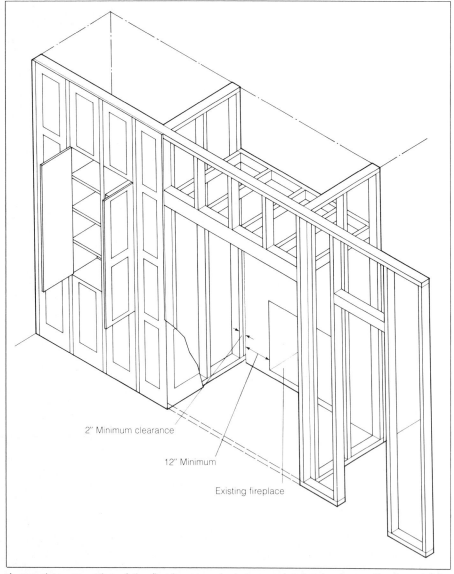

A complete renovation of the fireplace may include new framing to change the focus of the fireplace and provide storage shelves and/or a closet. Fireplace jambs must be at least 12 inches wide and there must be a 2 inch space between the masonry and the 2×4 framing.

resting against the far side of the flue, keeping it in place. Push up on it, and the iron will flip back over, opening the flue to use. The eyebolt may need to be adjusted to the correct length so it will work properly and sit tightly in place once closed.

If your fireplace already has a damper, but it is not closing tightly, replace the damper plate. The plate should lift up, tilt, and come out of the frame. This will be messy and you will probably get very dirty, since this job calls for kneeling in the firebox and reaching up to lift out the plate. Wear old clothing, glasses or goggles, and cover your nose and mouth to protect yourself against soot. Take the damper plate to a fireplace dealer, a metal fabricating plant, a sheet metal shop, or, if you have one, a blacksmith, for a duplicate replacement, then install.

Manufactured Device

Another way to install a fireplace damper is to use a "damper chimney hood", produced by G. W. Fisher and Associates. This device is a damper with a long extension rod handle that goes through the length of the chimney and up the flue. This rod will, with a push or pull, open or close the damper on top of the chimney. This gadget actually takes little time to install, no special tools or operations, and will act as both a damper to keep heated home air from escaping, and as a hood to keep outside elements out of the fireplace and chimney.

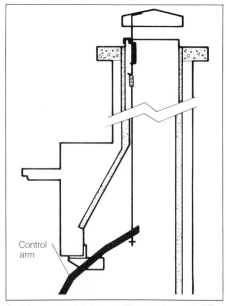

A chimney cap/damper will not only control fire drafts, seal out cold air and keep out debris and small animals.

6

BUILDING
A STONE FIREPLACE

A fireplace may seem like a costly investment, but in most cases the materials comprise only about half the cost—and when building with stone, the cost of materials may end up even less. By building it yourself, you can save a great deal of money.

The fireplace described in this chapter took less money to build than might be expected. The firebox, a prefabricated unit, cost $500. The materials for the foundation cost $700. The stone was available to the author/builder at no cost and other materials cost $200. Had a contractor built this same fireplace as described here, there would have been additional costs of at least $2,300. To determine current base costs, consult a fireplace dealer or a Sears Roebuck or Montgomery Ward catalog for the cost of the prefabricated metal liner; check with the appropriate builders supply company for the cost of block, concrete, support ties, mortar, brick, and flue tile.

Building a fireplace, regardless of whether you use stone or brick, is not a job to be undertaken casually. It requires a great deal of time, patience and determination. It will take a considerable amount of your time to construct a project such as the one shown in this chapter.

This stone fireplace is actually a stone-enclosed, prefabricated fireplace installed outside the house on a new, separate footing and foundation with an ashpit. The house wall was opened—and reframed to meet the required clearances—so the face of the prefabricated unit could fit a few inches inside the room. This type of installation was required because of the mass and weight of the stone.

Builders frequently suggest a masonry surround for a prefabricated fireplace rather than a masonry fireplace built from scratch because it is easier, more dependable in engineering and is subject to fewer structural limitations. This stone fireplace could have been included anywhere in the house—if it were all new construction. However, placing this stone-faced fireplace and chimney on an exterior base meant that there was no need for major reconstruction of the basement floor, floor/ceiling joists, or the roof.

This natural stone fireplace took about three months for the owner to build, working only an hour or two each day plus weekends. Because work began late in the fall, the fireplace itself was constructed first, as was the fireplace front on the inside. The block chimney was also completed early. However, the surrounding walls, raised rock hearth, air ductwork, and outside stone veneer were left until the following spring.

PLANNING

Careful planning is a must for building a fireplace. Unlike a bookcase or cabinet, you cannot move a fireplace once it is in position. The weight of even a small natural stone fireplace will run many tons, putting quite a load on the ground.

In most cases you will need to submit a plan to the building authorities and acquire a permit.

Complex construction is required for a traditional masonry fireplace built on the outside with an opening through the wall on an existing home. A fireplace and chimney in the center of a room—or even in the center of a house—may be easier to build and is much more heat efficient. An advantage of a fireplace on the outside and built flush to the interior wall is that you do not use up as much floor space;

cutting openings through the floor, ceiling and roof also is avoided. Assuring an adequate foundation for an inside fireplace can also be a problem in an existing home. The direction the floor joists run is another concern with an inside fireplace, requiring attention during the planning stage. If the joists run at right angles to the fireplace wall you will need a lot more supporting framing when cutting very far into the room floor. On the other hand, joists running parallel with the fireplace wall enable you to go farther into the room without as much support framing.

Size of the Opening

You will have to determine your dimensions depending upon your room and available space. One of the most important considerations when designing your own fireplace is the size of the opening. Here is a good rule of thumb for matching the opening width to the room size: (1) add the room length and width together for a total number of feet; (2) allow one inch of fireplace opening for each of the total—i.e., a 12x24 foot room would need a 36 inch wide (12+24=36) opening. The height of the opening will depend upon the width and the overall design of the firebox and the wall. Refer to chart in Chapter 3 for recommended

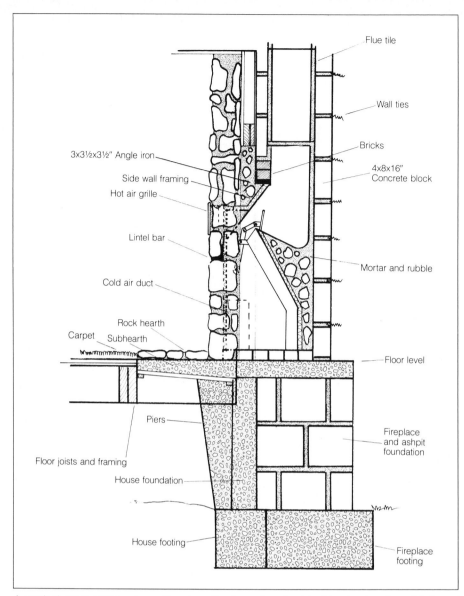

Flue tile

Wall ties

3x3½x3½" Angle iron

Side wall framing

Hot air grille

Bricks

4x8x16"
Concrete block

Lintel bar

Cold air duct

Mortar and rubble

Rock hearth

Carpet   Subhearth

Floor level

Piers

Floor joists and framing

House foundation

Fireplace
and ashpit
foundation

House footing

Fireplace
footing

A vertical cross-section shows the stone fireplace described in this chapter. A prefabricated firebox was used and set on a new foundation just outside the home.

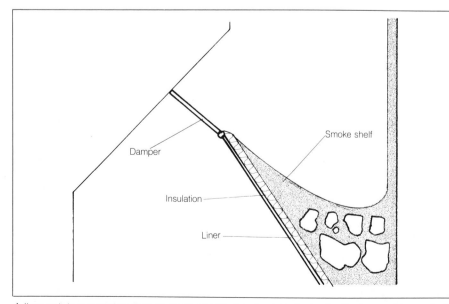

Damper

Smoke shelf

Insulation

Liner

A liner unit is a complete firebox. Back and front walls slope for heat reflection and to create the throat. Space behind back is filled and shaped into the smoke shelf.

proportions. A fireplace of this width can combine dramatically with other elements to create the dominant wall in the room.

Liner Unit

There are probably as many different ways to build fireplaces as there are masons, and there are many existing improperly constructed fireplaces, which are not only smoky, but dangerous. We recommend use of a preformed metal liner unit, whether doing construction yourself or hiring a contractor. The best types, such as the unit shown in this chapter, utilize an interior liner of ribbed boiler plate and an outside shell of metal. This provides an air-filled heat chamber around the firebox, which acts as a heat exchanger and sends the warmed air into the room. Side ducts bring in cool air, which is heated and then discharged into the dwelling. The ducts are fitted with fan motors to provide a more efficient exchange of air. The old-fashioned fireplace is only about 10 percent efficient, whereas this type is nearly 25 percent efficient. Heat can circulate to all corners of the room, and into other rooms, depending upon how the ductwork and vents are arranged.

There are additional advantages to use of a preformed unit. The double-walled steel unit comes complete with firebox, throat, smoke dome and a properly hinged and operating damper. Most also come complete with a construction guide that eliminates most confusion and should minimize installation errors.

Smoke shelf and damper. One of the problem areas when constructing a fireplace is the smoke shelf/damper, since these area dimensions and shapes are critical. By using a preshaped unit, these details are already constructed for you. The units are properly engineered and built with correct angles and dimensions. This eliminates construction mistakes. The damper is pivoted at the proper point and swings backward to an open position, providing a well-designed smoke shelf (preventing downdraft and smoke problems).

MATERIALS

A fireplace can be constructed from a wide choice of masonry materials, including many different kinds of brick as well as natural stone. The fireplace shown was constructed using a preformed unit, natural field stone for the front, the surrounding wall lining and the raised hearth, and around cold air ducts. The chimney was constructed of concrete block with a field stone veneer over this.

Natural Field Stone

Not just any rock will do. Natural field stones are the best choice for this type of job, and they are just what they sound like—stones that have been picked up from a field. To build a project as large as this takes a great many stones of many sizes—both large and small—of different shapes. For easiest handling, try to find stones 3 to 4 inches thick. In fact, for many homeowners the acquisition of enough good stone may be the biggest obstacle to the job. For others it will be quite simple.

In some parts of the country you could find enough stones out in your backyard. There are, however, many other places to acquire stone. If you live in an area where the stone is found naturally, you may be able to purchase the stone from a rural landowner for a fraction of the cost of what it normally costs from a building supply dealer. Many farmers would be willing to give them away. You will probably have to do the finding and hauling yourself, and that can be a hard task. Another likely spot to look for stone is a nearby construction site. Many developers will be glad to let you have the stones that have been dug up, since they have to pay to have them hauled away from the site.

Most larger cities have stone companies which specialize in stone used for this type of construction. A look in the yellow pages under "Stone" will give you an idea of what is in your area.

The best stones are field stones (most often round) with natural corners and good square edges, but a mixture of stones can also be used to create decorative effects. These also vary considerably in color; if properly selected they can create interesting effects. Use one type of stone primarily to keep the design from looking like a hodgepodge. Always have on hand plenty of square-corner rocks for use on corners. This makes the job much easier.

Hints on working with stone. Before getting into the actual construction methods, here are a few tips about working with stone. Stone masonry is addictive, and once you tackle and complete one project you will be looking for more. It is one of the most satisfying of construction jobs, yet at times it can also be one of the most frustrating. This is partly due to the weight of the stones and mortar, which means you can build only a little bit at a time. Then the mortar must set before you can proceed to the next layer or course of stones. In addition, it takes a fairly good eye to pick out the stones that will fit together properly for a good-looking, sturdy stone construction. Anyone who has laid stone knows that you can never have enough stones from which to choose. (However, this also means that when the job is over, there will be many stones to get rid of.)

Building with stone is a job almost anyone can do with a little practice. It takes few special tools. You may be amazed at how accomplished you become after only a little work on a project such as a fireplace. The main guideline for stone work is to stagger the courses, much like brickwork; the rule is that two stones go above one, and one above two. They should all overlap to provide strength. In addition, the method of pointing the joints (discussed later) will be important to the project's strength.

Synthetic stone is fireproof, usually lightweight, and relatively easy to handle. Do not combine it with real stone.

Synthetic Stone

An alternative is to utilize synthetic stone on areas that are far enough away from the firebox. If you do, make sure the stone is rated for use with fireplaces. Some are made of a lightweight mortar material, others from fiberglass. These can be mixed in with the natural field stones if the appearance of the materials is compatible; they usually do not combine well.

Mortar and Sand

It is hard to estimate the amount of sand and masonry cement needed, so just start out with a fixed amount and purchase more as you need it. Cement is hard to store for a long period and over time will lose its strength. If you decide to color the mortar, such as in the fireplace shown, you will also need mortar color. (See also Chapter 5.)

TOOLS

The tools that are needed for stonework are not complicated. Naturally, a powered cement mixer will make mixing the

When building with stone—either found stone or rubble-quarried stone—the most important consideration is finding stones that will fit together to make firm and secure courses.

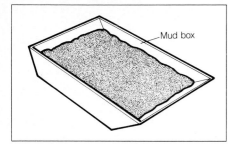

It is convenient to mix mortar in a mud box. The angled end allows you to pull a hoe through the mix and turn it easily.

mortar easier but it is not very difficult to do by hand. You usually can rent a power mixer. However, because of the time involved in building a project such as a stone fireplace, it might be less expensive to purchase one. On the other hand, the small batches of mortar that are required for this type of construction also can be mixed in a wheelbarrow, or in a mud box and shoveled into a wheelbarrow. If mixing in this manner, an old hoe with holes cut in the flat end makes a good mixing tool.

You will need a mortar board, which is nothing more than a board (approximately 16x16 inches) with a handle fastened in the center. You can create one easily from ¼ inch plywood. Cover it with a good paint to prevent moisture from being pulled out from the mortar by the wood. Attach a piece of a closet dowel, or 1¾x6 inch block, using a flathead countersunk wood screw. A small (24 inch x 24 inch) platform, resting on sawhorses or concrete blocks, also works well.

Because you will need a surface on which to set the mortar board while selecting stones, find an open-ended box, or even an old bucket, for this purpose. In addition, you will need a couple of pointed trowels, a carpenter's level, and carpenter's tools for framing in the open-

ing, a hacksaw for cutting reinforcing rod, a whisk broom, steel brush and plastic buckets for cleaning up, and an old round head bolt for pointing the joints (or you can buy an inexpensive joint tool). You will need access to clean water, and scaffolding to enable you to work safely on the chimney as you build upward.

FOOTING AND FOUNDATION
Opening the Wall

With all plans, materials and tools on hand, the first step is to lay out the wall opening or the floor openings, depending on fireplace locations. If your fireplace is built flush on an exterior wall, you can build the chimney along the exterior of the house and avoid any major cutting of the structural members that support the floor. Adjust the opening so you will not have to cut vertically down a wall stud. Locate the studs by tapping on the wall with a hammer. A hollow sound means no stud. A dull sound usually denotes a stud. Then either drive a long nail in place to determine if there is a stud, or use a portable electric drill to bore a hole through the wall to locate the stud. Lay out and plan the framing for the wall opening. The opening will have to be large enough to allow for clearances required by building codes as well as space for insulation and stone and mortar fill. Frame the opening to ensure that the structural strength in the wall is not weakened. Double the side studs and install a double header across the top of the opening, securing the header to the cut studs with nails (see page 56).

Supporting the Fireplace

Next, measure and mark the location of the foundation. If the foundation is not constructed correctly and on firm soil, the

fireplace can settle, shift, and pull away from the house. A typical stone fireplace can weigh 20 tons or more; a larger fireplace can weigh much more. A fireplace must be built on solid rock, or on a foundation strong enough to support it.

The size of the footing will vary according to local ground conditions, frost conditions, and local building codes. It must be at least six inches wider than the dimension of the outside faces of the fireplace; on some soils it may need to be more. The depth will vary. The fireplace shown features an extremely high two-story chimney, so the footing was poured two feet deep, even though the frost line is not that deep.

The first step in creating the footing is excavation. First mark off the footing area, using stakes. Make this area at least six inches larger all around than the finished chimney and fireplace dimensions. Make the excavation quite a bit larger than needed; it's easier to work in an open excavation rather than having to try and fit boards and form stakes in too small an area. Then excavate to the proper depth. Be sure to remove all loose dirt. In case the fireplace is to be installed next to a concrete slab, excavate up to the slab and slab footing, but leave it alone. If the fireplace is next to a continuous foundation wall, you may wish to excavate under the wall foundation to add additional strength, but in most cases this won't be necessary—merely excavate next to the wall foundation. You can then utilize a cantilevered hearth on the inside of the house portion of the fireplace.

Building Forms

Once you have excavated the area, set up corner batter boards with leveled string lines to locate the corners of the

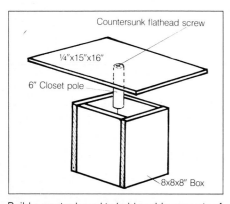

Build a mortar board to hold usable amounts of mortar while laying stone. You may hand-hold it or set it on small, hollow box.

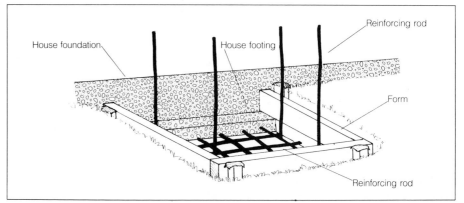

A fireplace requires a solid, reinforced footing and foundation adjacent to the house footing. Corner, vertical reinforcing will be carried up through to the top.

footing. Then drop a plumb bob from the junctions of the strings and mark the outer footing corners. Use 2x6 form boards to construct a form to hold the footing concrete in place during the pouring. Brace the form with supporting 2x4s. A footing must extend at least twelve inches below the frost line in any particular area.

Adding Reinforcing

Reinforce the foundation using ⅜ or ½ inch reinforcing rods tied into a grid pattern and spaced about eight inches apart. Support this about four to six inches from the bottom of the footing. Set it on rocks to hold it in place.

Mixing can be done by hand; however, because the volume needed to fill most footings, you may want to use ready-mix concrete. Vertical reinforcing rods should also be set into the footing while the concrete is still wet. These will help tie the fireplace to the footing. Set the vertical rods at each corner of the chimney (fireplace). Position them carefully, so they will be within the chimney walls yet not in the path of the preformed metal fireplace unit.

Correct Floor Level

One of the most important factors in planning the construction of the footing and foundation is determining proper heights. The floor of the hearth must come out level with the inside floor of the house. If the house floor is well above ground level, you will have to construct a rather high foundation; if the house utilizes a slab floor, the footing and foundation will be almost at ground level. In most cases you should measure down three inches from the desired firebox height (including firebrick); mark this level and build the masonry foundation to this height. If, as in the construction shown, the floor is much above ground level, you may wish to construct a foundation of concrete or concrete blocks filled with rubble and mortar to reach the correct height.

ASH PIT

The foundation can also contain an ash pit if you desire. In the example given here, the ash pit was eliminated because an outdoor deck was to be installed around the chimney. The drawing illustrates the proper method of constructing a masonry ash pit using concrete block and 2x6

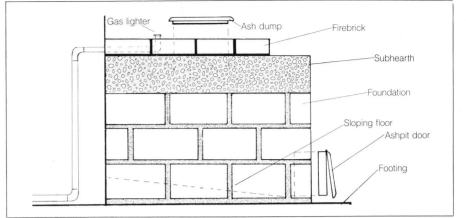

The foundation of the fireplace holds the ashpit with an exterior cleanout door. One useful feature added here is a gas pipe/fire lighter that will ignite any wood.

This fireplace was installed where an exterior deck was to be added. The foundation was filled with rubble. There is no ashpit.

After stripping off the house siding, cut through sheathing with a circular saw. Keep the saw guard on and wear protective gear.

forms. In this instance, the middle portion of the foundation or masonry-built-up foundation is left hollow, and the two sides are filled with rubble and mortar. A hole is framed with 2x6s for the ash pit door. The cleanout door is mortared firmly in place after the ash pit has cured and the 2x6s have been removed. The ash pit is poured at the same time as the subhearth. For an easy-to-clean ash pit, slope the concrete floor slightly from back to front so the ashes will slide down toward the door as you clean them out. The vertical reinforcing rods will continue up through the ash pit.

WALL AND FLOOR OPENINGS

Once the foundation has been constructed, the wall opening can be made. Because it will probably be some time before the opening is closed off, it is a good idea to have a tarp or some other covering on hand. The opening must be framed properly to support the weight. The rough opening must be much larger than the planned finished opening to allow for installing framing. Place sup-

port beams and plate as shown below to hold up the ceiling and the wall until the framing can be completed.

Cutting the Exterior

Wood or stucco. Mark the location of the opening on the outside and inside walls. Use a brace and bit with a long electrician's bit to bore through at each corner, creating corner marks. Then use a straightedge or a level to mark around the boundaries to be cut. The same method can be used to mark the opening of a stucco house. Then use a metal cutting blade in a circular saw (watch for nails) for the initial outside wall cut.

Brick. This is not an easy process, and may require hiring a professional. To cut through brick you will need to first determine the location on the outside wall, then bore the holes using a masonry bit. Use a brick hammer and brick chisel to remove the bricks between the lines. In most cases this means you will have to remove the bricks a little farther out than necessary, remortaring these bricks back in place after the chimney has been installed. In most instances you will not need reinforcing at the edges, but you should remove all bricks from floor to ceiling as you go up, to prevent sagging.

The Interior Cut

Remove the interior wallboard or plaster and lath (if in an old house) by first cutting the surface with a knife or key-hole saw and then pulling pieces away from the studs. Once the wall coverings on both sides have been removed, use a hand saw to cut out the studs at the top line. Pull the studs in and out to force them off the nails, which come up through the bottom plate. Using a hand saw and chisel, also cut through the plate on both sides, and remove it.

Build a new framing for the wall using double studs and a 2x6 double header as shown at the left and install it in place, carefully checking for plumb. Then toe-nail solidly in place.

Cutting the Flooring

After the wall has been opened and the opening framed properly, the next step is to cut away the flooring for the hearth. This also must be framed with double headers and joists, as shown. Steel joist hangers can be used instead to provide extra strength. In addition, you may wish to use concrete pier 4x4 posts to give even more support for the weight of the hearth and fireplace front. Since the fireplace shown utilizes natural stone for the side walls and cold air ducts, as well as the modified raised hearth, it was extremely heavy. Therefore, it was also supported with concrete piers poured against the foundation wall and down to the footing. If the floor joists run at right angles to the wall rather than parallel to the wall, you will need to place a heavy support beam underneath them as a preliminary step. You won't need a steel beam on a concrete slab, but over a crawl space or a basement sometimes the use of a beam can help eliminate sagging and settling.

SUBHEARTH

The actual hearth rests on a concrete subhearth. This is that portion over the foundation on which the fireplace unit sits, and which extends out into the room, underneath the hearth. The entire sub-hearth is poured concrete; the portion that fits into the room is most commonly cantilevered from the foundation. Again, make sure that the finished subhearth will allow for the firebrick portion of the hearth as well as whatever you use for the extension into the room. The ceramic tile, rock or brick used on the hearth should be flush with the floor, or come to the height you desire if building a raised hearth. The allowances are ¾ inch for tile and 2¼ inches for common brick. Dimensions for stone are based on your stone supply. Plan also on a bed of ½ inch mortar.

The subhearth should be at least six inches thick. Eight inches may be needed for a heavy fireplace. For a cantilevered forehearth, of the cantilevered portion of the hearth, install a wooden base form

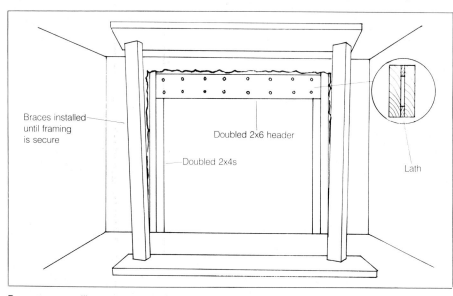

Braces installed until framing is secure

Doubled 2x6 header

Doubled 2x4s

Lath

Because you will remove supporting studs, install braces inside the house. To restore support strength to wall, install a doubled header across the top of new opening.

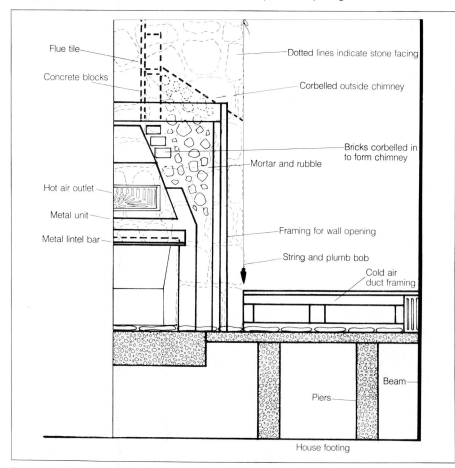

Flue tile

Concrete blocks

Dotted lines indicate stone facing

Corbelled outside chimney

Bricks corbelled in to form chimney

Mortar and rubble

Hot air outlet

Metal unit

Metal lintel bar

Framing for wall opening

String and plumb bob

Cold air duct framing

Beam

Piers

House footing

To support the increased weight on the floor joists, additional concrete piers were added to accept the stress of the concrete subhearth and stone facing on the fireplace.

Firebrick is laid on the firebox hearth area. Allow for the brick's thickness when bringing the subhearth to the level desired.

The concrete subhearth extends from below the firebox into the room as a base under the forehearth. Heavy steel rods increase the weight the concrete can support.

(see page 68) between the foundation and the doubled floor joists. This form may be left in place permanently.

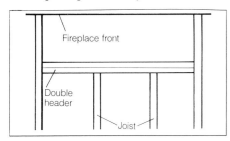

The size of the forehearth will depend to some extent upon how far into the room the fireplace unit will extend. The subhearth must provide support for a forehearth that extends a minimum of 16 inches in front of the fireplace opening. If the unit extends into the room 12 inches, the cantilevered subhearth must extend 28 inches from the house wall.

For the construction shown, the outside edge of the subhearth was framed using wood. This was left in place so it could later be used as support for a deck which would extend out from the fireplace. However, in most cases the outside will be framed with brick or block. In either case, check that all framing is level. The preformed unit must be installed level.

The area over the clean-out ash pit can be formed using wire mesh to prevent concrete from getting into that section. The subhearth must be reinforced with 3/8 inch steel rods spaced from six to eight inches apart and tied securely. These should be placed about three inches below the top of the pour, and supported securely on rocks or chunks of rubble before the concrete is poured.

Pouring the Concrete

With a little work you can mix your own. The formula for this concrete pour is: one part portland cement, two parts sand, and three parts gravel or small stone. Add only enough water to make the concrete fluid; mix well.

Allow the concrete to cure for at least seven days, preferably longer. Keep it covered with damp sacks to prevent its drying out too quickly. Note that the reinforcing vertical rods must also extend up through the subhearth, placed carefully so they will be inside the outer chimney wall with enough room left for the installation of the metal fireplace unit.

If an ash dump is to be installed in the ash pit, the ash dump door must be framed in during the framing of the forms for the subhearth.

HEARTH

After the concrete has set, you will be ready to lay the finished inside hearth. This must be installed using firebrick and special firebrick mortar which will withstand the heat of the firebox. Note that you need to install the firebrick only in the area of the firebox, and not entirely out to the sides; however, create a large firebrick-covered area on which the metal unit can sit. The firebricks are set onto a thin layer of mortar, with a thin layer in joints between bricks.

If you have planned to install an ash dump, the firebricks will be fitted around it. If you are including a gas log lighter, it also must be fitted in place at this time, using standard 1/2 inch gas pipe for a 20 inch log lighter unit with either natural or

LP gas orifices. An on-off control valve may be recessed in the hearth or the fireplace wall.

Laying the Firebrick

First, measure the area of the metal unit and mark its outline, with a pencil, onto the hearth. You must make sure all the firebricks will extend out past the outside edges of the metal unit. The mortar used is fireclay mortar, which is available at building supply dealers. Masonry cement mortar should not be used. The mortar seals the bottom of the heating unit to the firebrick, provides a means of leveling the unit, and prevents smoke from leaking out into the cold air ducts.

Mix the fireclay to the proper consistency as described on the mix package. Then trowel on a thin bed of mortar (approximately 1/4 inch thick). Then start laying the firebricks in place, positioning them in the mortar bed and leveling them by tapping lightly with a brick hammer. Keep placing a level on their tops to make sure you keep them all level and their surfaces flush. Butter between each brick as you go, again leaving about a 1/4 inch mortar joint. Once all the bricks have been laid, remove the excess with a trowel. Do not use a jointing tool to finish the joints or you will have depressions in the hearth that will be hard to clean. Instead, try to keep the hearth surface as smooth as possible.

INSTALLING THE METAL UNIT

After the firebrick has cured properly (about 24 hours) set the unit in place, centering it over the firebrick and making sure it protrudes into the room the proper amount for your particular face design. The unit can protrude as much as a foot into the room, or as little as two to three inches, depending on how far out into the room you wish the face to be. The normal distance would be about eight inches. The

When the firebrick has been laid, the prefabricated firebox may be set in position. Seal it to the firebrick with mortar.

hearth extension should be 16 inches into the room.

Placement of the larger units takes at least two people, so plan on asking for help. Be sure you install the unit level and plumb with the seal of fireclay mortar. This is extremely important; future construction will depend on the unit's being correctly positioned.

Insulation

Once the mortar has set, wrap fiberglass batt insulation around the entire unit. The insulation usually comes with the unit and is held in place with a thin coating of mortar. No metal surfaces should be allowed to contact the surrounding masonry. The insulation provides a cushion for the unit, handles expansion and contraction of the metal due to heating and cooling, and prevents cracks in the masonry. The procedure is a formidable one, but is stressed by the manufacturers

With the unit secured to the base, cover it with a layer of insulation to cushion expansion and to avoid cracking the masonry.

of the unit. Apply regular or fireclay mortar firmly over the metal unit until the unit is covered. Then press the fiberglass matting in place over the wet mortar. All corners and edges are given a double layer of the insulation to provide more protection in those areas. This is no problem, because the second outside layer of insulation will stick quite readily to the first layer already installed. The overlap should be about two inches. Let the mortar dry before continuing work on this area of the fireplace.

CHIMNEY

Once the entire unit has been placed and thoroughly covered with insulation, you can begin building the chimney. In most instances the chimney lies against the exterior wall of the house. The only area needing additional cutting is the roof overhang. However, this can be and is changed in some instances to provide for the chimney to run on the inside of the exterior wall or totally inside if you should choose to build a center fireplace. This application does not provide nearly the structural support as does the uncut wall method. It is easiest to lay the chimney with four-inch-thick concrete block and then veneer it with four inches of stone. However, the chimney could also be laid entirely of stone, as shown at lower right. In either case, this is a straight masonry job.

Use a mortar mix of one part mason's cement, three parts sand and enough water to make the mortar buttery, but still able to stand up on its own.

Laying the Blocks

The first step is to chalk an outline of the position of the outside line of the chimney, checking that it is square. Then place a bed of mortar around the perimeter of the chimney and on the foundation and, starting at each outside corner, set a block in place. Make sure these are level and plumb in all directions. Use a string line with mason's wooden corner blocks

Lay the concrete block around the unit. Fill the space between the walls and the fireplace unit with rubble and mortar.

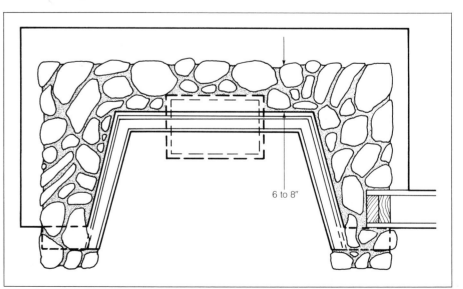

You can build the entire fireplace surround of stone and mortar, but the work must be done slowly to allow the mortar to set firmly. Placing too much at once can cause the stones to slip.

stretched from block to block, or a long level, to ensure that the corner blocks are level with each other as well. Then butter the ends of the rest of the blocks for the bottom course and position in place, again leveling in all directions. Once the first or bottom course has been laid, remove the string line and place mortar on top of this course. Again set the corner blocks, this time facing them in the

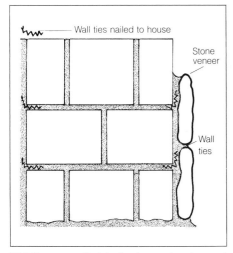

Wall ties are nailed to the house framing and tied to the block at mortar joints. Others are set in exterior joints and linked to the veneer in the mortar.

opposite direction (perpendicular to the first course so that the block overlaps and offsets). Use a level to make sure they are plumb with the blocks below them as well as level in all directions. Attach a string line to the blocks and lay the second course. Continue laying courses in this manner.

As you lay the chimney walls, install corrugated wall ties approximately every third horizontal mortar joint space 24 inches apart to tie the stone to the block. When the stone veneer is applied, fill in the space between the inside of the chimney and the metal unit with mortar and rubble, bringing the filling up as you bring the chimney up. The proportion should be about 75 percent rubble and 25 percent mortar. Use a level to make sure the chimney wall is built plumb straight, and a string to keep the walls straight.

FIREPLACE FRONT

Once blocks for the exterior chimney have been laid, the stones for covering the fireplace front and surrounding the cold air ducts must be added. Wall ties also are used in the stone courses to tie them securely together, as shown.

Laying the Stones

Choosing the correct stones is one of the most crucial steps in laying the stone for the fireplace front. Typically, they should be the largest you can fit into each space, and they should have at least one sharp corner to delineate the inside edge of the fireplace sides. After careful selection of the stones, trowel on a bed of mortar, and place the first stone. Position the stone in place on the mortar bed, then force the mortar in around it. Starting at a corner is a good idea. Again, use a level to keep the corners as plumb as possible, although it won't be nearly as necessary as with straight-line materials such as brick or block. The mortar joint can vary; however, try for a 1 inch joint (which usually squeezes down to a ¾ inch joint when finished). Tap each stone gently to firm it in place and to eliminate air bubbles in the mortar joints. Lay the entire first course in this manner. The stones should overlap in all cases to provide a bonding joint.

To lay the next course of stone, dry fit the first stone to make sure you have chosen one that will fit properly to give a relatively uniform mortar joint. Choose stones that are alternately large and small. The shapes should fit around each other. Then butter up the bottom course with mortar and position the next stone course in place just as you did the first one. The mortar should be flush with the faces of the stones. Pack it in firmly, but not so that it will ooze out when the next course is laid. Once the stones are in position, tap them lightly to settle them in place. Always check to make sure that the faces of the stones are plumb and that they are not tilted out or in at the top. Place rubble and mortar in any holes behind or between stones. Wearing gloves, use your

hands to force the mortar in and around the stones, removing all air pockets and filling all holes. Fill the gap between the chimney blocks and the exterior veneer as you proceed. Add wall ties to connect the stone fireplace front and the block chimney walls.

One important rule when doing stone work, particularly for walls and veneering, is to build only a little at a time. One course is a reasonable goal. Then wait and let the mortar set. Not only will too much stone laid at one time cause the mortar to slump, resulting in its squeezing out of the joints, but you can actually end up with the veneer falling apart. This did occur once during this project while the author was veneering the inside walls. After several courses were laid in relatively quick succession, the entire wall slowly slid off onto the floor—a mess of mortar and stones.

Interior stone work begins when the unit is in place. Insulation around it buffers the stone work from any metal expansion.

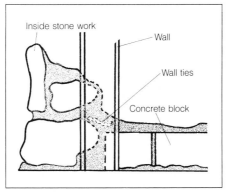

Wall ties are also used between the interior facing the block work. The ties fit between block joints and stone joints.

Stick props up wobbly stone until mortar sets up

Mortar does not set instantly; stones may slip unless held in place. Use a braced wood prop to keep stones up until mortar sets.

If a stone has a tendency to tip out at the top, prop it in place with a stick or another stone until the mortar sets. Once the mortar has been applied to the top of the stone (in buttering the next course) and the next course has been installed, the stone usually will be locked in place. The exception is a stone with too round a surface, which may allow it to slip out of the mortar joint.

Alternately work on each side of the fireplace a little at a time, bringing both sides up equally so you can keep them looking very much alike. This requires a large quantity of stones to choose from for the best results. Make sure you get the front faces of the stone fairly plumb and the side lines straight. A string dropped from a nail in the ceiling with a heavy weight can act as a plumb bob in the exact location of the side lines (at corners) as shown in drawing on page 56.

On the fireplace shown, the cold air ducts and inlets for the heat exchanger were placed at either side of the room at floor level where they would be most efficient at picking up the cold air. The ducts were temporarily formed with ½ inch plywood next to the fireplace firebox. These were later removed after the stones had been set in place over them. Forms were nailed together with 4d finishing nails. Once the masonry had set, the forms were pulled out of the sides by hooking behind them with a crowbar and pulling.

After the two sides had been brought up to the underside of the top of the metal unit, a ⅜ inch x 4 inch x 4 inch angle iron was placed as a lintel bar across the sides at the top of the opening. To set the lintel, first build up the sides to an equal distance

Bring stones up to the top of the opening. Place and level the lintel bar. Plan the stone work so it provides level support.

from the floor, just below the opening of the metal unit. Then position mortar in place on each end and lay the lintel bar across the opening, making sure it is kept level and embedded in the mortar on each end. Allow this to set up solidly. Then fill in on top of the lintel bar with a layer of mortar and start the stone course on top of it. The lintel must be absolutely level. Stop work and let everything set up, or head back outside and lay out some more of the chimney walls. Keeping yourself flexible, by going back and forth this way, can speed progress.

The metal grille for the hot-air vents needs a level course for support. Choose and lay stones that will provide a level position.

As noted above, once the lintel bar has been firmly set, place mortar across its top and lay some more stones. The stones directly on the lintel will probably have to be quite uniform in size. At this point, the work becomes a little more complicated because you will want to keep another level line just above the lintel bar for the warm air outlet. Pick out the stones carefully, working toward a level mortar line. Then, if using a purchased metal grille to provide the outlet cover, install it in place, keeping it level and plumb. Mortar it on both sides and bring the stone up next to it. Allow this to set thoroughly. Begin the next course; start on top of the metal grille and mortar the top securely in place. An alternative is to use stones in a "soldier" course—stones set up on end, spacing them about 1½ inches apart to provide the openings for the outlet. If you choose this arrangement, it is a good idea to add a small steel lintel over the top of the stones for more strength. When you have reached this point, it is merely a matter of continuing to place the stones until you reach within

about four to six inches of the ceiling. Finish this space with molding if you wish. You will have difficulty finding stones that will fit in this small space.

Finishing the Mortar Joints

One of the most important facets of stone work is the cleaning up of the joints once the stones have been laid. With a little practice you will soon have a finished job that really looks professional and neat, and shows off the stones to their best advantage.

There are many different thoughts on how the mortar joints should look. In most instances you will wish to point the joints, or to remove a little of the mortar between the stones. This gives more light and shadow to help show off the stones. The amount of material removed is a matter of personal choice, but do not remove too much mortar (½ or ¾ inch maximum) or you will weaken the joint. If the veneer is thin (one inch), take out less mortar. The amount of set the mortar has at the time you work the joints is crucial. If the mortar has dried too hard before you begin work, you will not be able to clean out the joints properly. If the mortar still is too wet, you will force out too much mortar. Wait about half an hour to an hour after applying the mortar, continually testing the mortar to see how it comes out of the joint. This operation can only be perfected with experience and by learning to recognize the feel of the mortar. Weather and temperature conditions will affect how fast the mortar sets.

For a rustic look, using the finger of a gloved hand does a good job of compacting and finishing a mortar joint. As an alternative, the tool used to clean out the joints may be nothing more than a ⅜x6 inch round head bolt. The large round head can be used to scrape the excess mortar out of the larger joints, while the smaller end of the bolt can be used to get into smaller spaces. Once you have scraped out the excess and have made a smooth, rounded joint, use a small whisk broom to remove any loosened mortar chunks. Smooth the surface of any scrape marks left by the pointing tool, also using the whisk broom. The surface left after brooming gives an indication of how fast the mortar is setting; you should still be able to smooth the surface down with the whisk broom at this stage.

Follow the brooming with a steel bristle brush to remove any excess mortar that has gotten onto the faces of the stones. Later, after the mortar has set for several days, many stone masons like to clean the stone faces with water, to which a bit of muriatic acid has been added. However, if the mortar is cleaned as you go, a light washing with pure water and the steel bristle brush (a couple of days later) will clean away any mortar dust left from the first cleaning job.

Cold Air Ducts

In the fireplace shown, the next step was to construct a wooden frame for the cold air ducts which run to either side of the room. This was made of 2x4s nailed in place to the wall studs and to the floor joists. Then a ¾ inch plywood covering was installed.

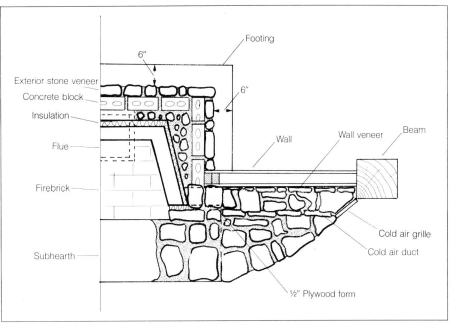

Cold air ducts reach to the edge of the wide forehearth and are covered with decorative grilles. The vertical beam at right was added for support and decorative unity.

Vents for cold air are built on the sides of the fireplace face. Cover these plywood boxes with stone and mortar.

Insulation must extend from the firebox between the vents and stone to protect the stone and mortar from expansion pressure.

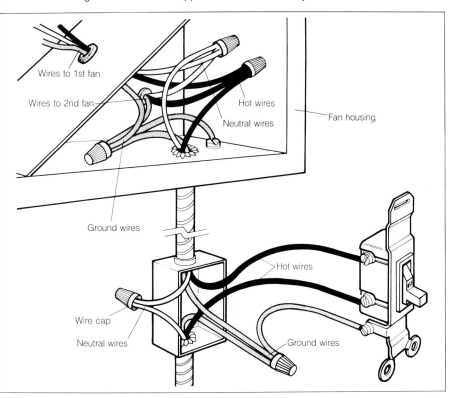

For greatest heat exchange, fans must pull cold air into the fireplace unit and blow out warmed air. The wiring is not difficult, but shut off power before connecting wires.

Wiring. The fan motors on the metal grille units were wired by running a wire over the fireplace to the fan motors, then bringing a wire up through the floor for the incoming power lead and wiring to a switch box mortared in place on the adjoining stone faced wall. The wiring diagram is illustrated above. A wooden channel was built on both sides to run the wires through; however, in some locations you may need to install conduit for the wiring to suit local codes.

After the wiring was completed, the framed air ducts were covered with stone and the metal grilles were mortared in place.

Veneering the Walls

Veneer the walls using thin, flat, field stones. This is probably one of the most difficult aspects of the job. Because of their thin shapes, the stones have a tendency to tip out or slide down out of position until the mortar sets. Concrete block wall ties were nailed up to each stud about eight inches in height to help hold mortar and stone veneer to the wall. An alternative would be to knock indentations into the existing plasterboard behind the stone veneer and to use these pockets to help lock the stones into place. A method often used by professionals is to first nail expanded metal to the wall. (Expanded metal is a specific material used in the trade. It is a form of wire mesh formed by stamping sheet metal into a pattern of open grids. Ask for "expanded metal"; otherwise, it might be confused with lightweight mesh such as chickenwire mesh, which is not recommended.) When the mortar has settled into this, the metal helps hold the stone and mortar in place.

If a stone tips and won't hold securely in place, use a wooden prop until the mortar under the stone sets up. Then remove the prop; once the mortar and next course have been installed, the stone normally will be securely locked in place. Veneer the wall to within about six inches of the ceiling, and then stop.

If you wish to place support bars or hangers for items on the veneered stone wall, do this while the mortar is still wet. Almost any item can be inserted in the damp mortar, including the hooked rods, or long screws inserted into the damp mortar to hold other types of brackets. Insert the item in place; prop it or tape it in position with duct tape. Push and turn roundhead wood screws into the mortar for items that have holes in them and are actually meant to be fastened to a wall other than masonry— such as a fireplace tool kit. Allow mortar to set thoroughly before removing the tape.

Adding the Beams

In the fireplace shown, two massive 12x12 inch beams, each 12 feet long, were installed on either side of the fireplace wall during construction of the house. However, these also could be boxed in.

After completing the masonry section, fit the box beam around the projecting portion of the fireplace front and back up against the veneered side walls. Hold this in place with 2x2s bolted to the ceiling. If the joists in the ceiling run with the supports instead of across them you will have to use hollow wall anchors or Molly bolts to secure the wooden supports in place. Then cut the beam from 1x12 rough-sawn white cedar lumber. Fasten the beam together with angle irons at each corner.

The beams shown were all stained a grey color to simulate weathered barn wood. Here are the steps involved.

1. Apply a full wash coat of light grey paint made by mixing black acrylic with white latex paint.
2. Allow this to dry; then apply a somewhat darker coat over this. Do not work the second coat into the grain quite as thoroughly.
3. Follow with an even darker coat of an oil-based dark brown stain, lightly rubbed over the surface after the paint has dried, to create dark highlights. You will probably wish to experiment on a piece of scrap before tackling the entire beam.
4. When the beam has dried properly, find someone to help you hold it up. Fasten it in place with 8d finishing nails driven into the supports already attached to the ceiling.
5. Once it has been securely fastened in place, cut the bottom pieces to fit on the underside.
6. Scribe and cut them to fit around the rocks. Stain and fasten them behind the lower front edge of the beam.

The Smoke Shelf Area

Now go back outside again for more work on the chimney. Fill the slanted area between the metal unit and the inside of the chimney wall with rubble and mortar as you bring up the walls. Place a wall tie into the inside as well as one to the outside, as shown. This rubble fill should reach to about six inches below the damper. Bricks or rocks should be used to corbel (offset) the sides in as shown.

Corbeling is a method of angling in the sides from the width of the fireplace opening to the width where the sides must meet the chimney flue. Corbeling is done by setting one stone over the other and extending it just a bit past the edge of the one below it. This is probably the hardest job in building the fireplace. You cannot work very quickly because the weight of

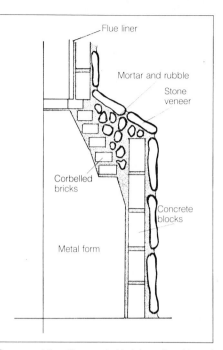

To support flue tiles, corbel brick up the sides of the unit. Fill area between wall and unit with mortar and rubble.

the stones extending out over those below them can cause the wet mortar to sag, or the stones can even fall out before the mortar has a chance to set. Many masons like to use bricks for this job since they're easier to use. They won't show at all, so it really doesn't matter. The reinforcing rods also are bent around those corbeled sides at this time so they can be extended up through the corners of the fireplace chimney. On short chimneys you may only need to use one set of rods. However, on two-story chimneys you will probably need a second set, placing them right next to the ends of the first ones as you build up.

Construction of the masonry smoke shelf. This shelf ensures that air current downdrafts are sent back up the chimney and prevents downdraft smoking problems when the fireplace is being used. The shelf must be rounded and smooth, constructed of ordinary mortar, placed about six inches below the damper blade as shown on page 63. Use your hands to create a rounded surface. Then a small triangular trowel can be used for the final surface smoothing.

Let the downdraft shelf set overnight until the mortar has set up thoroughly. If you do not wait, any mortar or debris dropped onto the shelf will stick and create a roughened surface. Once the mortar has hardened you are ready to finish both the side and rear walls of the

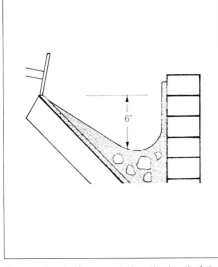

The smoke shelf curves below the level of the damper to a depth of 6 inches. The shelf mixes downdraft air with rising smoke.

Flue tiles weigh 65 lbs each; scaffolding aids exterior construction. Reinforcing rods show at each corner of flue tile.

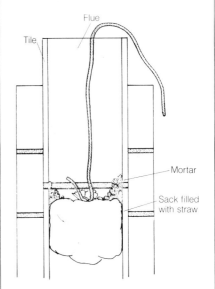

When the chimney is completed, pour mortar into the chimney and pull up a straw-filled bag to seal joints.

fireplace unit. You can continue to use concrete blocks on the outside chimney walls, but bricks should be used to form the corbeling, gradually laying them inwards on both sides of the metal unit to form a support for the tile flue liner. The corbeling in this case follows the outside shape of the metal fireplace unit, from the outside dimensions of the lower fireplace section up to the location of the start of the chimney area. Again, bricks are substituted for stones, since they are much easier to use for the corbeling. They also create a more even area for attaching the stone veneer. Fill in with rubble and mortar, in a three to one ratio of rubble to mortar. Check as you go along to make sure the outside edges of the chimney blocks are plumb and straight. Continue laying the bricks in place until you can cover the top edge of the metal unit, as shown.

Flue Liner

Now install another ¼x3½x3½ inch angle iron to act as a support for the tile flue liner. Tile flue liners are used in the chimney because not as much creosote will stick to the tile as to brick, rough stones, mortar, or concrete blocks. The tile should be at least ⅝ inch thick. This helps reduce fire hazard. Be sure to place the first tile of the flue liner so that it does not fall over a joint of the concrete block course. Otherwise you could have a crack through which a spark could leak back to the exposed woodwork of the house.

Flue tiles are quite heavy and require a great deal of support to hold them in place, so you can work only a little bit at a time. Butter up the edge of one tile; lift it in place carefully (this usually takes two people); check level and plumb.

Concrete blocks have already been laid to just below a flue tile joint. After the first tile has been installed, continue the concrete blocks on up around that tile, again filling the spaces between the tile and blocks with mortar and small pieces of rubble. Continue until you reach just below the next joint of flue tile, then mortar that flue tile in place and continue the blocks up around it. Install the blocks around the tile and fill between them with rubble and mortar. Allow it all to set up before installing the next flue-tile-and-block courses. The flue tiles are very heavy—as much as 65 pounds each—and the weight of one tile may force wet mortar out of the joint under the next lower tile. Professional masons are able to set several tile and block courses in a single day, but the homeowner building a chimney in this manner is better off doing one tile and block section a day—or two sets, one in the morning and one in the afternoon. Spacing the laying time will allow the mortar to set and give the homeowner a chance to regain his (or her) strength.

Mortar drips. One common problem when installing flue tiles is the mortar that drops down inside the chimney onto the downdraft shelf. To prevent this, fill an old sack with straw or rags, tie a strong rope on it and force it down inside the previously laid flue tile and up against the edge to be mortared. Then apply the mortar to the tile. Set the new flue tile in place, and smooth it. Pull the sack up, removing dropped mortar as you raise it. This also helps give smooth mortar joints on the inside of the flue tile liner. Make sure you have a strong rope on the sack, however, as the author spent a great deal of time trying to fish out a sack from which the rope had broken.

Corbel sides of chimney. Once the tile flue liners have been installed, you will probably wish to corbel in the sides of the chimney (see page 70). Corbeling usually starts at the outside corners just above the smoke chamber and runs to just above the joint of the metal unit and chimney or flue tile. However, it could be started higher and run farther if desired, creating a better-looking chimney for a two-story house. Leave just enough space around the flue tile to fill with mortar, but work out the spacing so that you can cut the concrete blocks to fit. As mentioned earlier, you may wish to use brick instead, since it is easier to handle. Lay blocks; install flue tiles; fill between the two with rubble and mortar until the top of the chimney is reached. As you go up, install additional metal reinforcing rods by setting them firmly in the mortar if the

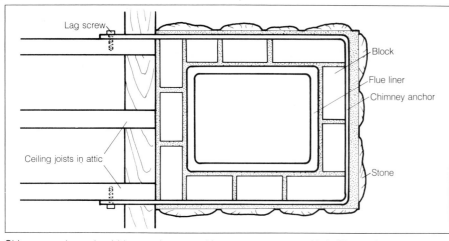

Chimney anchors should be used on any chimney over one story high. The anchor protects the chimney from excessive pressures during high wind and prevents pulling on the wall.

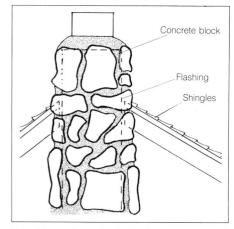

The chimney is made of flue tile, concrete block and stone veneer. Flashing at the roof keeps water away from the chimney.

previously set rods do not extend to the top.

Chimney anchors should be used to help hold the chimney securely to the house. They may be required by some local building codes. The chimney anchor is a metal strap that wraps around the chimney blocks (between the blocks and the stone veneer). It is then brought into the house just above the ceiling joists through small holes bored in the sheathing (the siding will have already been removed in this area) and fastened to the ceiling joists, using lag screws in the holes provided in the straps. You can also use wall anchors, to anchor each course of block to the walls.

Preparing the Roof

The next problem occurs where the chimney reaches the roof overhang and starts through it. Build the chimney up to the underside of the roof line, using a level. Then mark on the underside of the roof overhang, as well as on top of it, the exact location of the chimney as it comes through the overhang. Remove the shingles or composition roof to an area about six inches larger than the chimney opening. Mark the area to be cut away for the chimney on the roof sheathing; cut with a hand saw. This should be cut about two inches wider than the fireplace dimensions for clearance. Cut through rafters and remove rafter pieces or ridgepole ends that may be in the way.

Rafter or ridgepole cuts. If a rafter or the ridgepole end has to be cut, first secure it on the inside of the house by nailing a brace to the end of the cut rafter and to the nearest ceiling joists.

Flashing. After the concrete block

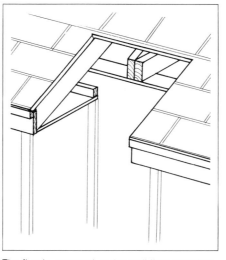

The flue is centered at the wall line; therefore, you must cut through the roof and eaves to allow it to extend straight up.

chimney has been brought through the roof, metal flashing is cut and installed around the chimney to seal off the area from water. The flashing is installed in two layers. The first layer of metal is bent and installed on the wooden sheathing and against the blocks. Then the shingles and roofing material are laid down over the flashing and a second outside layer of flashing is installed over the roofing material. All this is cemented and caulked in place using roofing compound. After installing the chimney, lay the shingles back in place and seal with flashing as shown. Later, when the stone veneer is in position, this will complete the sealing job and keep out seeping water. Check with local building codes for the distance the chimney must protrude above the roof line. Normally this is a three to four foot minimum.

The cap. The last tile for the top of the flue liner extends up above the concrete or

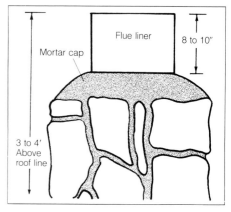

For safety, the liner should rise above the chimney veneer by 8 inches or more. A mortar cap directs water away from the tile.

stone veneer to form a cap. To finish the cap, shape the mortar with your hands into a well-rounded form, then use a small fine trowel. An alternative would be a formed cap made by constructing a hollow wooden form on the top of the chimney and pouring mortar mix into the form. A cap not only has aesthetic value, but lets rain water run off rather than seep down between the blocks and the flue liner.

Veneering Outside Chimney

Veneer the outside of the chimney with stone, just as for the inside. In most instances the foundation would not be exposed—except in a case such as this, where the floor level is so high above the ground level. The foundation usually would also be covered with the stone veneer or, in the case of a brick fireplace, with brick. On the fireplace shown, a deck was installed at floor level to cover the exposed foundation, as planned.

7

BUILDING
A BRICK FIREPLACE

If you prefer a brick facing on your fireplace instead of a stone one, it can be created using one of two methods that are similar to those for building the stone fireplace in Chapter 6. The first method is to build the concrete block chimney and to merely veneer it with brick in much the same manner as constructing the stone fireplace of concrete block and veneering the outside surface with stone. Or you may prefer to construct the fireplace entirely of brick. In some cases, you may even wish to build the entire unit of brick, eliminating the metal liner unit. This requires careful brickwork as well as a good understanding of fireplace design. A series of steps, with photographs, is provided at the end of this chapter. However, most home craftsmen find it simpler to utilize the metal unit rather than to construct the basic firebox. This technique was shown and discussed in Chapter 6.

First, check all your local building codes governing the construction of a fireplace and acquire any permits needed.

ENERGY EFFICIENT FIREPLACE
Footing and Foundation

A footing of reinforced concrete should extend at least 6 inches beyond the outside outline of the fireplace in all directions. You will have to establish the exact inside dimensions of the chimney corners so you can install vertical reinforcing rods in the wet concrete in these areas.

When building a fireplace during construction of a new home, you will probably have the fireplace footing, house footing and foundation excavated, formed and poured at the same time. If your home has a basement, the base of the

Brick is the most common and most familiar facing material for fireplaces. Depending on the brick you choose, a fireplace may look formal or casual or be of any period design.

This Victorian fireplace is faced with wood and ceramic tile and the chimney breast is covered with damask wallpaper, but underneath it is brick.

Mantel
Sheetrock
Metal liner unit
Concrete block
Opening lintel
Firebrick
Brick facing
Brick hearth
Brick veneer
Cantilevered subhearth
Concrete block
Footing

This brick fireplace is very much like the stone veneered fireplace in the previous chapter. This fireplace was veneered with brick. The basic installation is the same.

fireplace will be part of the foundation of your home. If your house is on a slab, you will have to provide a foundation for your fireplace at least as deep as the footings for your house. You will need extra-strong footings to hold the weight of several stories of brick. However, if you are adding a fireplace to an existing building, you will have to excavate for the fireplace footing and then cut through the wall of the house for the fireplace and chimney (as discussed in Chapter 6). You will also have to cut through the flooring and frame-in with doubled headers around the hearth. Again, this is done in exactly the same way as in building the stone fireplace.

The Ashpit

If the house sits on a slab, you will not be able to utilize an ash pit. In a house with crawl space or basement, where the house floor is at least 16 to 24 inches above the ground level, you probably will wish to build an ash pit.

Step one: laying the brick. Once the footing and foundation have been framed, poured and cured (refer to Chapter 6), clean all dust and debris from the concrete footing. The first area of the fireplace to be built is the ashpit/air intake pit. Using a large square, a straightedge and a piece of chalk or crayon, mark the outlines of the outside of the ashpit area on the founda-

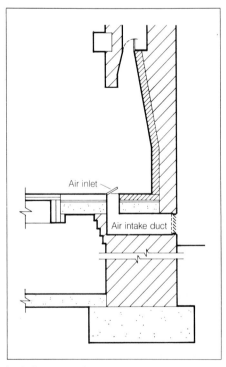

Air inlet
Air intake duct

Include an outside air intake. This provides combustion air directly to the fire.

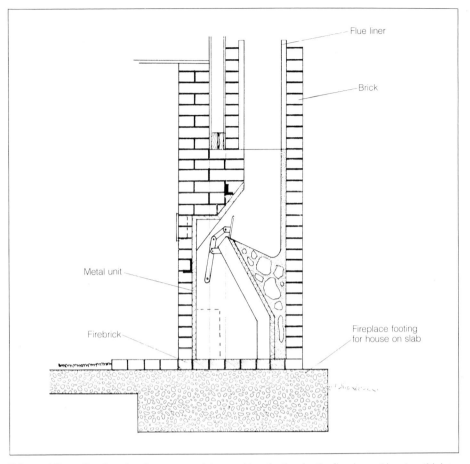

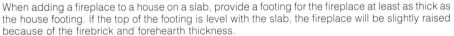

When adding a fireplace to a house on a slab, provide a footing for the fireplace at least as thick as the house footing. If the top of the footing is level with the slab, the fireplace will be slightly raised because of the firebrick and forehearth thickness.

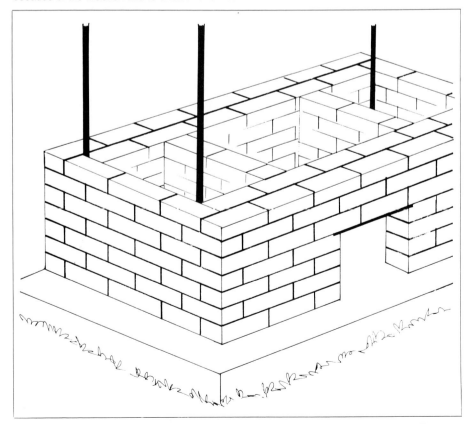

An ashpit may have interior divisions to allow for separate ash disposal and air intakes. The inner walls provide some hearth support. Reinforcing rods run up the corners.

tion floor. Mix a batch of mortar as described for the stone work. Dampen the bricks with a fine spray from a hose. Spread a layer of mortar inside the marked line and start laying the brick—keep the brick level by checking with a carpenter's level and tapping with the trowel handle. The mortar joints should be ¼ inch for the greatest strength. Make sure the bricks are level in all directions.

Step two: building the walls. Build the front and back walls two bricks wide to create double-thick walls. The end walls are left single thickness. In addition you will also have to lay up two interior walls dividing the unit into the ashpit and air intake areas.

Step three: creating an air inlet. The ashpit and air intake pit should be separate units in the base for safety. The air intake should have an opening (air inlet) 4½ inches by 13 inches built into the floor of the firebox. Locate the inlet in the exact center of the fireplace opening with the outside, long edge of the inlet even with the outside face of the fireplace. Cover the inlet with an adjustable damper/door. The damper should open so the air is deflected into the firebox. Run an enclosed duct from the inlet through the pit to the air intake vent on the exterior wall.

Using wall ties. Although the interior dividing walls do not have to be tied into the side walls, wall ties should be used on the outside (supporting) walls. Lay the ties in the mortar of these walls; the courses will secure the ties solidly in place.

Step four: finishing the ash pit. After you have laid up enough courses that the mortar in the first course or two has set up enough to just take a thumb print, clean all excess mortar from the joints with a joint cleaning tool. Knock off sharp edges with the side of the trowel. Mortar the metal ash pit cleanout door unit securely in place. Install a metal lintel bar across the top of the opening to provide support and to prevent the weight from above crushing the door. Mortar the door tightly in place so no sparks can escape around it. Mortar the vertical reinforcing rods securely by placing bricks across the corners and adding mortar in and around the rods. Fill in the side spaces with mortar and rubble.

Step five: supporting the forehearth. In order to support the forehearth that

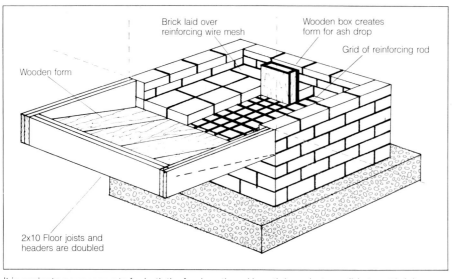

It is easier to pour concrete for both the forehearth and hearth base but possible to set brick over a reinforcing mesh in main hearth area. Pour concrete for the forehearth.

extends out from the face of the fireplace, the front wall of the ashpit must be extended forward in a series of steps called "corbels". As the front wall is built up toward the upper floor, the wall is "stepped out".

How to corbel. Begin corbeling above the ashpit cleanout door and lay each successive course so that it projects beyond the course below. The amount that a brick may be corbeled is no more than one-half the height (thickness) or one-third the width of the brick. This means that a brick $2\frac{1}{4}$ inches thick and 4 inches wide may not project more than $1\frac{1}{8}$ inches beyond the brick course directly below. The corbeled wall is reinforced with wall ties every 16 inches vertically

and 32 inches horizontally and the wall is tied into the side walls by a row of headers at least every third course. Check local codes for specific requirements.

The corbeled wall provides bracing and support for the cantilevered forehearth. The distance the wall must be corbeled is approximately one-third the depth of the forehearth. Most forehearths extend sixteen inches from the face of the fireplace; therefore, the ashpit wall should be corbeled out approximately five inches for a sixteen inch forehearth. The number of the corbeled courses and the spacing of the courses will depend upon how far you must corbel the wall forward and how high you must build the ashpit/fireplace support.

The Subhearth

The subhearth, which is made of poured concrete, is formed on top of the ashpit.

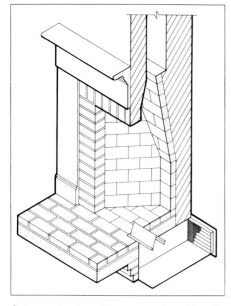

Cutaway drawing shows concrete subhearth, layer of bed mortar for the bricks, and bricks. The firebrick is set with close joints.

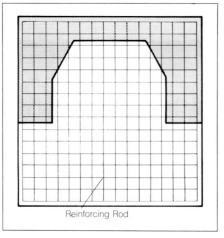

Good reinforcing is needed in the hearth slab. The rods tie the hearth and the forehearth together for a durable surface.

Probably the most important point is framing-in the forms for the subhearth to provide the correct height for the top of the hearth (including the firebrick). The hearth must end up the height you want in relation to the finished flooring of the house. Above all, you do not want the firebrick and finished forehearth to be below the flooring (unless you are planning a sunken hearth). In most instances the hearth will be planned at least $\frac{1}{4}$ to $\frac{1}{2}$ inch above the finished flooring, including carpeting if it is to be installed. In some cases you may wish to install the fireplace higher than the floor level and create a raised hearth. In all cases, you must determine the planned height of the hearth, then subtract the thickness of the firebrick, mortar, and sheet metal base for the firebox. Bring the walls of the ashpit to the proper level and lay sheet metal as a base form for the poured concrete subhearth of the firebox.

Forehearth. The forehearth that will extend out in the room should be framed in to a height that is lower than the desired finished level by the thickness of the base plywood, the concrete and the finishing material, whether brick, stone, or tile.

The forehearth is cantilevered out from the ashpit and should not be attached directly to the floor joists. If the floor joists run perpendicular to the face of the fireplace, you must install a doubled header parallel to the face of the fireplace as support for the floor joist(s) that must be cut to provide a clear space for the forehearth. If the joists run parallel to the face of the fireplace, there may be sufficient clearance for the forehearth if your joists are on sixteen inch centers. If the joists have narrower centers than sixteen inches, you will have to cut at least one joist and use doubled headers on each side of the forehearth area for joist supports. These doubled headers will run from the house framing to the next set of joists.

Construct a form for the forehearth from 2x4 stock and attach it temporarily to the joists. Lay a piece of $\frac{3}{4}$ inch plywood (fire-resistant if possible) over the form with one edge resting on the corbeled brick wall.

The firebox area must be covered with heavy gauge galvanized sheet metal or heavy mesh to support the concrete. Build box forms for both the ashdump and the air intake. Cut openings in either the mesh or the sheet metal to accommodate these spaces. Reinforcing rods must be positioned approximately 6 inches apart, running from the back of the firebox to the front of the forehearth. Another set of rods is placed at right angles to the first set. These sets are supported at least one inch above the bottom of the forms and are tied together. The concrete is poured over these. There should be no less than 6 inches of concrete in the firebox area and no less than 4 inches in the forehearth area.

After the concrete has set, remove the wooden forms below the forehearth so it is not connected in any manner to the house flooring. Remove the box forms for the ashdump and air intake also.

Build up the outside walls of the firebox two courses above the height of the finished hearth, then install the firebrick on the inner hearth, laying each in place with fireclay mortar. As shown in the drawing, the entire hearth area need not be covered with firebrick, only that portion that will be enclosed in the firebox—or in the case of the metal unit, the portion on which the metal unit sits and the firebox area.

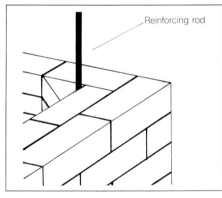

Vertical reinforcing rods extend through the construction at corners.

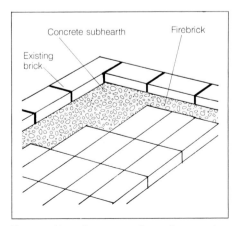

The exterior walls serve as form when pouring concrete subhearth. Firebrick completes the hearth, surface.

You may lay the finished forehearth of brick or tile now, or you may leave this for later. Any exposed brick or other materials on the hearth should be covered with a thin layer of sand to prevent dropped mortar from adhering to the surface, or there will be a hard clean up job once the fireplace has been finished. It helps also to line the firebox floor surface with building paper or a drop cloth.

Placing the Metal Unit and Accessories

Install the metal liner unit, placing it on a thin bed of mortar as specified by the manufacturer of your specific unit. Make sure the unit is installed level and plumb, and that the face of the unit is set inside the wall by the distance necessary to allow for facing the fireplace with the brick. Again, this measurement will vary and will be given in the specific directions for your particular unit.

Apply a thin layer of mortar to all exposed surfaces of the metal unit and use this as a glue to apply the fiberglass batting insulation that comes with the unit. This provides a cushion for contraction and expansion of the metal unit in relation to the masonry. All surfaces that touch the masonry must be covered. The corners and edges must have two layers for additional protection. This step is important; if it is not carried out properly, the fireplace masonry may crack and break from the pressure of the metal unit as it heats and cools.

Now lay the masonry surround for the metal unit. Bring the inside facing and the outside masonry up a course at a time. When you have laid brick to near the top of the vertical reinforcing rods, tie new ones to the existing ones by sinking new rods into mortar and wiring the rods together. Continue running the rods up in the corners of the chimney as you work.

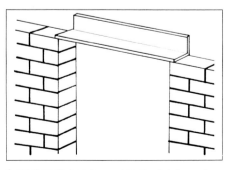

A steel angle iron is used as the lintel opening. It must support the masonry above the opening.

When you reach the top edge of the unit front opening, install a metal lintel bar by mortaring it in place on the top edges of the side bricks. The ends of the lintel bar should be protected with insulation like that placed around the metal liner. Next lay brick over the front top of the bar to continue the facing. If the fireplace unit has a hot air grille for the front, work this in as you take the front facing up. Keep cleaning out the joints in the bricks.

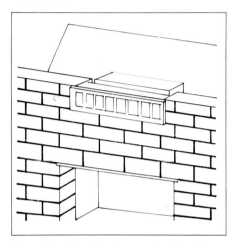

A heat circulating fireplace requires hot air vent above the lintel. You may have to cut brick to fit the opening.

Create cold-air ducts of brick as you lay the front facing of the fireplace. These channels are masonry construction, but for best efficiency the inside surfaces must be parged—the surfaces coated with a smooth layer of mortar. If using brick coverings for these opening channels, add a grid of ½ inch reinforcing rods set in mortar over the top of the channels to support the top bricks. Then mortar the metal grille/fan units in place and hook up the wiring following manufacturer's directions.

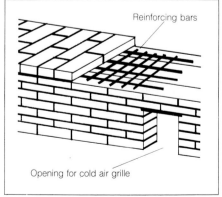

A lintel bar above the opening and a network of reinforcing rods in upper mortar bed supports courses above cold air duct.

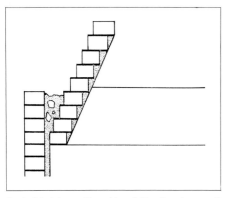

Corbel brick up the side of the fireplace unit throat. This will provide support for the flue tile at the chimney.

The Chimney

After completing the air chambers inside and facing the front up to the top of the damper unit, the outside masonry is brought up to this point as well. Fill in with mortar and rubble between the brick walls and the unit. At this time do not go higher than the bottom portion of the masonry downdraft shelf. Proper construction of this particular part of the fireplace is very critical. The void, slanted area behind the unit must be filled with broken rocks, bricks and rubble to about 6 inches below the damper. Corbel the bricks inward up the sides to create a support shelf for the throat of the fireplace. Then build up the outside of the walls of the fireplace to about the height of the damper.

Downdraft shelf. Construct the masonry downdraft shelf by creating a rounded masonry shelf. Use your hands to roughly establish the rounded area. The shelf should be higher at the front than at the back to guide the draft back up the chimney. Use a trowel to make the area as smooth as possible; it must be well rounded to provide a good air draft. The bottom of the shelf falls about 6 inches below the damper blade for proper air draft currents down the chimney and to avoid downdraft smoking problems. Now continue working on the exterior sides and back.

Corbel top of the fireplace throat. Carefully corbel on both sides to create a support for the tile flue liner that will be installed in the chimney. The space must be carefully adjusted so that the edge of the shelf and the flue tile are flush. If the edge of the flue tile projects, it will catch the rising smoke and gases and interfere with the updraft. If the shelf is wider than the tile, the opening will be too small for

good draw and settling smoke debris will accumulate.

Checking level. Use a string level and string blocks or a long carpenter's level to make sure you keep the masonry construction level and plumb.

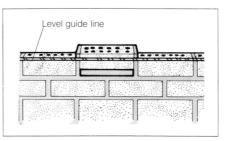

Masonry work is only strong when it is laid level and plumb. Use a level guide line to make sure that your courses are level.

Installing the flue liner. Allow the corbeling to set solidly before installing the flue liner. Bend in the metal reinforcing rods so they are inside the finished brick of the chimney but outside the flue tile. You also may install a metal lintel bar at the back of the unit for more support for the heavy flue tile. Build up the outside wall of the chimney two layers above the shelf where the flue tile will rest; let the mortar set thoroughly.

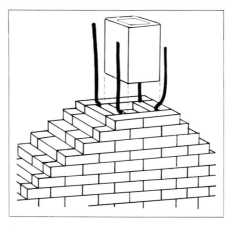

The first flue tile sits on the brick support. Opening in the brick must match the opening of the inside of the flue tile.

At this point corbel in the sides of the fireplace (unless you want a chimney as wide as your fireplace) and fill the area with mortar and rubble as you work. Then place a layer of mortar on the shelf and set the first flue tile in place. Make sure it is perfectly level. Fill all open spaces between the exterior chimney wall and the rising flue tile with mortar.

With the first flue tile set in place, lay up the bricks around the tile to create the chimney. As you pass the top edge of the first flue tile, lay two more courses of

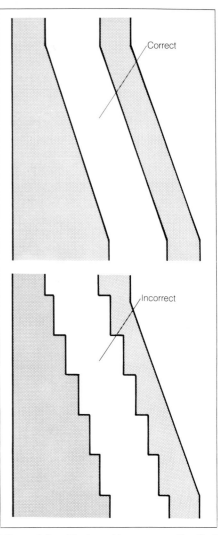

Mitre-cut flue tile to achieve a smooth offset flue. A stepped flue will not draw well and accumulate soot quickly.

brick, then allow all to cure. The next day, install another flue tile and again lay the bricks up around it. Check corners for square and bricks for level and plumb.

The Roofline. Make the cut through the roof overhang to allow the chimney to pass through. Where the chimney penetrates the roof line, install approved chimney anchor straps. Run them around the flue tile, through the house wall, into the attic. Fasten them to the ceiling joists with lag screws. The opening into the house should be sealed with caulk. However, the opening will also be covered by the entire masonry chimney.

Install flashing where the chimney penetrates the roofline. Two layers are installed; the first is L-shaped and is laid against the chimney and under the shingles immediately surrounding the chimney. These shingles must be loosened and lifted up; the flashing fits underneath them and glues to the chimney and roof.

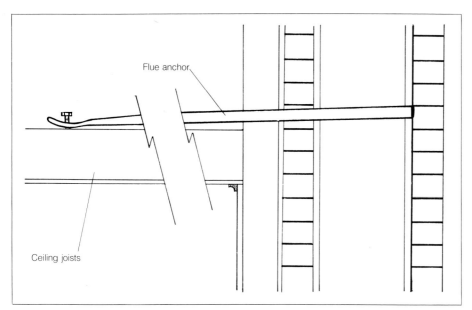

When the chimney reaches attic level, install a chimney strap (flue anchor). Bring it through the house wall, around the flue tile, and bolt it to a joist. The anchor prevents chimney sway.

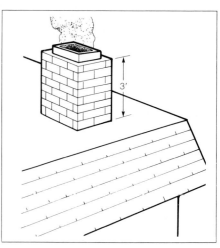

A chimney passing through a flat roof must rise 3 feet above the flat surface. Add a spark arrester for safety.

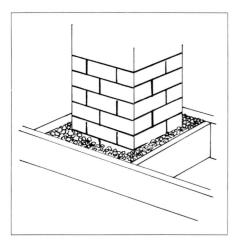

If the chimney is within interior framing, it cannot be closer than 2 inches from the wood. The space is filled with insulation.

When the shingles are back in place, secure them with fresh roofing cement and install the upper (and outer) layer of flashing. This layer has an edge that inserts into the mortar joints of the chimney. The flashing fits down over the chimney and the shingles. Adhere it in place with asphalt cement over the shingles. You can leave the mortar joints in which the flashing will fit partially open during construction of the chimney, and later seal the chimney flashing in place with caulking compound.

Always utilize the proper amount of reinforcing, as stated by local codes. Some codes, for instance, require a 1/4 to 1/2 inch piece of metal rod called "pencil rod" to be laid vertically in the mortar every 24 inches.

Continue building the chimney up until it is the proper height above the roofline of the house. Install the flue liners and lay the brick courses around the chimney as you work upward. The last flue liner should protrude about eight inches above the top row of bricks.

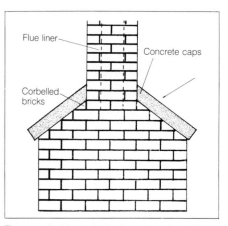

The exterior is corbelled to the width of the chimney. To finish, fill corbel steps with mortar and cover with concrete caps.

The cap. Mix up a batch of mortar and spread it on top of the bricks, sloping from the flue tile to the outside of the chimney; form a cap. The cap not only has aesthetic value, it allows water to run away from the flue and it deflects wind at an angle to prevent downdraft problems. Rake all joints and clean as needed. Then finish off the top portion of the inside of the fireplace using a mantel of your choice.

Interior-wall chimney. If the chimney is built on the inside wall of a house (for example, when a fireplace is constructed on an interior wall or as a center

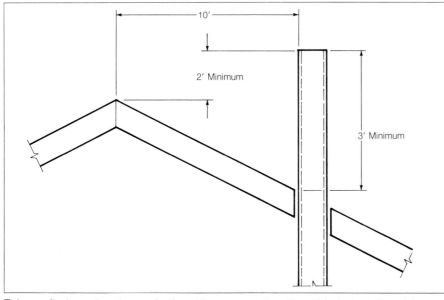

To lessen fire hazard, codes require that chimneys must rise at least 3 feet above the point where it passes through the roof and 2 feet above the highest roof point within 10 feet.

portion of a house), keep the wooden framing where the chimney penetrates the ceiling joists at least 2 inches away from the masonry. After the sheetrock ceiling is installed, fill these open spaces with a non-combustible material such as loose gravel or plaster chips. Never fill in this area solid with mortar.

BRICK VS. PREFABRICATED FIREBOX

You may feel that you definitely do not want a steel liner unit for your fireplace. If so, you must build the entire firebox and throat of masonry. This is difficult unless you have considerable masonry experience and understand fireplace design. The construction of the fireplace up to the finished hearth is basically the same as with a prefab unit. From that point on, until the finishing of the firebox, the construction is considerably different from merely sliding a metal unit in place.

Masons usually lay the inner walls of firebrick while they bring up exterior walls and front facing of the fireplace. The firebricks are laid using fireclay mortar. The mortar is applied a little thinner than is the mortar for the other bricks, usually about ⅛ to ¼ inch thick. The side walls of the firebox are usually angled a total of 4 to 6 inches. As the side pockets are created between the interior and the exterior walls, fill with rubble and mortar. This not only strengthens the firebox walls but gives more bulk to hold heat longer.

The back wall usually is laid straight up and down for the first foot. Then it slopes or slants inward to create a heat-reflecting wall. The degree of slope will depend on the size of the fireplace you are building (discussed in Chapter 3). The sidewalls of the fireplace butt against the sloping back wall. The area between this sloping wall and the exterior walls also is filled with mortar and rubble, but only after mortar in the sloping reflecting wall has set up properly.

Getting all these dimensions and proportions just right requires care, patience, planning and work; the chart shown gives the basic relationships.

After the fireplace is built up to smoke-shelf height, install a metal damper. There are a great variety of damper styles and types. Follow the instructions that come with your particular damper.

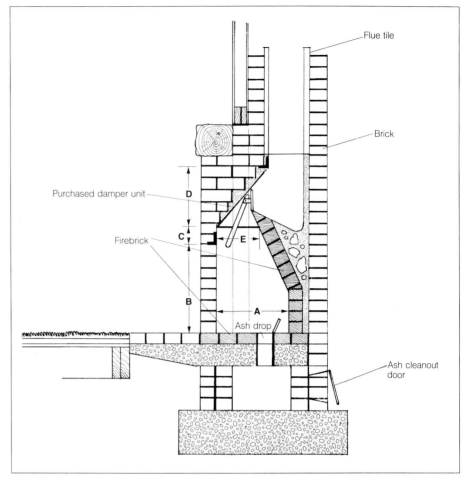

If you build a masonry firebox rather than use a prefabricated unit, keep the proportions noted in the accompanying chart. Major changes in these proportions may create combustion problems.

INTERIOR AND EXTERIOR DIMENSIONS

A	B	C	D	Front Width	Inside Width	E
16″	24–27″	6″	13½″	24″	11″	10″
16	24–27	6	13½	29	16	10
20	27–30	6	13½	35	22	10
20	30–33	6	13½	41	28	10
23	33–36	9	13½	47	34	10
23	36–42	9	13½	53	40	10
26	36–42	9	13½	59	46	10
26	36–48	9	13½	71	58	10

Use the flue tile size recommended by the manufacturer of the damper.
Height should be ⅔ to ¾ of the width.
Depth should be ½ to ⅔ of the height.

To construct the throat (the point at which the fireplace narrows down to the chimney opening) follow the same procedures as given in Chapter 6 for the stone fireplace. If a dome damper unit is installed, corbel the bricks up to fit the chimney width. Note that the chimney will usually be the same depth front to back from its start to finish, although the sides of the firebox will have to be brought in to the chimney width. From then on, construction is the same as for chimneys discussed previously.

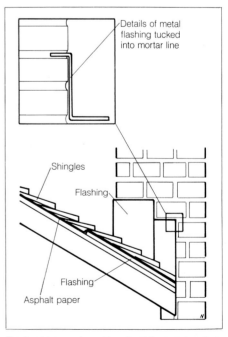

Flash chimney for safe, durable construction. Properly flashed chimney will not leak.

BUILDING A RUMFORD FIREPLACE

Most of today's fireplaces utilize large, deep fireboxes which, when laid with a pile of logs, put out considerable amounts of heat and look warming as well. However, older fireplaces patterned after the Rumford design utilize a shallower firebox with a larger hearth and a higher and wider opening in relation to the depth of the fireplace. These shallow fireplaces often need to be filled up more often, but they throw more heat into the room.

The basic differences between the new designs and the Rumford is that the Rumford consists of a firebox with a height that is twice the depth of the firebox. The width is also twice the depth. Therefore, the width and height are always equal. In addition, the point where the reflecting wall begins to slope is always 12 inches or less. This sloping back protrudes farther into the firebox than does a standard modern design, creating a narrow throat opening of about 4 inches. This throat is kept as wide as the firebox up to the smokeshelf, from which it is corbeled in. The smokeshelf is usually about 12 to 16 inches deep. The flue size is $1/10$th the area of the fireplace opening. These dimensions create a firebox whose higher and more deeply angled back wall reflect more heat.

This demonstration fireplace shows brick corbelled to support the forehearth. Corbelling normally occurs near basement ceiling.

The louvered exterior air intake will close when the fireplace is not in use. Ashpit cleanout door is near the intake.

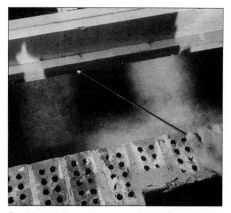
Double header supports the forms for concrete subhearth. Plywood base spans the gap between the corbelled brick to header.

Firebox hearth base is heavy gauge sheet metal cut to fit around the air intake and ashdump cover forms.

Reinforcing rods extend from firebox onto forehearth area. These are tied together where they cross and supported by small pieces of brick.

Concrete is poured level over the entire hearth area to a depth of 3 or 4 inches—depending on local codes.

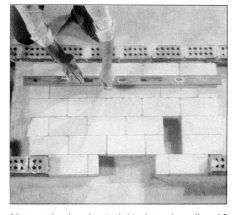
Use a plumb rule straightedge; draw line 16 inches from the inside of the front face. This is your guide for laying the back wall.

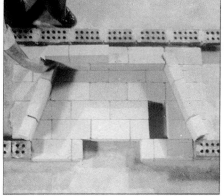
Dry lay the first course of firebrick along the guidelines. Then cut firebrick to fit and lay the courses.

The air inlet opens at front edge of firebox. It directs cool, outside air into the fire, not into the room.

Fit building (tar) paper into firebox while constructing the interior masonry walls. This protects the hearth to make cleanup easy.

The back of the firebox walls should be mortar coated—parged—for protection. Lay two wythes of brick behind the firebrick wall.

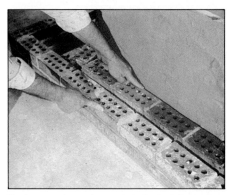

Codes require at least eight inches (two standard brick wythes) of brick masonry behind the firebrick back wall.

Raise the front face to smoke shelf level. Fill voids with rubble and mortar. Wall ties join face brick to the lining courses.

Raise back wall equal to firebox depth. Corbel in small steps. Slope half of depth for smoke shelf. Parge shelf smooth.

Install a metal lintel across the fireplace opening. Opening should be no higher than it is wide; in this fireplace—24 inches.

A second angle iron supports the slanting wall that forms the smoke chamber and supports the flue tiles.

The smoke chamber is corbelled to a small opening the same size as the inside of the flue tile as a secure base for the liner tile.

Base flashing fits against the chimney and under the shingles. The overlapping joints send water over joints and not into them.

Counterflashing fits over the base flashing and into mortar joints. The combination gives good weather protection.

Counterflashing matches roof angle. Install from low chimney face. Overlap joints are caulked; mortar joints tuckpointed.

Corbel chimney to form a projecting lip. Sloping cement wash cap directs rain water away from flue.

8
INSTALLING PREFABRICATED UNITS

Adding a traditional masonry fireplace involves expense, inconvenience, and in many cases, a long wait for the warm weather needed before beginning construction. (You cannot cast a slab if the soil has frozen.) The introduction of the prefabricated fireplace discussed in depth in Chapter 2 has reduced these difficulties. They come ready to install, constructed out of heavy sheet metal or cast iron. If you have had some experience with light house framing, the installation of a prefabricated fireplace could be completed and in operation after only a weekend of work. For those with less experience, plan on a week. The work itself is not tedious, but patience and care in the construction are essential. Step-by-step instructions included with the fireplace explain how to assemble the building materials into a framework into which the pieces of the fireplace fit together. The instructions not only describe the assembly of the fireplace but the requirements for the enclosing framework. If you are in doubt about your ability to install a prefab fireplace, pay a visit to your local supplier and request a sample instruction manual. The home-assembled fireplace is within the capabilities of anyone who can read and can use a saw, hammer and nails.

THE ZERO-CLEARANCE UNIT

The zero-clearance looks like a standard fireplace; however, it is a metal shell which is set in place and then covered with a framework and suitable fascia. The fireplaces are called "zero-clearance" because their insulation permits installation next to combustible walls or, in a new home, in the framework of the structure but without a masonry foundation. The units are usually firebrick-lined,

A prefabricated, zero-clearance fireplace can be installed in any room and matched to any period style or decor. The unit is hidden by the surround and covered as needed.

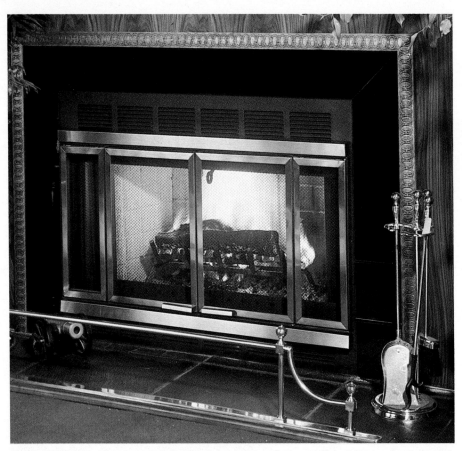

Many prefabricated fireplaces are also heat circulating and energy efficient. Vents allow heated air into the room. Glass screens prevent air from being drawn back into the fire.

A free-standing fireplace may also have heat-circulating features. This unit offers both a view of the fire and heat exchange.

relatively lightweight, and available in designs that resemble the standard fire-place. In addition to the conventional single-opening fireplace, recent design innovations have resulted in improved heat production. Model styles range from a standard fireplace to those with built-in heat exchange systems. These systems use fresh-air intakes to feed the fire combustion and interior-air intakes to collect cool room air, heat it, and circu-late it back into the room and/or dwelling. There are models that can be connected to the existing furnace ductwork. These have thermostatic controls that cause the furnace to take over when the fireplace heat drops too low. There are other units that hook up to the dwelling's hot water system. A word of caution on these units. Most state and local codes require very strict installation and operation proce-dures for the add-on to the furnace. It is strongly recommended that if you are contemplating this type of fireplace, you select a qualified installer.

When installing a zero-clearance unit in your home, several options are avail-able to you. The first, and probably the easiest, is to install the entire fireplace on the outside of an exterior wall. This means that an opening from the interior space to the outside will be required. A framework for the chimney is then built on the outside of the wall. The second option is to install the fireplace entirely inside the home, against an interior wall. The chimney framework is then built up through the roof from the interior, using considerable interior space. No matter which option you choose for a zero-clearance fireplace, you will have to build a 2x4 framework to house the fireplace and chimney. Once the framwork is completed, exterior and interior finishes of your selection can then be applied.

Buying the Unit

When choosing a zero-clearance, check for the U.L. label. This is a must! It will ensure that certain safety features have been built into the unit. This also means that it has been tested and inspected, and is a reputable, stable and safe product.

If you do not want to do the extra work of connecting a unit to the existing heating system, but you want to get the most out of a standard unit, then purchase one with a built-in heat exchanger and an outside air intake option to improve combustion. When purchasing a unit, make sure that the fireplace will permit installation of a protective glass firescreen to keep the warm air in the rooms. Many units have this option; however, there are prefab fireplaces which cannot accept glass firescreen panels.

The major concern in choosing a fire-place should be the size of the firebox opening in relation to the room where it will be installed. To determine the correct size, measure the room, the length and width together. You should have one inch of fireplace opening width for every foot total. If the room is 15 by 17 feet, you will need a fireplace with a 32 inch opening. It is important to buy the cor-rectly sized unit, because if it is too small, it will not product enough heat. A unit that is too large will mean a waste of energy.

Position of the Unit

You must also plan the location of the fireplace. Consider the construction of the fireplace location. It is unwise and im-practical to cut through joists and floors for the chimney. It is more desirable to choose the shortest route for the chimney, cutting a minimum number of framing members in the walls or ceilings. No load bearing members can be cut.

Prefabricated units even come in opposite-faced models. This unit draws cool air from floor level and directs it upward.

A free-standing fireplace may be located at any position convenient in a room. The chimney may be jogged to keep it from passing directly through a room above.

Examine the traffic patterns in the room. Putting a unit in an area that will force people to walk between the furniture and the hearth could make the fireplace a nuisance or in some cases may assist in developing a clear traffic pattern in the room. Furniture itself is a consideration. It is a good idea to plan the furniture arrangement while you plan the fireplace so you will have an idea of how the room will look. Plan the location so the fireplace may enhance that look.

Consider any possible problems on the outside of the dwelling also. If there is a neighboring house adjacent to the wall where you hope to install the fireplace, you may want to consider another location. A house or even a tree can disrupt the draft pulling of the chimney at the cap level. You may be able to position the unit where it can be ducted into the furnace chimney, if you will have an unused separate flue.

Bearing in mind that even zero-clearance units take up some space in a room, you may wish to install one on an outside wall with the face flush with the inside wall surface. This is possible if your house has a brick foundation and walls, although a building permit may be required. Buy more brick and build a foundation and wall for the unit and the chimney chase. The chase refers to the space that is created by the enclosing framework; it is a shallow recess in which the chimney is set. Make the fireplace flush with the inside of the exterior wall and avoid interior work of framing such as cutting into the framing or through the ceiling joist and roof.

You should now decide whether you want a raised hearth. If you do want a raised hearth, it can be created by building a framework of 2x4s to the desired height, and covering the framework with plywood. This raised hearth should extend beyond the front and sides of the unit to meet the minium clearance requirements of the unit's manufacturer. Be sure that the raised hearth complies with local and state building codes. One requirement will be the installation of a 6 to 8 inch wide piece of galvanized sheet metal that is slightly greater in length than the fireplace. The strip will be tacked down so that 3 to 4 inches project out from the face of the installed fireplace. If the unit is off balance, level with shims until it is even on the floor or raised hearth.

Installation

Once you have determined the proper location of the hearth and prepared the chimney opening, place your unit in position and construct the necessary framework around it. Keep in mind that the chimney opening should have at least three inches clearance from a vertical wall or surface. If the unit is to be installed on a combustible floor, take a 6 or 8 inch wide strip of sheet metal and tack it down so that 3 to 4 inches of the metal will extend out as a hearth area in front of the unit. This will keep sparks from falling onto the combustible floor material.

Following the manufacturer's directions, nail the unit in place, using the wall tabs that are provided on the sides of the unit. Nail holes will be punched out already. Use small 2x4 blocks at the four

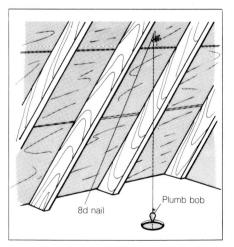

8d nail   Plumb bob

Use a plumb bob to position the chimney pipe. This will ensure accurate cuts through your ceiling and roof line.

corners of the base, nailing them firmly to the unit and against the floor. Installation of the chimney may be begun after the fireplace has been set in position. To have better access to the chimney, all the enclosing chimney framework should be installed after the chimney installation has been completed. Once the fireplace has been set in place, the chimney openings through the floor, ceiling, or roof must be cut. The best way to locate the openings is to suspend a plumb line with plumb bob from the ceiling until the plumb bob is centered over the flue opening of the fireplace below. Mark the spot on the ceiling. The opening through the floor or roof will be in exact alignment with the flue opening. If the chimney opening is to be located at a point in the roof or ceiling that does not align itself with the center of the flue collar, an offset chimney flue is required. Most manufacturers supply a combination of chimney sections and elbows required to meet most offsets. To determine the offset between the fireplace flue collar and the roof or floor opening, you must provide two dimensions; vertical offset and the horizontal offset. The procedure is similar to that employed in determining the position of the chimney opening in the roof. Drop a plumb line and bob from the ceiling to the centerline of the flue collar. Drop another line from

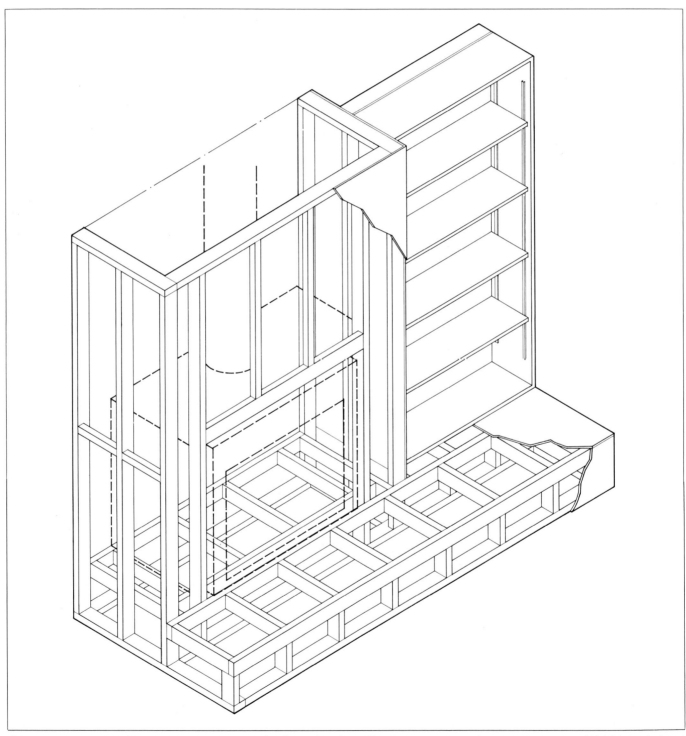

Although codes require a 2-inch clearance between any fireplace unit and wood framing, there are no other restrictions that would inhibit the design of your surround, which may be plain or include storage, bookcases or display shelves.

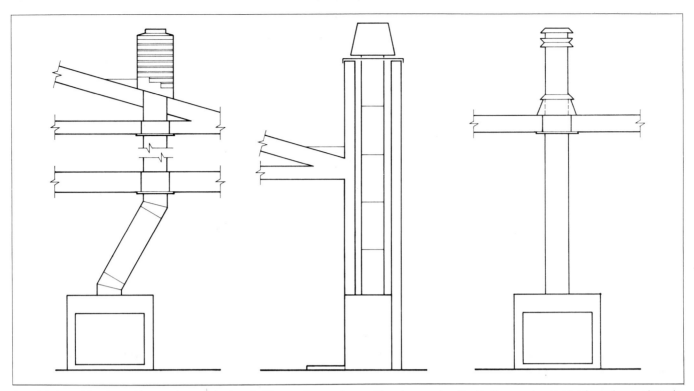

A prefabricated fireplace chimney pipe may be installed in one of several ways. The pipe may be offset to fit around a structural member or obstacle, run up the outside of the house and enclosed, or left exposed to run straight up through the roof.

the roof opening to the floor. Measure the distance between the two. This is the horizontal offset. From the top of the flue collar to the bottom of the roof opening represents the vertical offset dimension. Your fireplace supplier will provide you with the necessary sections to meet those offset dimensions.

Connecting the flue. The flue comes in three sections: inner pipe, intermediate, and outer. Attach the inner pipe first, then the intermediate and outer pipe. The inner pipe will fit inside the sections, while the other two fit over or outside this section. The intermediate and outside sections should be installed with the folded edge end up and the crimped end down. At each opening in either the ceiling or the roof, a firestop-spacer must be installed. The firestop-spacer is required by most state and local codes when chimney flues are installed. The firestop-spacer also provides a stable connection for the flue as it passes through the floor or ceiling. Run the flue pipe through openings all the way up to and through the roof of the house in this manner. However, do not yet assemble the flue pipe section that will run through the final roof opening.

Exterior framing and finishing. Finish the framing work around the chimney flue and fireplace using 2x4s. Do this according to the manufacturer's specifica-

tions because each model has a different height dimension from the base of the unit to the point above the firebox opening. For a unit such as Superior's, there must be 56 inches of minimum clearance from the bottom of the header to the fireplace base. There should be 2x4 studs adjacent to each side of the fireplace opening, representing the jambs. Between these 2x4s should be another 2x4 spanning the top of the fireplace opening. This piece acts as a header and as a cross brace.

The framing around the unit can be designed in any shape to suit any taste or atmosphere desired. If requested, the Z-Brick Corporation will send you any of four or five plans in various styles for woodwork around the units. The usual frame plan that is provided in most prefab fireplace instructions is for a simple box-shape extending from the floor or raised hearth to the ceiling. With a little imagination, you can add more to the sides and include set in bookshelves, television or stereo space, or even wood storage. However, the simplest is that which runs out from one existing wall, across the front of the unit, and to the wall on the other side, extending all the way up to the ceiling.

If you have decided to run the chimney flue out through an exterior wall and then up, you will also have to build a frame-

work up the side of the house around the flue pipe for an outside chimney. You will have to use supports on the chimney flue pipe to keep it against the wall, build the framework, and wall it off with plywood. Use exterior grade plywood, which is the only grade that will resist outdoor conditions.

Some units come complete with cold air intakes, a warm air vent, and heat-resistant glass screens for energy saving.

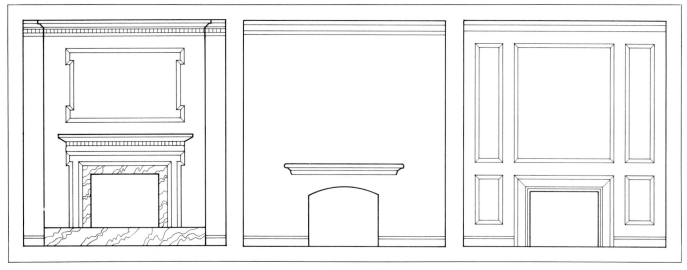

After covering framing with wallboard, you may create any style surround you desire. A marble forehearth and edging may require professional installation. Simple moldings or a plain mantel shelf may be added by the homeowner to give a period touch to the face.

An electric fireplace may be installed where wood burning is not possible. In most areas it is cost effective and trouble free.

To surface the chimney, you can use simulated brick, flagstone or rock. It is a simple task to apply mastic to the plywood, and apply the ''brick'' or ''stone''. The end result will appear to be a masonry chimney.

Finishing the interior. Face the frame with plywood or other suitable material. If the unit has inside heat-exchange intake vents, be sure not to cover them. This would cause the units to overheat once a fire was built and damage the fireplace. Once the plywood is up, you can see that you have built a wall around the fireplace. All that is needed now is a finish on the plywood.

Just as you must choose the style for your framework, you must choose the style of finish the fireplace face will have. It can be something as simple as wall paneling to match the rest of the room, a coat of plaster, Z-Brick, or even decorative tiles, which may be cemented in place. If you do use a Z-Brick type material, be sure to grout between all the joints to complete the masonry effect. Once the bricks have set and dried, apply sealer for protection.

Installing at the roofline. Now prepare the chimney from the roof up. This includes the roof flashing, storm collar, and termination or cap. The roof flashing must be centered carefully over the roof passage hole. Tack nail it in position so it will not slide off center. If you use conical style flashing, which is wider at its base, thus providing an easier connection on a pitched roof, be sure the base has the proper pitch by sliding the outer section down into the flashing cone. Make sure that there is proper alignment with the flue pipe below and that the flue pipe will fit in a full vertical position as it passes through the flashing. Do not lock the outer pipe section into position with the lower flue pipe. First check the vertical alignment of the outer flue pipe section with a level and, if necessary, adjust the position of the flashing until each is plumb vertically.

Remove the outer section from the flashing cone. Secure the flashing in place by nailing along the perimeter of the flashing into the roof. If you have a shingled roof, cover the upper half of the flashing with the shingles, but allow the lower half of the flashing to rest on the roofing. Cover the nail heads with roofing

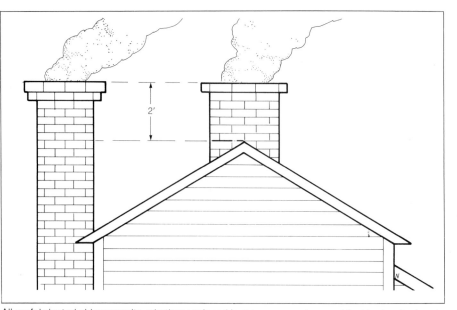

All prefabricated chimney units, whether enclosed in masonry or not, are subject to standard code restrictions, requirements, and clearance regulations.

cement. Then begin assembling the chimney parts by placing the inner pipe section through the flashing, and then add the intermediate and outside sections to bring the pipe up through the roof and flashing.

It must be remembered that, in compliance with the National Fire Protection Agency's rules, the extension of the chimney above the roof ''shall be at least three feet above the highest point where it passes through the roof of the building, and also shall be at least two feet higher than any part of the building, including the roof, within ten feet of the stack.''

Once the chimney has been built to the correct height, the last procedure is to install the termination or cap. Center the inner lips of the cap into each flue pipe section. Push down until the units lock into place. Test the connection by pulling up lightly. Your fireplace is finished.

FREE-STANDING FIREPLACE

The second type of pre-fabricated unit, the free-standing fireplace, is a light, modern version of a stove, but it includes some of the features of a fireplace. It can be placed in most rooms, installed with or without a hearth, depending on the interior floor finish. An exposed wood floor directly in front of the fireplace, for example, will require a protective metal

plate in front of the opening in order to protect the floor. Many units are open on one side only. Some models of free-standing fireplaces can be put near a wall, where only five or six inches clearance is needed. This means that they can be used in nearly the same manner as a zero-clearance fireplace and there is less work involved.

Heat-producing options of the free-standing unit have been developed much

This free-standing unit has a combination glass door/screen and a damper control built into the front below the firebox.

like those of the zero-clearance type. Built-in heat exchangers and connectors to the heat and hot water supplies are available.

Positioning the Unit

For the most part, the free-standing fireplace should be centrally located in the room or in the house, since one of its advantages is that it will radiate the heat in nearly all directions—which a zero-

This round unit could be installed anywhere. Tempered glass surrounds the firebox and provides a clear view of the blaze.

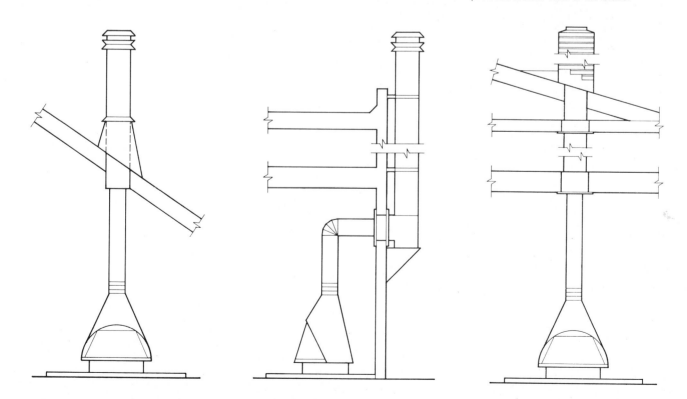

Chimney units for free-standing fireplaces come in many styles. A special flashing cone is made for steeply pitched roofs. Another chimney unit cuts through an outside wall rather than the ceiling. Prefabricated units can give brick-like finish to chimney tops.

Free-standing units come in a variety of styles and finishes. Units frequently appear in settings to which they are color matched.

clearance or masonry fireplace cannot do. This is because a free-standing unit is open on more sides than are the other types. The free-standing fireplace requires more floor area around it because of the heat it generates. It is important to keep all combustibles away from the chimney and sides.

Installation

There is very little construction involved for a free-standing fireplace except for cutting the hole for the chimney. The normal household workbench tools will be all that is required to do the job.

Fireproofing the floor. If the flooring under and around the unit is made of combustible material, you will have to fireproof the floor. Fireproofing may be anything from a heavy gauge galvanized sheet metal (which can be painted the same color as the unit) to a raised platform with a Z-Brick, brick, stone or other noncombustible covering. You can do anything that meets the protection specifications of the manufacturer of the unit to fireproof the floor.

Hookup. The unit is now put together and placed onto the ''hearth'' you have provided. The chimney sections run just the same as those for a zero-clearance unit or a stove, working from the top down, using plumb lines to make sure all is lined up correctly. Where the chimney will come in contact with combustible materials at the second floor, it is advisable to enclose the chimney flue in a similar manner as the zero-clearance fireplace.

BREAKING IN A PREFAB FIREPLACE

Before you fire-up your new fireplace, there are several things you should consider. The first is the type of fire grate you should purchase. Cast iron, wrought iron and some prefabricated steel special designs are currently available on the market. The grate will protect the refractory lining of the firebox. The brick lining is easily broken, so that the installation of a grate is strongly recommended. The second is the type of fireplace tool you are planning to use. The tool set can be a decorative addition or an accent to the fireplace. Always select tools that are sturdy and well constructed. Third is probably the most important; that is the 'burning-in' of the firebox. If the firebox is properly fired, your fireplace will provide you with a long life. If improperly done, the life of the refractory brick will be reduced by half.

The proper burn-in of a fireplace requires patience. Start off by building very small fires. The smaller fire will evenly ''cure'' the brick. When the brick is properly cured, all the moisture that the brick has absorbed will be released. The brick will then change color and take on a darker hue. Keep the underside of the grate clear of ashes so that the brick will be exposed to the flame. After the first five or six fires, gradually increase the size of the fire until you arrive at a size that is suitable for your needs.

9

PREVENTING HEAT LOSS

The words "fuel efficiency" go hand in hand with the word "money". The less fuel used; the more money saved. Everyone is conscious of it, from the higher income to the lower income brackets. The greatest efficiency permits the homeowner to get the maximum amount of heat from every bit of fuel. A fireplace that is thirty or forty years old often is both a heat loser and a money loser. This should be of special interest to those who are buying or have purchased an older home with a fireplace. Just as old wiring or plumbing needs to be updated and replaced, so the fireplace will need special attention.

An efficient fireplace uses fresh air from outside for efficient combustion, circulates heated warm air, and shuts off chimney draft quickly when the fire dies down. A combination of an outside air duct leading to the firebox, interior vents, ducting, blowers to circulate heated air, and glass doors to seal the fireplace opening as the fire dies can offer a considerable improvement of the efficiency of the fireplace.

Although energy conservation is a contemporary concern, even the Victorians cared about stopping drafts. They built iron doors on their fireplaces to keep heat in.

STRUCTURAL CONSIDERATIONS

There are many ways to obtain heat from the fireplace. The key is to have a fireplace that was built correctly, and placed in a position from which it will spread heat evenly throughout the room. If the fireplace was not built correctly, or has been built into an awkward part of the room, it will waste valuable heat. Improper firebox proportions may prevent your getting the best and fullest heating potential from the fireplace. The best proportions were discussed in Chapters 3 and 7. Although there should always be ample clearances and correct sizing in order to have a functional unit, you may still be able to correct some problems— not by reconstruction, but by installing one or more heat-efficiency additions to the fireplace.

If your existing fireplace has no mantel, thought should be given to adding one, as described in Chapter 4. A mantel over the opening aids heat retention from the firebox. A mantel of any size acts as a heat deflector, so that much of the heat rising from the fireplace opening will not float straight to the ceiling area and be wasted.

Air Intake Vents

A fire in conventionally built masonry fireplace, when measured in BTU's (British Thermal Units, a form of measuring heat), results in an output of a negative 5 percent of heat. You may feel heat being thrown out of the opening into the room, but at the same time, great quantities of heated interior air are being stolen away by the fire if the fireplace draws air from inside sources only. Unless you turn off your furnace each time you plan to use the fireplace, you are sending warm air up the chimney. Without an outside draft, the

Electric fireplaces are "artificial"; since no flue draws off heated air they give more BTUs than do most wood burning units.

fireplace will draw only on the air which your home utility has already heated. The provision for outside air lowers the pull of air from the room. To preserve the home's heated air supply, install outside air intake vents to fuel the fire. Remember, a fire needs air to make it burn.

A fireplace will benefit most from the installation of an outside air intake passage with an outlet at the front of the firebox, just inside the opening. However, outside air intake vents may be installed directly through the back firebrick wall of the firebox. Venting kits come ready for installation and are available from several firms. To install a direct vent, use a small hard chisel to lightly chip away at the mortar on a lower brick of the firebox. Remove the brick and insert the vented metal plate in its place. Next, drill a hole through to the outside brick wall with a masonry bit. Insert and cement into place the small piece of

This unit has an exterior air duct. It is meant to be installed in an existing fireplace, and is set through the back wall.

tubing from the kit. These vent kits also have the shut-off valves built into them. Once the fire has gone out, and the fireplace has cooled, these allow you to reach in and close off the vent, just as you should close the damper.

Some homeowners have simply drilled a small hole through the back wall of the firebox and then inserted and cemented in a pipe to gain outside air. This will save heated air while the fire burns. However, unless there is a way to shut off this piping, heated air will be lost once the fire dies, for it will be drawn out the pipe as air is drawn up a flue without a damper. When inserting your own piping or a manufactured vent, seal up all cracks and spaces between piping, the vent, and the surrounding brick. Use a heavy paste of portland cement on the outside wall and a high-temperature cement on the firebox side. Tuck and pack it firmly into the cracks and gaps with a small trowel.

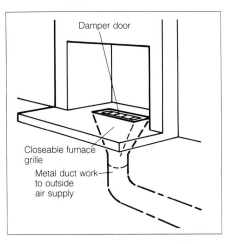

Damper door

Closeable furnace grille

Metal duct work to outside air supply

To add a grille to an existing fireplace for incoming air, route the duct work through the ashpit to an exterior wall.

Floor venting from outside. The addition of the exterior airway into the floor of the fireplace was discussed in Chapters 6 and 7; refer to that chapter for general directions. Any fireplace with an ashpit can be adapted to bring air from outside into the hearth. Even if no other adaptation is made, you can prop open the ashpit cleanout door if it is on the exterior wall or on an interior wall in an unheated basement. When you build your fire, prop open the ash dump; cover with fine screen; cool air will be drawn in to the fire.

The Fireplace as Furnace

There are other methods and devices which will further add to the efficiency of a fireplace. One alternative is to provide

ducts around your fireplace or under the firebox floor so that air can be pulled through the area of the fireplace, heated, and released into the room.

Attached to furnace. Call in a professional to run ductwork off of the fireplace, connecting it to the home's existing furnace ductwork and heating the entire house with the fireplace. The system can be thermostatically controlled so it will shut off the furnace when not needed and let it cut back in once the fire has gone out. With a masonry fireplace, especially an older model, this conversion is costly and difficult. If you are adding a fireplace to the home, the system can be installed at less expense and with less work.

Any design using ductwork should be done with the help of a consultant (either architect or engineer) so that ducting does not interfere with the outside air intake or alter the basic efficient design of the fireplace unit.

Ducts next to fireplace. It is possible, and easier, to build ducts on either side of the fireplace so that air is drawn from the floor, then heated, and finally released through upper vents. This should occur naturally because warm air rises; as the fireplace heats the air in the ducts, it should move upward and out the vents creating a moving stream of air.

Installing the vents for these ducts on an upper floor will give heat to that floor. Assuming that you have an open stairway so that air will circulate freely through the house, you should get a flow of warmed air moving through your system. The addition of a built-in fan/blower will speed up and/or control this natural flow. If you add a blower to your system, be

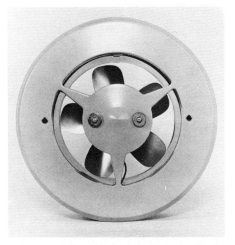

Some fan units are designed to work with the heat exchanger in a fireplace in order to increase efficiency and distribution.

This wall-mounted unit pulls warm air down from the ceiling level to the floor level, where it is recirculated.

Andirons work well in this very small fireplace; however, in most cases, a grate will be more effective in maintaining a blaze.

sure that you provide convenient access to the unit for upkeep and repairs.

A raised hearth can be adapted to include a duct which pulls cool air across the warm hearth surface and blows it into the room at the other side. A blower can be built in next to the fireplace wall to circulate the air heated by the bricks or masonry.

HELPFUL PRODUCTS

Use of either andirons or a grate is a necessity. These items promote a well-burning fire, for they let the ash fall to the floor, allowing the fire to burn unhindered. Otherwise, ashes will tend to smother and suffocate the breathing capacities of the fire, creating less heat.

Grates, Andirons, Alternatives

The grate is more efficient. A grate helps circulate a draft for the fire, resulting in a stronger, hotter blaze. The grate should always be the correct size for the fireplace. Buying just any grate size is not a good idea. If possible, the grate should be as wide as the firebox. A grate that is too small provides a blaze that will not utilize the entire back wall of the firebox, which means less radiation of heat.

Andirons should generally be placed a foot to a foot and a half apart. The distance will depend on the size of the fireplace, for the smaller the width of the firebox, the shorter the distance between the andirons. Andirons are not as efficient as a grate because often a log will burn

Convection grates without power fans circulate air around the fire through tubes. Heated air rises and comes back into the room.

and break in half, falling and settling down into the ashes. This reduces the blaze, and cuts short the burning time of the wood.

Convection grate. In the past decade many products have been designed and manufactured to help turn the fireplace into a more fuel-efficient heat source. The simplest, least expensive product to help retain fireplace heat is one that replaces the common steel grate. It is a grate made of hollow tubing and it works on a convection principle. The tubing is formed in a U with the open ends facing the room. The tubing runs below the logs, around the back, and over the top of the burning fuel. Once the fire is going, the grate will draw in air through the bottom and circulate it around the fire. This forces out heated air, through the top and back into the room. This type of heat exchanger has, using the power of natural physics, the potential to create 10 to 20 percent more heat from the hearth. There are no installation procedures required.

Heat exchanger. There are also similarly designed heat exchangers available, with the added option of an electrically operated blower that rests on the fore-hearth to the side of the fireplace opening, where it plugs into an adjacent common household socket. Like the simpler version, the working part rests in the hearth. The blower helps increase the air intake and output, causing more heat to be

Power-assisted heat exchangers often come as combined units with a grate and glass screens. Fan units on hearth pull air through the grate and send heated air into the room.

thrown into the room and house, but these are fairly visible contraptions. This means you will have an eight- or ten-inch square boxlike blower motor housing on display. If you wish to hide this, some firms make heat exchangers that can be built into the walls of the fireplace. The exchanger is then wired into the main electrical supply. This usually is only incorporated into a fireplace when it is being built, not for existing fireplaces. There are also glass fireplace screens with built-in heat exchangers and blowers.

Heat Reflector

Another method of improving the efficiency of a fireplace is to increase the reflectivity of the walls. Colonial fireplaces often had "fire backs". These were pieces of metal attached to the back walls of the fireplaces. While some were quite decorative, a plain sheet of copper was often used. A piece of polished, reflective metal will not only direct the heat toward the fireplace opening, but it may also ncrease the reflected light.

Today several types of heat reflectors, such as that made by Kronos, are available. One device is nothing more than a wide, slightly curved piece of metal which rests against the back of the firebox. The metal absorbs and then reflects the heat out into the room. It also shortens the space in the firebox. Since many older models of masonry fireplaces were built too deep to radiate heat efficiently, a heat reflector will help correct this problem. These products are installed without any hard work, for the reflector is placed directly behind the fireplace grate, resting on its own pedestal. Although this type of heat reflector will not add great amounts of heat, it will contribute somewhat to the warmth and comfort of the home.

The Physicist's Fireplace. This grate, called a Texas Fireframe, was designed by Dr. Lawrence Cranberg. It supports the logs so that maximum heat is created for efficient combustion. The design also sends more heat directly into the room, providing maximum heat to the home although still sending the smoke and gasses up the chimney.

Glass Firescreen

A glass-door firescreen, which is shut once the fire is out, prevents heated air from going up the chimney. One of the problems for any fireplace owner is how to retain heat while the coals are still smoldering. The damper must remain

A relic from earlier days the fireback—a reflective metal attached to the back wall of the fireplace—sends a little more heat into the room than the firebrick wall.

Designed by a physicist to hold logs to create as hot a fire as possible, this grate sends more heat into the room than do ordinary grates. The design also aids ingition.

Styling of heat exchanger grate/glass screen units varies enough to provide attractive and practical models for any decor.

A fireplace insert is one answer to increasing heat efficiency. This unit includes a powered heat exchanger in the base.

open and, at this point, great amounts of heated air will be then circulating back through the fireplace and out the chimney. With a glass-door firescreen, the damper can remain open, because the closed glass doors shut off most of the air supply and let the fire go out without waste or danger. If the glass doors remain closed while the fire burns, you will still retain visibility of the flames. The glass also reflects heat out into the room, much like windows do with direct sunlight. It is a variation of passive solar energy. If you have a choice between the old-fashioned wire mesh screening or a glass-door screen, choose the glass version.

Combination firescreen/heat exchanger. Combining the best features of the two items, there are combination glass-door/heat exchanger firescreen systems. These not only have a glass door, but also a heat exchanger/grate attachment. Some come with electrical blowers built into the bottom of the glass doors, hidden from sight. The blower plugs into a nearby socket. In this arrangement, the

glass doors remain closed at all times, reducing the amount of burning time and fuel used, yet forcing out great amounts of heat. Such glass-door firescreen heat exchangers can considerably cut costs.

Fireplace Inserts

For those who are even more energy conscious, there is a device that can convert the fireplace into a nearly airtight wood burning stove. The unit is called a fireplace insert. Manufactured by several firms from either heavy steel or cast iron, these units are built along the same principle as a stove. Some are shaped to fit directly into the fireplace opening, all the way to the back wall. Many have broad doors, inserted with viewing glass, which cover the entire mouth of the opening. These airtight inserts use draft controls, just as a stove does, so you can control heat output and burning rates. Just as with the stove, they have ''baffled'' walls that circulate the gases, smoke and heat around the outer perimeters of the fire, yet allow only the smoke to go up the

flue at the same time, the system pushes large amounts of heat into the house. It is said that these units can burn one armload of wood for eight to ten hours.

Fireplace inserts are relatively easy to install since, for the most part, they slip into the firebox and are cemented in along the front edges and around the flue using a fireproof cement. Some patience is necessary, however, because the first step is to cut templates out of sheets of the fireproof material supplied with the unit, according to the instructions. This is done after removing the existing damper, since the inserts have built-in dampers. After making a template to fit up in the flue, you use the fireproof cement to set in the damper section, known as a collar. Then you take the sealing plate and screw or pop-rivet it around the collar. The collar and sealing plate are glued into final position around the lintel and flue. The joints and gaps between the sealing plate and existing brick are caulked with fireproof caulking. The flanges on the insert fit around the collar and are caulked. The insert is

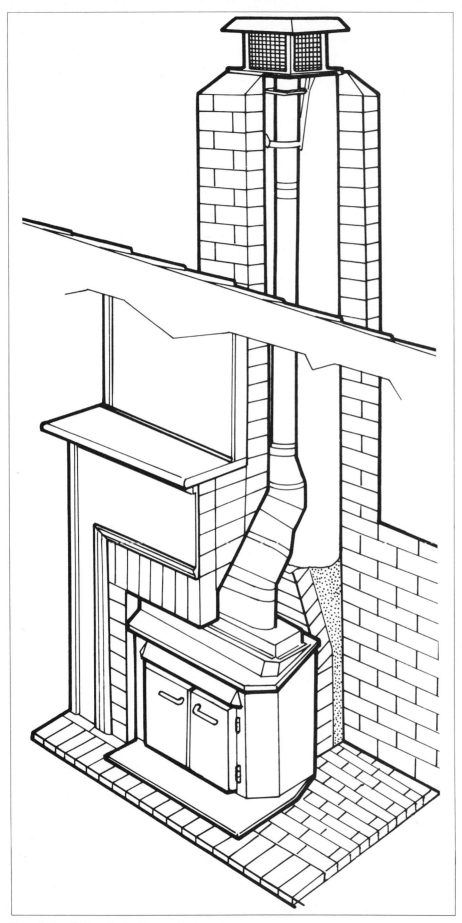

placed in the opening and caulked around the edges on the front of the unit.

There are a few drawbacks to these units. For example, you have lost the use of your ashpit. But these units burn at such a high temperature that there will be less ash, and an occasional cleanout should not prove too large a problem.

Other fireplace inserts are designed to sit farther forward. This means the heat from the unit is radiated directly into the room. Like the free-standing wood stove, these units must stand on a large, fireproof pad. It is even better to provide a raised hearth larger than the unit by at least 12 to 18 inches all around. This will serve as a warning to anyone approaching the stove. Any heat-radiating unit will cause severe burns if touched.

The units that stand out into the room usually require that the fireplace opening be sealed with a stoveboard cover, normally supplied or integral with the unit. The exhaust is vented up the fireplace chimney. It is best to provide piping up through the flue, but most will work acceptably with connections either up to the flue or even just into the firebox.

The insert model shown resembles a stove that uses a fireplace. The heat-resistant board in front of the insert extends the hearth.

If you do not use your fireplace often, seal it with a temporary covering. This helps keep the room heat from escaping.

For safe installation of a fireplace insert, install a complete flue insert that seals to the unit to keep creosote from collecting on or behind the insert and igniting.

10

WOOD STOVES

STOVE VS. FIREPLACE

Much can be said for the benefits and beauty of a fireplace, and the same holds true for the "old-fashioned" wood burning stove. Like the more elaborately ducted fireplaces, the wood burning stove has been developed to a point where it can heat an entire dwelling, especially if electrical blowers help distribute heat. Optional connections to the home's hot water supply and furnace system are possible if carefully planned and properly installed. Thermostatic controls help regulate the heat in the home—much as you would control the furnace in the basement. In fact, there are many units available that are designed to take the place of a furnace. Other units can be installed next to the furnace to operate in conjunction with it, using the same thermostatic control. Thus, the furnace uses less fuel because the wood stove gives supplementary heat to the home. If installing this type of system, it must be properly designed and connected, with all local codes and manufacturers' requirements met.

A modern stove is an economical purchase because updated design and new engineering principles allow a wood burning stove to supply great amounts of heat using only six to ten logs daily. The cost of a stove, compared to that of a fireplace—even of a free-standing type fireplace—is appreciably less. If you decide against a fireplace because your budget will not allow it, consider buying a good wood stove.

Approach buying a stove with some forethought. While efficiency is a recognized factor generally considered by both manufacturers and purchasers, safety may not be. Most incorporated areas now have codes requiring standards or limiting stove installation. Underwriters Laboratory seals are required for most stove codes. Not all stoves meet UL standards, however, and you must be wary. Deal with businesses you know and trust. Ask questions and do not rush.

In the past few years the consumer has been responsible for many of the problems with stoves. Improper locations, unsafe installations and questionable maintenance procedures have all contributed to home fires and other accidents. Remember that stoves radiate their heat! Novels set in the 19th Century often refer to pot-bellied stoves glowing red hot in schools and stores—a stove in use is always hot. Follow installation directions and never cheat on clearances. Locate your stove out of the major traffic ways. Set it high enough on a pad or a hearth so you cannot walk directly into it. Use a ceiling fan near the stove to keep the air moving and to avoid heat buildup in one

Modern wood stoves are more efficent heating units than most of the old-fashioned stoves. They not only offer a great deal of heat, but can be maintained with moderate care.

room. Above all, read the instructions that come with your stove and follow all directions regarding loading, burning and cleaning.

A stove, especially a modern, airtight, thermostatically controlled stove, burns hot enough to ignite the wood gases that usually lead to a creosote deposit. If you burn a slow, cool fire a few consecutive times, the next large, hot fire may ignite the creosote in the stove pipe. A well-

Some stoves look like free-standing fireplaces. This stove has thick-tempered glass sides that allow a full view of the fire.

"Caution: do not touch. Keep children, clothing and furniture away. Contact causes skin burns." Remember that stoves are hot.

insulated pipe will retain enough heat and prevent creosote buildup. Even if you are buying a stove in order to save money, do not try to save money on your stove pipe. Check seals on pipe joints regularly; exhaust smoke and gases can asphyxiate. It is also advisable to install smoke alarms and provide yourself with fire extinguishers as a safety aid.

However, do not panic. Thousands of people heat their homes safely and eco-

Many old homes have stove flues. They should be checked before installing a new stove. Pipe and flues must be cleaned regularly.

European homes have been heated by stoves for centuries. This Scandanavian stove is very popular because of its efficiency.

nomically using efficient, attractive modern stoves.

HEAT AND EFFICIENCY CONTROL

The original stove was, in most cases, a simple one. It consisted of either a cast-iron box or upright cylinder, with a vented door on hinges, a small draft control, and legs to keep it off the floor. The stove was placed in the middle of a room, then fueled, and fired. The metal body heated up, retaining and radiating heat throughout the room more effectively than any fireplace could. Air for combustion was regulated and admitted through openings in the front or top, or both, and the smoke and gases were then exhausted through a vent and up through the chimney. This same principle is still true in the modern-day stove, but the stove is no longer a simple metal box with doors.

Airtight design. Today's stove, unlike the original, is airtight, sealed with strips around any and all possible openings, including the doors. Combustion air is let in through carefully designed air intakes. Although some stoves are made with solid doors, many are manufactured with heat-resistant glass doors, allowing a view of the fire. This airtight design greatly adds to the stove's heat-producing efficiency, and also results in better control of the amount of heat in the home.

Internal smoke baffle. Stoves now have an integral smoke baffle. This produces more heat and air movement around the fire. The wood gases burn off more completely, which means all of the fuel is consumed to give the maximum amount of heat. This also reduces the amount of creosote these gases will deposit in the flue, if the airtight stove is properly operated. A slow burn in an airtight stove can create a great deal of creosote.

Damper controls. Damper controls are now built into the unit. The older models only had dampers in the stove's pipe, an arrangement that was much less efficient. Many stoves also have thermostats built into the dampers, so they will automatically open and close the damper to maintain the level of warmth desired. Electrical blowers force air out the bottom of the stove and push this heated air to the floor instead of letting it drift up to the ceiling, where it is wasted. These

Stoves often are attractive. The glass door option appeals to many people, and the top surface can be used for heating water.

Soapstone stoves absorb and radiate more heat for longer periods than do other stoves. This stove replicates an older design.

The doors on this stove rotate to reveal the firebox inside. This unit may serve as a stove or as a free-standing fireplace.

additions to the stove's design, along with other specialized features, help cut down the amount of wood necessary, reducing the overall amount of fuel required.

STOVE STYLES AND FEATURES
Design Features

The stove is no longer plain, black, large, round, and one-dimensional. In fact, the styles are so varied that it may take a considerable amount of time to select the right one. Stoves range from the octagonal shape that has no legs but hangs from the ceiling by a heavy chain (an Octagon Stove), to a horizontal, half-moon shape with large, full glass doors, (a Greenbriar model). For those who wish a traditional, old-fashioned look, there are many modern replicas of old style stoves available from many dealers. These include a chrome-accented parlor stove with an optional fire screen to replace the airtight doors (for a better view of the fire) and a soapstone stove identical to 19th Century predecessors created by the same manufacturer. It will hold and radiate heat for a long period of time.

If a view of the fire is a primary consideration, there are many stoves that offer tempered-glass doors, and some with full-glass sides and front, much like the three-faced fireplace. If elegance is desired, there are stoves styled more subtly and decoratively than the conventional cast-iron wood burning stove; one

Although not as heat efficient as an airtight stove, this simple stove will serve to heat a room in cold weather but will, however, use more fuel than would a modern stove.

There are stoves for every need. A small stove provides more than enough heat for a single room and takes up little space.

A larger fireplace can heat several rooms as long as proper circulation of air is provided to move heated air from room to room.

This stove, air-tight and fuel efficient, serves as a free-standing fireplace. The door lifts up for a view of the fire. This answers the need for heat efficiency and the natural desire for a view of the flames.

is available with heat retaining decorative tiles—similar to European tile stoves.

Modern stoves are made from cast iron or steel. Some have firebrick linings that retain heat and radiate it long after the fire has died down.

The Radiant Stove

The radiant stove is the basic stove form. It radiates heat from its walls and out into the room. This type of heat travels in direct lines from the heated surface of the stove to the surfaces of any object nearby. Such simple stoves are best used in the basement, garage, or any other work-bench type of area that is otherwise unheated.

The Franklin Stove

The Franklin stove, or versions of it, was a non-airtight stove that actually was a free-standing fireplace, with double doors that opened outward. Although the original models were not airtight, some current models are now airtight when the doors are closed. The Franklin stove has one major drawback: since it usually is not airtight, it will burn wood at a much faster rate than will airtight models.

The Franklin stove was actually the first free-standing fireplace. It is attractive with the doors open for viewing the fire, but is more heat efficient with the doors closed.

A heat reflector placed behind the stove protects the nearby wood paneled wall and directs warm air into the room.

Codes require that stoves be surrounded by a noncombustible material, or that they be kept well away from stud walls.

A stone surround has been provided for this stove. There are many stoves that can burn either wood or coal, as this one does.

The Circulating Stove

A circulating stove has two walls, with the inner walls surrounded by a small space, followed by an outer wall. These are almost always airtight, and often have electrical blower systems to force large amounts of heat to circulate into the dwelling. This type of stove is suitable for use anyplace in the home where greater amounts of warmth and heat retention are required.

THE BEST LOCATION

As with a fireplace, the first step before buying or installing a stove is choosing the best location. The spaces available for placement of the stove determine the stove size. Placement also affects heat distribution. Putting a stove in the center of the room means heat will reach all four corners of the room. With current home designs, it is not always feasible to locate a stove in the center of a room. However, it must be located at least 36 inches from any wall or the ceiling. This is mandatory if the wall is constructed of a combustible material, for a stove does radiate quite a substantial amount of heat. This is one of the design limitations of a wood-burning stove. It cannot be designed for a zero-clearance operation. Although building codes and the recommendations for each individual style of unit will differ slightly, it is always best to have a three foot clearance, or better, between the stove and any combustible material. If the wall of the dwelling is constructed of brick, stone, or protected by some suitable

noncombustible materials, then the unit may be placed closer if codes allow.

Stoves may be used in conjunction with an existing fireplace flue, using the chimney for its exhaust. To do this the fireplace opening must be shut off completely with either brick, block or a fireproof stove board, or metal sheeting—such as copper, brass, stainless steel, or galvanized sheet metal.

Heating Area

Your decision on the location of your stove will depend to some extent on how much of the house you want it to heat. If

the stove will heat only one room, purchase a simple, small radiating or circulating stove. Locate it where nothing will block the heat. If you want to heat the entire house, consider buying a large circulating stove that can be connected to your existing furnace ductwork. If you cannot do this, then place the stove in a room near the middle of the house. The room should have several doors so heat will disperse evenly throughout the house. A room with only one doorway will hold most of the heat. Remember that you will have to run chimney connectors and sections out through a wall or through

A stove board hearth of pebbles embedded in cement sits under this stove, which is positioned well away from the combustible walls of the room.

the ceiling to the exterior—be sure you have chosen a spot where this can be accomplished easily.

INSTALLATION

Although installation of a stove is relatively simple, and much like that of a free-standing fireplace, the National Fire Protection Association often recommends that a stove be installed by the dealer from whom you bought the unit. This is a service nearly all dealers provide. In several states in the East, local and state laws require that dealers install each stove they sell. This is because incorrect stove installations by homeowners in recent years have led to many problems and created many hazards. People have been injured or killed in home fires, because stove pipes in use have disconnected during the late night hours, or creosote has been allowed to build up too long in a stove pipe section. There are now schools that instruct dealers and employees in the correct, safe installation of stoves. Many states have laws that specify how a stove may be installed—even where and how it may be installed in a home.

If you do the installation yourself, follow the manufacturer's instructions very closely. Do not use shortcuts to

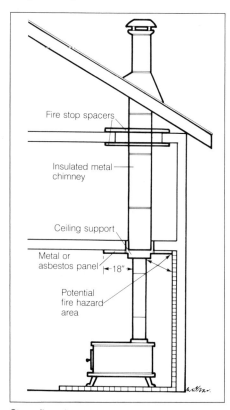

Stove flues become very hot—even when they are insulated. Extensive fire protection is required in installation.

speed up the process. A stove may look easy to install and instructions seem self-explanatory, but it can be very dangerous if installed incorrectly.

Step One: Fire Protection

Lay down a noncombustible protective pad, a stove board that is a minimum of 3/8-inch thick. Although a stove has legs to keep it above the flooring, there is still a lot of heat, which is the reason for the pad. The pad can be of brick, stone, or sheet metal—or you may buy a ready-to-use stove board from companies such as Kemstone, which also produces protectors for the wall behind the stove. Such boards will allow you to drastically reduce the clearance between the stove and the combustible wall. The pad under the stove must create a forehearth area (much like that for the fireplace) that is at least 18 inches in front of the stove, and extends a minimum of eight inches on each side. Again, a thicker pad provides a better warning for unaware passersby.

Step Two: Chimney Connection

The stove *must* have its own flue. The chimney should be made either of masonry (using an existing fireplace), or a Class A-rated, insulated, prefabricated series of pipe that will extend above the roofline to meet the same requirements as those specified for installation of prefabricated fireplace units.

There are certain parallels between the free-standing fireplace and the wood burning stove, and this is evident in the installation of the chimney. After placing the stove on the protective pad, you begin to build the stove pipe upward, beginning

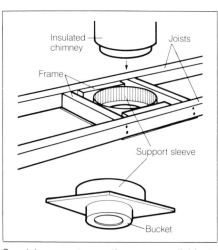

Special connector sections are available to ease and ensure proper installation of a stove pipe through a ceiling.

at the connection in the stove. Place the uninsulated, single-wall flue pipe or chimney connector on the stove's flue pipe. These connectors come in the same colors and metals as that of the stove, and are made of 24-gauge steel. It must be a noncorrosive steel, for the flue gases will soon eat holes in ordinary metal. Check also that it is designated an "all fuel" metal, so that you can, if necessary, burn coal as well as wood.

There are several pieces to the chimney connector. You will need: collars, which cover the wall openings for the flue pipes; support boxes, used to support and center the stove pipe as it passes through walls or ceiling; tees, which are used to connect the horizontal connector pipes to the outside double-walled chimney material; brackets, necessary to support the chimney as it runs up along the outside wall.

There are several ways to arrange the stove chimney system. One method involves running it straight up through the ceiling and through roofing, where the chimney begins. Another system has the chimney reach to within 36 inches of the ceiling, make a 90 degree turn and run parallel to the ceiling. It then passes through an outside wall, where it connects to the chimney. A third alternative calls for the connector to run directly out the back end of the stove, through a wall, where it connects to a tee, from which the chimney begins and goes up, tied to the outside wall.

There are rules you must follow no matter how you choose to install the exhaust system.

(1) A connector should never have more than two bends, of any degree.
(2) If the connector pipe is installed horizontally, the pipe must be sloped at an upward angle, with no less than 1/4 inch per foot.
(3) No pipe should ever be longer than three-quarters of the length of the height of the chimney, measuring from the connector.
(4) A connector cannot run through a combustible wall without a collar support box and fireclay thimble; connectors conduct heat that could ignite the combustible wall.

Step Three: Connector Installation

To install the connector, cut it to the right

length; slip the pieces together, fastening them with sheet metal screws. You may use rivets, but then you will not be able to take the pipe apart in order to fix any problem or clean it out.

For tight joints between sections, install sections with crimped ends away from stove. Attach with screws and seal with cement.

The ends of the connectors fit over the flue outlet of the stove and that of the chimney. If the connectors run horizontally along the ceiling, use straps or wires at regular intervals (2–3 feet apart) to brace the pipes; keep each section in position. Everything else, including the cutting out of the wall or ceiling to allow passage of the piping, the insertion of the supports, and the collars, all are the same as for installation of a free-standing fireplace (see Chapter 8).

USEFUL SPECIAL ACCESSORIES

There are many items which can add to the beauty and usefulness of a wood-burning stove. One is the Stovepipe Shelf by Cedar Creek Homestead, which replaces part of the stove piping a few feet above the stove, and is secured with small machine screws. The result is a metal platform from which you hang cooking utensils (to use on the cooking and heating surface most stoves have), and on which to place food dishes to keep them warm while the rest of the meal may still be cooking. You can even dry mittens or gloves on it during a wet, snowy day. Another item that is utilized with the stove piping is a baking oven. This is a metal box, double walled to allow the smoke and heat to pass around its perimeters.

Also available for use with the stove-piping is the Chimfin radiator, a specially designed circular piece of metal that straps to the stovepipe, collects heat, and desperses it into the room. It effectively transfers heat without causing the stovepipe to cool or allowing creosote to build up.

There are other products that collect heat from the stove pipe. They come equipped with electrical blowers that plug into an outlet, forcing the collected stovepipe heat back into the room. You can install an old-fashioned parlor fan in the ceiling to push heated air from the ceiling

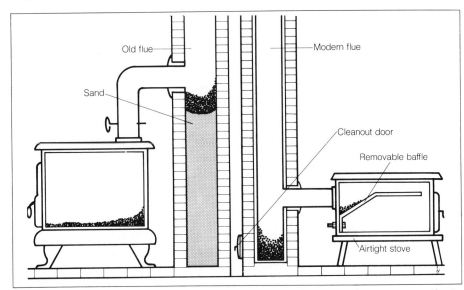

If you connect a stove to an old flue, fill the flue with sand to just below the stove connection to make cleanout easier. You will have to disconnect the pipe for cleanout.

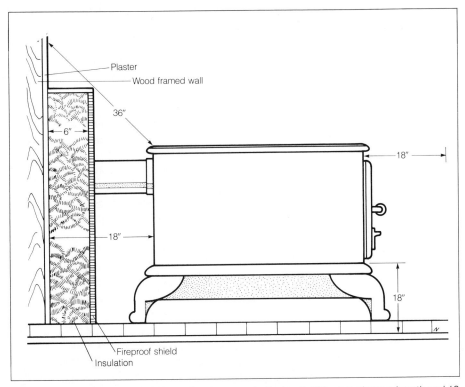

Codes require clearances of 36 inches from an unprotected wall, 18 inches above a hearth and 18 inches from a protected wall. There are various methods of protection.

This coal or wood burning stove is attached to a modern wood-stove flue, with a cleanout door positioned just above floor level.

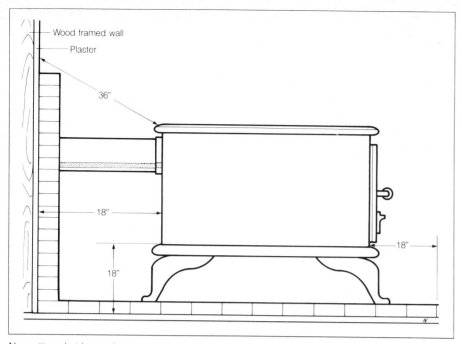

No matter what is used to protect combustible walls, the same clearances are required, including the requirement of keeping all furniture 36 inches away from the stove.

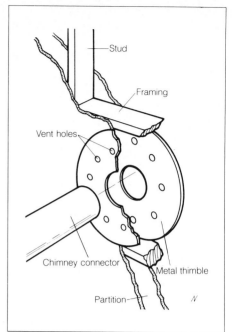

A thimble is used as pipe passes through walls. Framing and insulation are needed.

down to the lower floor level. This usually is an attractive addition to a room and will improve the heating efficiency of the stove.

Tips for Safe Operation

Again, it should be stressed that a wood stove used properly is safe, but remember to keep the pipe sections clean and joints tight. If you vent your stove through a closed fireplace, the cool air from the flue will cause unburned gases to condense quickly. Line the firebox area with sand, or vermiculite and clay to absorb this creosote. Unseal the fireplace and change this material annually for your safety.

If you enjoy a relatively warm heating season and do not burn hot fires regularly, clean the pipes frequently or you will have a chimney fire.

Use insulated pipe. It will retain heat and exhaust gases before they have a chance to cool and condense.

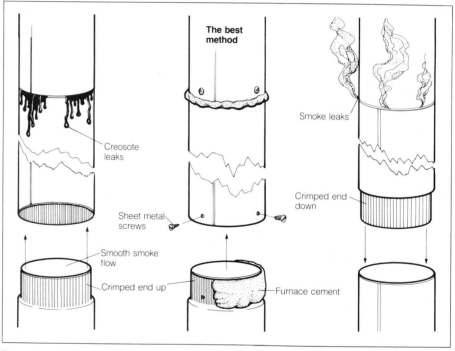

Proper connection and sealing of a stove pipe is necessary to avoid problems. Without proper sealing a pipe connection will leak—either messy creosote or dangerous smoke.

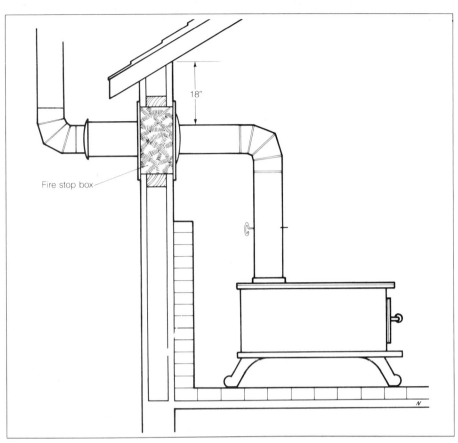

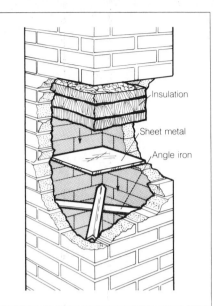

When a pipe connection passes through a wall near the ceiling level, the same 18-inch clearance must be maintained. The firestop box is insulated and sealed with a thimble.

To install stove pipe through an old chimney space, create an insulated support platform on which the pipe can rest.

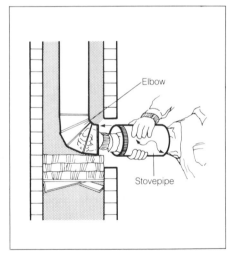

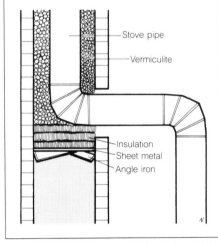

To join pipe sections in walls, place each one on a helper's arm and guide it in.

When pipe is in place on the insulation, fill the chimney space with vermiculite.

The solution to conflicting needs may be a stove in a fireplace. This versatile stove has heat-circulation and swing-out-doors.

Stove insert can be used to heat water or to cook. Note the additional stove board hearth needed to meet code requirements.

11

CHOOSING
AND USING WOOD

Whether you have decided to install or to renovate a fireplace, or to purchase a woodburning stove, you must concern yourself with the fuel involved. Burning wood as an alternative to or supplement for oil, gas or coal is logical if wood produces cheaper heat and is readily available.

One cord of air-dried oak has approximately the same heating capability of 150 gallons of Number 2 fuel oil, or 220 therms (one therm is 100 cubic feet) of natural gas. Wood burning savings can be compared easily to your cost for gas, oil or electricity. Check with your oil supplier or the gas or electric utility and find the cost of 100 cubic feet of gas, or a gallon of heating oil, or of one kilowatt hour of electricity. With this information, multiply the kilowatt hour price by 35, the heating oil price by 1.4 and the gas price by 1.8. The figures you get will be very close to the cost for an equal amount of heat from a cord of hardwood. Compare these costs to that of a cord of wood in your area, and you will see what your

The most important feature of a fireplace is the capacity to burn wood. A good fire requires an efficient firebox and good wood.

savings would be if you used nothing but wood fuel to heat your home.

CHOOSING WOOD
To be certain of high quality in the wood you are either purchasing or cutting, you need to recognize the wood qualities that help create a good fire. These include variations in the heating and burning characteristics of each type of wood, and even differences in their aromas.

Hardwood vs. Softwood
Softwoods have a different set of characteristics than hardwoods. A softwood, such as pine, fir or spruce, ignites more easily than a hardwood because it contains a great deal of resin. If you cut down a pine, look at its bark. You will see sap bubbling out of the crevices here and there. Once this type of tree has been felled and allowed to dry, the oozed substance turns hard and becomes even more flammable, which is why forest fires occur so much more frequently and seriously in the western coniferous forests than in the hardwood forests in the eastern regions of the United States. However, softwood burns only for a short time. Therefore, pine is better when used for a fast, warming fire or as a starter for a lengthy, hot fire fueled primarily with one of the hardwoods.

For a consistent, longer-burning fire, choose a hardwood such as oak, ash, hickory, or even elm. Elm burns well when added to an existing fire, but it is difficult to use to start as an initial fuel. Because hardwood is not as porous as a softwood, it resists burning longer. Once a blaze catches, however, a hardwood fire will burn for hours. It is said that oak burns with the most consistent fire of all

the hardwoods, although the wood of the eucalyptus, available mostly to Californians and Hawaiians, is known to burn for even longer periods of time. Eucalyptus also gives off a sweet, menthol odor.

Burning Qualities of Woods
For a pleasant smell while heating the house, try wood from fruit trees. If wood from apple or cherry trees is available, by all means get a half cord or so to supplement your wood pile. This type of wood sells for more per cord than either the ordinary hard or soft woods, but it adds an extra, pleasurable dimension. Fruitwood is fragrant and, even when dried, will burn with colorful flames.

The ideal wood to burn is one that gives the most heat per cord. However, this wood may be difficult to find if you are cutting your own wood and expensive if you are buying your wood. The ideal combination of traits is a wood that gives high heat, is easy to split, is easy to ignite and does not spark or smoke heavily. No one wood meets all of these criteria.

The highest heat will be given off by apple, ash, beech, birch, hard maple, hickory, locust, oak and pecan woods. These woods also give off the least smoke. Woods that offer good heat range include alder, cherry, soft maple, walnut, elm, gum, and sycamore—all hardwood—and Douglas-fir, yellow pine, larch and tamarack—all softwoods. The hardwoods in this list are more difficult to ignite than the softwoods, but they all give about the same amount of heat and they are all easy to split. The alder, cherry, soft maple, and walnut also give off little smoke and do not spark heavily. The other woods give off considerable smoke. If your area has stringent air

BURNING CHARACTERISTICS OF WOOD

Hardwood	Heat Production	Ignition quality	Splitting quality	Smoke	Sparks	Comments
Apple, ash, beech, birch, dogwood, hard maple, hickory, locust, mesquite, oaks, Pacific madrone, pecan.	High	Difficult	Moderately easy	Light	If disturbed	High quality firewood
Alder, cherry, soft maple, walnut	Moderate	Moderate	Easy	Light	Few	Good quality firewood
Elm, gum, sycamore	Moderate	Moderate	Difficult	Moderate	Few	Good if well seasoned
Aspen, basswood, cottonwood, yellow poplar	Little	Easy	Easy	Moderate	Few	Good as kindling and first logs in fire
Softwood						
Douglas-fir, southern yellow pine	Moderate	Easy	Easy	Heavy	Few	Best of softwoods, but smoke a potential chimney problem
Cypress, redwood	Little	Easy	Easy	Moderate	Few	Usable
Eastern red cedar, western red cedar, white cedar	Little	Easy	Easy	Moderate	Heavy	Usable, best softwood kindling
Eastern white pine, ponderosa pine, sugar pine, western white pine, true firs	Little	Easy	Easy	Moderate	Few	Usable, good kindling
Larch, tamarack	Moderate	Easy	Easy	Heavy	Heavy	Usable
Spruce	Little	Easy	Easy	Moderate	Heavy	Usable, seasoned wood good kindling

pollution regulations, you may not be permitted to burn wood that smokes heavily.

A fire built with a combination of hard and soft woods will ignite more easily, and once going well, will burn without difficulty any hardwoods added to the blaze. If cutting your own wood, plan to cut cords of several types of wood. If you are buying wood, especially if you are using wood as supplementary heat and need only a cord or two, specify cords of mixed hard and softwoods. Shop around until you find someone who will sell you a combination of wood that offers the highest heat and lowest smoke and spark qualities.

What to Ask about Firewood

If you are buying your firewood, look for dry wood. Be sure that the wood you buy is not wet or green. This is especially true if you are buying wood by the ton instead of by the cord. A wet cord of wood will weigh anywhere from 400 to 1400 pounds more than a dry cord. A wet cord will use much more of its own fuel energy burning off the moisture before providing heat. Probably the only way to determine wetness or greenness is to take a log and split it. If the wood splits easily without binding the axe, it is green, wet wood. Wet wood splits very easily; dry wood is

hard to split. Green wood also will have bark that feels damp.

Stacking. There are those who will sell you a cord of wood and dump it in your yard when they deliver it. Not only does this mean extra work for you, but you will have to stack the wood before you know that you have received a legitimately measured, standard cord of wood. When you order wood, specify that the price includes a cord delivered, stacked and, if necessary, carried across the yard to the stacking location.

By the cord or by the ton. To make sure that you have received the amount of wood you paid for, it is best to know how stacked wood is measured. There are two ways to measure out wood, either by the cord or by the ton. Most wood is sold by the cord. A cord is a stack of wood which, when piled in a rectangular pattern, measures eight feet long by four feet high by four feet wide. There are variations of the cord; a ''face cord'' measures much less in volume than an actual cord. A face cord is a unit of cut wood that measures four feet high by eight feet long by the length of the cut logs—usually 16 to 24 inches. If you buy a face cord, you will be getting only a third to a half cord. Check the description of the cord you are buying as well as the price. Order by the full cord, if you have the yard space for

protected storage, from someone who will stack the wood. If you are capable of cutting and splitting the wood yourself, it will be cheaper to buy a cord in logs of either four or eight foot lengths.

In some parts of the country, wood is sold by the ton. If this is the case, remember that a ton of air-dried hardwood will only measure out to about half a cord, and even less if it is wet wood. If you must buy wood by the ton, purchase the driest wood possible.

CUTTING YOUR OWN WOOD

If you are strong, have a great deal of free time and like the outdoors, you may be able to cut your own wood. However, felling a tree and cutting it into firewood takes more time, skill, strength, foresight, and equipment than most people realize. If you happen to own a piece of rural property with a good size woodlot, you probably should be periodically cutting wood to properly manage the forested land. However, if you simply think that it would be a pleasant experience to spend an afternoon in the forest gathering wood for winter, you will be better off buying your firewood.

Felling a tree is dangerous. Even accomplished foresters approach cutting a tree with respectful caution. Before you attempt cutting firewood for a winter supply to handle all the home's heating needs, consider that a medium-size home with good circulation of air will require at least seven cords of wood to maintain a comfortable living temperature during a moderate northern winter. One tree, suitable for firewood, will yield one-half cord. Therefore, if you propose to cut enough wood for the winter, you will be felling, trimming, cutting, hauling and stacking wood from 14 trees. A fully equipped, professional woodcutter can handle several trees a day, but the amateur—even if equipped with good basic equipment—will probably be able to fell and cut only one tree (two, with luck) per weekend.

You may, of course, be able to supplement the wood you have purchased with wood you find, cut and prepare, and this may add enough to make wood cutting worthwhile.

If someone in your family owns a piece of property with a good woodlot or at least a good stand of trees and is willing to let you clear deadwood, you are lucky, and should consider taking advantage of it. In addition, many state and national forests have provisions for the public to clear areas of dead trees and brush. If you can obtain the use of a small pickup truck for a weekend, you may be able to clean and trim enough dead wood for a small truck load. This helps keep the forest clear and improves the condition of the growing trees, as well as providing you with good, dry wood.

Before attempting serious wood cutting, you should take a forestry course through your area extension service, technical school or college, or forest service. Often such a course can be taken at night, for a very small tuition fee. You will learn to recognize the character of a forest or woodlot, learn which trees should be cut, learn what equipment is needed and how to use it, and how to—as safely as possible—fell a tree and prepare your firewood.

Equipment

If you are serious about cutting wood, you will need a bow saw and an axe for quiet, slow cutting or a chain saw and an axe for fast but noisier cutting. It is possible that you may need all three to handle some trees. You should also have a sledge and maul for splitting wood or one of the newer, more mechanical wood-splitting devices. For someone planning on major woodcutting, motorized wood splitters are available, but these cost from $800 to $2500.

You should also have a heavy rod—a sturdy staff with a curved hook built into one end. You will need this to pull trees and logs free of obstructions. You should also have a set of wedges to support cuts and free tools stuck in partially felled trees.

Wearing apparel. Personal gear required ranges from a hard hat to rubber soled safety boots. If you are using a chain saw, you should invest in ear plugs or a set of the selective sound-muffler ear covers available at most gun shops. You will need heavy work gloves, goggles and pants and a jacket with protective padding. Your clothing should allow you to move freely, but you must not wear anything that will be loose and will catch on branches. When a tree goes down, you have to get out of the way fast. If your sleeve catches on a branch, you may find yourself under a felled tree.

The chain saw. While it is an obvious boon to the woodcutter, a chain saw is a potentially lethal weapon. Choose one that is large enough to cut trees for firewood but not so heavy and cumbersome that you have trouble controlling it. Remember that you will have to heft your chain saw all day; do not buy one you cannot carry and use without strain.

Carry and use your chain saw carefully. Never support it with your body when you start it. Put it on the ground. Keep it sharp. Follow manufacturer's instructions exactly for use and maintenance and have it professionally checked and sharpened at regular intervals of use. A chain saw in less than perfect working condition is hard to handle and more dangerous than usual.

A last reminder: when a tree starts to fall, you have to get clear of the area fast. Your chain saw will be running. Learn to run with the chain saw turned off before trying to run with it still on. You must carry the saw with the blade away from your body. The saw blade cannot contact any trees as you move.

Motor transport. If you are handling considerable quantities of wood, you will need a pickup truck—at least ¾ ton—to carry the cut wood out of the woodlot or forest. It is also useful to have a tractor available to drag felled trees out of the woodlot, as well as to provide power for freeing trees that have gotten "hung up" on other trees during the felling process.

Which Tree to Cut

The choice of tree depends on how much time you have before you will want to use the wood, and how much wood you desire. If it is already late summer or early fall, and you do not have any wood for the upcoming months, you will do best cutting a dead or nearly dead tree. Dead wood requires less time to season once felled compared to a healthy tree that takes six or eight months to a year to dry out and season. There is no need to try to cut a really large tree, either. A tree that has a trunk 12 to 24 inches in diameter at five feet above ground level will provide enough wood for a half cord and is easier to cut down and trim clean.

Cutting the Tree

Never attempt to fell a tree alone or on a windy or wet day. Felling a tree is not a job to take lightly. If felled incorrectly, a tree can do serious damage to the woodcutter and to the surrounding trees. For safety you should choose a tree that is easily accessible and in a reasonably clear area. For a first try, have an experienced forester with you and cut a tree near the edge of the woodlot.

Before cutting the large tree for firewood, you will have to clear the area around the tree for access and safety. If you plan to bring a truck or tractor in to carry out the load of wood, you have to clear a large enough path for the vehicle. In any case, prepare the area around the tree so that you can run clear of the tree when it starts to fall. Cut all saplings off even with the ground. If you leave small stumps, you can trip over them as you move away from the tree. Since you may be carrying a running chain saw, you need the clearest, easiest path possible.

In addition, if you are driving a vehicle, the saplings must be cut off level with the ground or they will puncture your tires. A sapling stump will penetrate a tractor tire as if the rubber tread were tissue paper.

Uncut saplings will act as springs if your felled tree falls on any. While the weight of the entire tree may hold the saplings bent to the ground, as soon as you start to clean the trunk of branches or cut the trunk into lengths, the weight will be lessened and the saplings will start to spring back. At some point the sapling strength will equal or exceed the weight of the cut tree, and your felled tree section will be catapulted free. If you cut the sapling after the tree has fallen on it, there will be a different release of the tension and your felled tree will fall farther. This will probably be a sudden action. Have a good grip on the saw or axe and be ready to move clear or you may find the tree on your foot—or even your chest.

Once you have chosen a tree, step back and look at it. A tree should be felled in the direction it leans. Most trees have a distinctive lean; the tree should fall in that direction. If the tree does not seem to have such a lean, look to see if one side has larger and heavier limbs; this is also the direction in which it should fall.

Clear the area of brush as well as saplings for your retreat path. Protect yourself as much as possible. A felled tree will not necessarily fall as you expect. It may catch on a nearby tree and be thrown in an unpredictable direction by the spring effect. A sudden gust of wind may twist it or push it backward. A well-cleared area path offers easy escape.

Before beginning to cut, check that the guide bar on the chain saw is large enough to cut through the width of the trunk. Make your first cut on the leaning or heavy side of the tree, about a foot or so above ground level. Make a straight, horizontal cut about a third of the way through the tree. Another foot or so above this cut, begin a downward-angled cut towards the first cut, until it meets the horizontal cut. Remove the notch you have just created; save it for the fireplace. After the notch has been removed, the tree can begin to fall at any time, so beware. Now that there is a notch on the side the tree should fall toward, go to the opposite side of the tree. Begin a horizontal cut about three inches above the base cut of the notch. This will leave enough wood between the new cut and the notch to create a hinge. As you cut this horizontal line in the back, the tree should begin to bend on that hinge in its downward fall. Once you reach the point where it begins to topple, move clear of the tree.

Using an ax instead of a chain saw. If you prefer to use an ax, it is better to use a heavier one than a lighter model. The weight gives power to the cut. Cut a notch on the side which is heaviest or already leaning. As before, make sure of

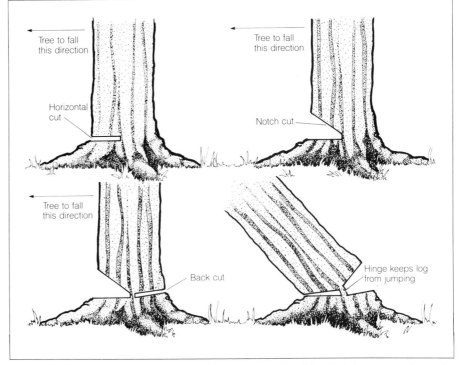

The art of cutting a tree is getting it to fall where you expect it to fall. This is harder than it sounds. Careful cutting preparation is essential for safe tree felling.

Once the tree is down where you want it, you must trim off the branches. Trim upper branches first, cutting so that the weight will pull the branch away from the saw.

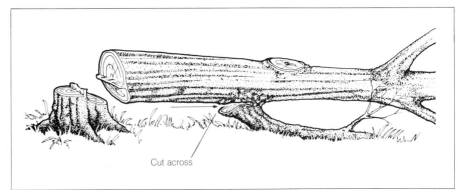

Cut branches underneath the tree later. Cut from bottom so that the weight of the tree on the branch will keep the cut from binding against the saw, causing an accident.

your retreat path. Notch the tree about a third of its thickness, and then go to the back of the tree. Begin a wide cut there, making sure the cut will be a little above the middle of the notch. The more you cut, the more the tree will lean, until it begins to fall.

Beware of falling trees. No matter how carefully you have prepared, your tree may not fall in the direction you anticipate. Another messy problem is that the saw may be trapped or pulled out of your hands.

Your tree may catch on the way down. It can become so securely caught that you must leave it. You may be able to pull it free with a winch—in which case it could flop forward suddenly onto you or your equipment. The falling tree may hit another tree and cause it to bend sharply and then spring back like a slingshot and send your tree flying through the air as much as 50 yards.

For your own protection, work up to a large tree by practicing on smaller ones. Work with someone who knows the forest, and learn before doing.

Preparing the Wood

When the tree is down, before you try to move it, trim all the branches off, cutting downward letting the chain saw do the work. It is the best tool for this. Cut off the branches right next to the trunk level. These branches will likewise be cut up, trimmed of their leaves and twigs, and used as wood and kindling.

Once the tree is bare of branches, you can cut the main trunk into four-foot (or shorter) lengths. Try to place supports under the tree trunk, or cut the trunk into a few sections, raising each section off the ground and then cutting these sections into four-foot lengths. Four-foot lengths are easier to stack as a measured cord, and can be cut in half and split after having been seasoned in your backyard. When cutting down into the tree as it rests on the ground, do so carefully. Don't let the saw bite into the ground. This will dull the teeth, and may result in injury.

Stacking wood. Stacking the wood allows it to dry out and season. It usually takes wood anywhere from six to ten months before it is dry enough for use. If you should be in a hurry, remember that split wood will dry much more quickly than whole logs. The easiest way to stack wood, though, is to lay it out in a cord measurement. The four-foot lengths make this a simple task. By planting four-foot high posts at each end of a row of logs that is eight feet long, you will then be able to stack the logs four feet or higher as long as the braces are tall enough to hold the top layer of logs. You will then have a cord, or some fraction thereof, lying all in a row—easy to pull out and cut and split.

Wood should be stacked in a protected outdoor area, such as under the eaves, or some other form of constructed overhang. You can also use a large, protective cover such as canvas or heavy plastic tarps. These are a good idea, for they will keep out the wet, cold weather, allowing wood to dry out faster, and to stay dry. Coverings are manufactured by many firms. Such covers are especially helpful if your wood is split already, because split wood is more susceptible to moisture.

Splitting Logs

Splitting the wood is the next step, and the chain saw is of no help here. Ideally, firewood should be cut into two-foot lengths, although it is harder to stack correctly in this manner. Short lengths will dry more quickly than the four-foot lengths. Two-foot lengths will give a better fire than one-foot pieces.

The old-fashioned way to split a log is to use a sledge hammer and a maul, a heavy steel wedge. On a log of average width (16 to 24 inches in diameter), one wedge is placed in the middle and firmly hit to split the log in half. Repeat the procedure for the halves. A quartered log produces a more effective fire. However, swinging a sledge at a maul is hard,

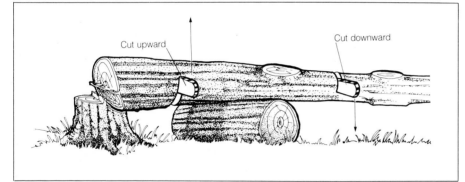

Always cut so that the weight of the tree will pull the cut open or you will find yourself fighting to free a jammed saw. Even a chain saw will jam under enough pressure.

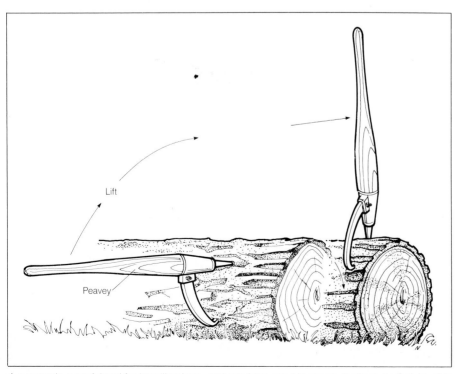

A peavey is a useful tool for handling logs, and provides good leverage. It allows an individual to turn a log that would otherwise be far too cumbersome to handle and cut.

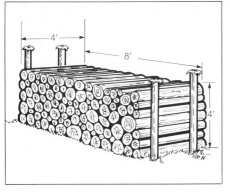

A standard cord of wood is 4 feet high, 8 feet long, and 4 feet deep. Any cord you buy should stack to this measurement.

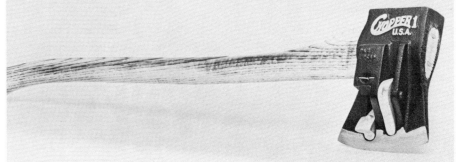

This tool combines both an ax and a maul. It is designed to split wood as simply and as easily as possible. You need only one tool, rather than two.

Another modern innovation is a spring-powered maul. The spring increases the power applied and makes splitting easier.

demanding work. A slip of the wrist may cause the sledge hammer handle to break. There are many products on the market today that make log splitting easier and less time consuming.

The Chopper-One ax-splitter is a combination ax and maul. It not only cuts into the log, but because of the rotating levers in the ax head, it turns the downward stroke into outward, log-splitting force. It can and will allow the user to split wood in half the usual time.

There are other tools, such as fully portable prefabricated metal frames with a built-in wedge on the bottom, that reduce splitting time and effort. Place the log on the wedge; tap it in place with a sledge; neatly hit the top of the log, splitting it easily from the bottom up. This tool makes splitting with a sledge and maul much safer, for it nearly eliminates the possibility of a bad hit, or flying steel wedge.

To cut long logs into shorter, more manageable lengths, it is best to use a sawhorse. This will keep the log off the ground, protecting the teeth of any saw you use, and will allow a controlled, nonpinched cut.

Transporting Logs to the Fire

There are several products on the market that simplify carrying split logs into the house without making a mess. The Log Wheeler, a combination hand cart and log holder, lets you wheel a stack of wood right up to the fireplace. It has retractable handles, so you can also use it as a fireside log holder. Canvas and leather "bags" are available in which you can pack an armload of wood. You then carry the bag, just as you would a suitcase, into the house. One such product has the added feature of an aluminum handle, making it easier to carry when it is full of wood. These and many other aids help simplify stacking, cutting and splitting the wood.

BUILDING A GOOD FIRE

Fire requires three natural elements: air, fuel and heat. Laying a good fire involves the proper combination of these three. Positioning the logs to create drafts helps them to burn once they have been ignited. This is one good reason for using a grate in the fireplace; elevation of the logs allows sufficient draft under them to encourage burning, allowing them to burn hotter.

The best fire uses only three or four logs—never more than four. The first log, the "backlog", should be the largest. It is placed on the grate at the very back of the firebox. This backlog will help radiate more heat into the room, at the same time providing a heat source for the other logs. After the backlog, place another log in front. Between these two lay any newspaper and kindling, dry twigs, bark or lumber scraps. Then lay one or two more logs over these.

Before lighting the kindling, open the damper. When the kindling has been lit, heat will rise and be forced into the narrow spaces between the logs. It will concentrate the hot air and keep the fire going. If the fire refuses to burn steadily, add more kindling and/or newspaper. Then gently reposition the logs with a poker. Once the fire is burning, try not to adjust the logs too often. A well-built fire will cause its own good draft, sustaining the fire until the logs are spent. To add new logs, first rake the coals toward the front of the grate. Place (do not toss) one or two more logs on the fire. Always rejuvenate the fire while there is still a sufficient amount of flame left in the other logs. This will avoid your having to restart the fire. Keeping a layer of ashes is one way to retain enough heat to rekindle the fire, yet too much will smother it. A two-inch layer of ashes in the firebox is usually best. Clean out the ashes regularly, but only down to a two-inch layer.

Here is one more hint for those who want a long-lasting fire: if your wood pile happens to be a mixture of softwoods, hardwoods and fruitwood, use hardwood only for the backlog. Use softwoods for the rest. Once the fire is going, keep adding hardwoods for a hot fire, with an occasional log of fruitwood for its aromatic, colorful benefits.

12

SAFETY
AND TROUBLE SHOOTING

Homeowners welcome all the enjoyable aspects of having a fireplace or wood stove, but nearly always overlook the potential safety and fire hazards presented by these heating units. For the most part, people seem to feel that once the fireplace is built or installed, nothing else need be done but to continually fuel and fire it. Unfortunately, this is not true.

Most of these safety hazards are recognized by local and Federal governments, and by private organizations devoted to safety such as Underwriters' Laboratories (UL), the International Conference of Building Officials (I.C.B.O.) and the National Fire Protection Association, Inc. (NFPA). All are concerned with the public's safe and sensible use of fireplaces and stoves, from installation through assembly. They also watchdog the manufacturers to ensure they produce safe products. This attention includes a check of each unit as it comes off of the assembly line. For this reason, do not buy a fireplace, a stove, or even an item to be added onto either product, unless it is stamped with a label from a reputable laboratory or association.

Without regular maintenance and certain precautions, the same fireplace or

Even an electric fireplace must have a routine annual maintenance, although it is the wiring that needs to be checked. Do not neglect this safety precaution; conduct checks before and after fire-burning seasons.

stove that offers warmth and beauty can become a danger to the homeowner. Because of these very real potential hazards, the National Fire Protection Association (NFPA) has set certain standards for the use of both fireplaces and stoves. They have also made studies of the many safety factors that affect fireplaces and stoves, from their installation to their correct, daily use. Here are hazards to watch for and the rules to use and live by when using the fireplace or stove.

EXISTING FIREPLACE AND CHIMNEY

If buying a home with an existing fireplace, first thoroughly inspect it from the hearth to the chimney cap. Question the previous homeowner extensively on how much the fireplace was used, and how often (or, if ever) it was cleaned. Inspect the outside brickwork closely for cracks and breakages. If you find too much loose mortar and brickwork, call in a professional mason to inspect it from top to bottom. He will let you know if there are significant structural problems.

If you feel there may be cracks that leak smoke or gases, you can check for these by building a brief, small, smoky fire and loosely covering the chimney cap to slightly impede the exhausting of the smoke. Keep windows open for ventilation. Have several people equipped with chalk or tape stationed at the chimney

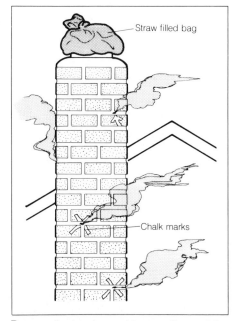

Temporarily stopping a chimney will reveal the location of leaks, which must be sealed before the fireplace can be used again.

walls on all floors. If any smoke at all leaks from the chimney, mark the leaks from the chimney, and do not use the fireplace or stove until you have the chimney repaired. If there are no leaks on the exterior walls of the chimney but there are two or more flues within the chimney, check that no smoke rises from an adjacent flue when the smoke is blocked in the flue that serves the fire.

Check the damper. First, make sure that there is a damper. Some of the older model masonry fireplaces were constructed without dampers. If this is the case, you should install one (see Chapter 5). If the fireplace does have a damper, open and close it a number of times to make sure it works correctly and closes completely. If it rattles, or if it is loose, lift out the old damper plate. Then insert a new one.

Check for any alterations which may have been made on or near the fireplace. Any modifications should have been built in compliance with the local building codes. One example of damage that can

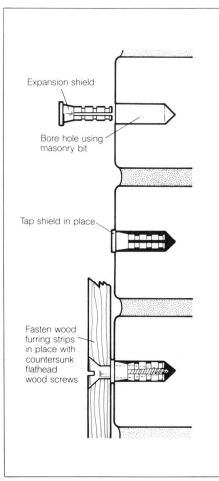

Application of wood paneling to a fireplace surround requires expansion shields and screws that do not reach through masonry.

result from incorrect workmanship is illustrated by a case where a homeowner paneled the fireplace masonry work. Wood furring strips were attached to the brick with large, long cement nails. Paneling was applied over these strips. The long nails used to hold the wood furring strips to the masonry became overheated after prolonged use of the fireplace, and the paneling caught fire. Always keep this risk in mind when building cabinets or bookcases near the fireplace.

Across the country building codes insist on minimum clearances of 2 inches between firebox walls (which consist of eight inches of regular masonry plus four inches of firebrick) and any combustible material.

This means that wood framing around the face of a fireplace must have a 2 inch air-space gap between the masonry and the combustible framing. You may want to apply fiberglass insulation over the masonry and then build framing of metal lath.

WOOD-BURNING STOVES

The same cautions that apply to use of an existing fireplace and chimney are also crucial to the operation and installation of a new or used wood-burning stove. If you have purchased a home all or partially heated by a stove, examine the stove closely for any of these defects: cracks in the metal, broken door hinges, warped or loose fitting doors, or dented and warped metal. Be certain the legs are in good shape. Look at the condition of the grate, and inspect for draft dampers and regulators that may not operate correctly. Cracks in the metal must be repaired before using the stove. Cracks can be welded or brazed by a professional. Should the stove be dented or warped, you should replace the entire unit, since the material will continue to weaken through normal use.

If you are purchasing a new stove, be sure it is listed by UL, I.C.B.O., or another reputable testing lab. Shop around. Find a reputable dealer who not only will sell the stove, but will install it and will demonstrate how to use it correctly.

The National Fire Protection Agency has taken a careful look at the minimum standards for stove clearances and is taking a firm stand on stove clearances from combustible surfaces. Placement of tables, chairs, couches, and other furniture pieces has caused many problems and hazards. A stove gives off a great deal of heat; it is not necessary to place furniture pieces close to the unit. If too close, they will smolder and catch fire. The minimum clearance from a stove in use is 36 inches. This includes furniture, carpeting, draperies, curtains, wallhangings and other household items as well as combustible walls.

SAFETY HINTS

Hazards mentioned above are of the utmost concern, yet sometimes the simpler problems present even more danger. Care should be exercised in the every day fireplace use.

When using the fireplace, never store paper, wood, or any other combustible materials in front of the firebox or hearth. Keep these a safe distance away. Use a firescreen, either metal or glass, which prevents sparks from popping out into the living area of the room. If you use a wire mesh firescreen, it is advisable to also use a fireproof throw rug in front of the hearth. This will help to protect the room's carpeting or wood veneer flooring if a spark does land on these surfaces.

Starting the Fire

Never saturate wood with a flammable liquid to start or rekindle the fire. It is always better to let the fire take hold naturally than to induce it with a flammable liquid. Never store such liquids on or near the hearth area.

There are a few products available that use flammable liquids as firestarters. The classic example is the Cape Cod firelighter. This is a covered bowl that holds approximately one cup of kerosene or charcoal lighter. The cover has a small notch cut out to accommodate the metal handle of the lighter. The lighter has a knob of soapstone, a porous rock, which absorbs the kerosene or charcoal lighter over a period of a day or more. When the user wishes to start the fire, he removes the lighter from the bowl, ignites the kerosene soaked soapstone, and puts the soapstone end beneath the grate to start the fire. There is also a block of soapstone fitted and strapped into a cast iron box; this assembly works in the same way as the Cape Cod lighter.

Both these devices can be used to light a fire safely, but only if correctly used. Do not use too much fluid; the soapstone acts as a wick so that only the fluid at the surface burns, and it is difficult (and

A Cape Cod firelighter is a handy device for starting a fire, but never leave it this close to the fire while a fire is going.

dangerous) to attempt to snuff out the lighter flame. A heavily soaked lighter can—and will—burn for hours. Even if the bowl appears to be empty, there will be a residue of kerosene on the surface. You cannot ever return the lighter to the bowl directly from the fire or you will have an explosion in the bowl. The lighter must cool several hours before it can be put back in the bowl.

Never store the lighter unit near the fireplace opening. It is advisable to store the bowl or block out of doors when not in use. Matches, likewise, must be kept a safe distance from the fire—in a hanger on an adjacent wall, or in a basket well away from the hearth.

Banking the Fire

If it is late in the evening, and you are going to bed, do not leave the fire still blazing. A log could suddenly roll forward, breaking ·or knocking over the screening—or a spark could fly out. Bank the fire by raking the hot coals to the back, spreading them around to let them burn off individually and more rapidly. Using your tongs, stand the logs on end in the back corners of the firebox at an angle that prevents their falling over. This will help the logs to burn out quicker. Save them for the rekindling a fire the next day. Never pour water on the fire. It will create too much smoke for the draft to handle and smoke will billow out into the house.

Putting out a fire quickly. If you are called away from home unexpectedly and have a roaring blaze in your fireplace, or if a fire gets out of hand, you will have to extinguish it before you leave. It is a good idea, in any case, to be prepared to handle a too vigorous fire. Smother the flames with baking soda, sand, dirt, or plain clay cat litter. Shovel the material onto the fire quickly but in a controlled and steady manner. Sudden action and careless shoveling may spread rather than reduce the

When a stove is in the center of a room, clearances apply to floors and furniture. Keep protected surfaces 18 inches away from the stove—unprotected surfaces 36 inches away.

flames. It should take only a minute or two to put out the fire.

A nearby fireplace dealer may also carry fire snuffers. These are bottomless sheetmetal boxes in various sizes that can be lowered over the entire grate. They work on the same principle as a candle snuffer—cutting off combustion air to the fire. It is always advisable to have a pair of fireproof/heat resistant gloves to wear when handling such a box or adding wood to a good size fire.

A SMOKING FIREPLACE

There are many possible causes for a smoking fireplace. It could be that the chimney, especially an old one, is dirty and needs a good cleaning before it will draw correctly. It could also be a construction problem: for example, the chimney may be too low to catch the breeze that is needed to help pull the air up the chimney so the fireplace functions and draws correctly. A chimney should be able to catch a breeze from all sides.

If the chimney is the correct height, the lack of draft could be caused by a nearby tree limb that is too close to the cap—or a nearby and newly built house next door can interfere with the normal flow of the breeze. Even a nearby hill can prevent air flow and limit the necessary chimney draft. To correct this problem you will have to clear the obstruction in some way. You can easily trim nearby trees, but

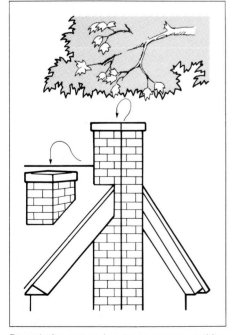

Downdrafts occur when trees grow over chimneys or new caps are built to low. Trim nearby trees. Add courses to the chimney.

other obstructions may require adding to the height of your chimney. Adding a tile for a higher chimney cap is not particularly difficult. It will require removing the cap finishing, cementing in a new tile and refinishing the cap with a tight seal and sloping cement wash—a thin layer of mortar.

Study the slope of the nearby land, prevailing wind direction and heights of adjacent trees and building. If these are appreciably higher than your chimney, you will have to add more than one flue tile and then cover it with brick surround. Depending on your skills and needs, you may want or need to have this done by a mason or chimney service.

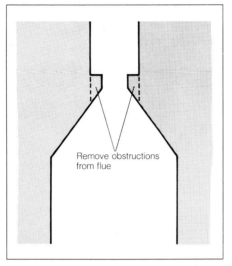

The too-wide flue supports in this unit hinder updraft so that soot collects in the flue. These supports should be trimmed.

Structural Problems

There is also the possibility that the smoke shelf of the chimney was built incorrectly or that an incorrectly sized fireplace opening is not allowing the fireplace to achieve the draft it needs.

If your smoke shelf is too small to allow the correct movement of air or proper amount of draft, or if it is too far forward in the flue, then there may be a need for major surgery by a qualified masonry contractor. If you should find the opening to the fireplace is too large, or that the firebox is itself too large for the unit to work correctly, there are a few solutions you can try. One is to lay another layer or two of brick on top of the hearth and forehearth. (Refer to Chapter 4.) This will decrease the height of the opening, and probably create a better draft. To shorten the depth of the firebox, purchase a heat reflector sheet, as men-

tioned in Chapter 9. As well as improving the draft of the fireplace, it adds to the heat output of the fireplace.

Creating a draft. A smoke puller installed at the top of the chimney (fan or blower) not only creates a draft, but also helps keep leaves, dirt, wind, and animals from going down the chimney, since it serves as a cap. Pullers are easily installed, because they are placed directly on top of the chimney, cemented in position on top of the brickwork, and then sealed. Pullers or caps will create a draw because of their designs, or because a built-in electrical exhaust fan pulls the smoke up the chimney. However, do not run the cable down through the chimney; eventually it will be burned and turn into a potential hazard. Instead, run weatherproof cable down the roof and over the eaves. Then run it into the attic—in the same way you run a television antenna cable into your house—and connect to an electrical power source. As an alternative, drill a hole in the roof at the base of the chimney; then connect the wiring to the power supply. If the cable runs through a hole drilled in the roof, you will need to provide a watertight silicone sealer to keep the water from dripping through the roof into the house.

A smoking fireplace can also occur if your house does not have enough moving air to provide a draft and you have no built-in outside air duct in your fireplace. If this is the case, you may need to open one or two windows slightly in order to provide air for a draft. In this situation

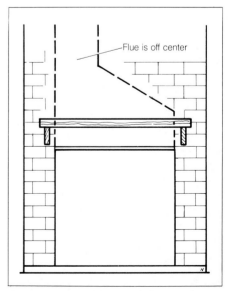

An off-set chimney will draw unevenly in most cases. A smoke puller increases the draft and provides better burning conditions.

you will be wasting valuable heated air. Follow directions in Chapters 6, 7, and 9 to provide combustion air for the fire. The draft will improve, your fireplace will not smoke, and you will have better, warmer fires.

Cleaning the Chimney

A dirty chimney can cause or contribute to a smoking fireplace. A fireplace or stove used on a fairly regular basis for more than two or three months of the year should be cleaned out every year before the heating season. This is required not only because of the dirt and soot that collect, but because creosote can build up to dangerous amounts over a period of time and after extensive use. This is especially true if you have a slow-drawing and burning fireplace or stove. Creosote buildup results from a chemical reaction in a slow-burning and cool fire. A cool fire produces acetic and pyroligneous acids, smoke and water vapor. These are expelled in considerable amounts as the low fire burns. The vapor condenses in the flue area of the chimney, accumulating as a black, gooey residue. This residue is very volatile and flammable and can seep into small cracks in the interior masonry work of the flue and chimney. If a hot spark hit an accumulation of the creosote residue, especially where it has penetrated into a crack in the bricks, it will ignite and burn hotly, spreading flames and damaging the brickwork.

There are a number of ways to clean a chimney. One good method is to hire a competent chimney sweep.

If you prefer to try the job yourself, buy a chimney cleaning kit, which includes: various sized brushes to fit any size flue opening; long, flexible extension rods to run the length of the flue; drop cloths to help collect the falling debris at the hearth. For those with a little more money, you can also purchase a vacuum cleaner device that sucks up the falling debris and ensures that there will be little or no mess.

Begin the cleaning by lining the firebox with disposable dropcloth and sealing the front of the fireplace with heavy paper taped securely to the hearth, jamb and lintel.

To clean the flue, start at the top with the brushes. Work down the flue, scrubbing lightly. Keep the damper shut tight during this operation to collect any soot and ash that could fall down. Once your cleaning has progressed down to the damper area, go inside the house and, if you have left it closed, carefully open the damper, allowing the debris to fall. Once the soot and ash has all settled, carefully scoop up the cloth and dispose of it. Then vacuum out the rest. No matter how careful you are, however, it will be a messy project. Remember that much of the debris will have caught on the smoke shelf. Clean that too, sweeping it with a brush with an angled handle.

One time-tested method of cleaning a chimney calls for you to take a few bricks, wrap a lot of cloth around them, tie a rope to the cloth bag, and dangle it down the chimney. Swing it about, knocking all the soot, ash and creosote to the bottom. This entails serious risks, however, with too hard a swing, especially in an older masonry fireplace, and even a padded, dangling brick can crack the interior masonry work, causing untold future problems. So either hire the profes-

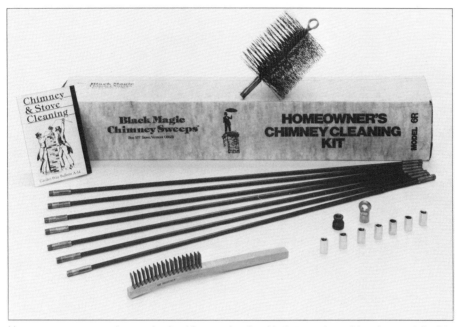

Homeowners can purchase a basic chimney cleaning kit that consists of brushes and flexible extension rods to push brush down the chimney. A simple kit will clean a small flue.

Chimney cleaning requires the "sweep" to work from the roof down. Before attempting such a job, you should understand the dangers and provide yourself with a safety harness.

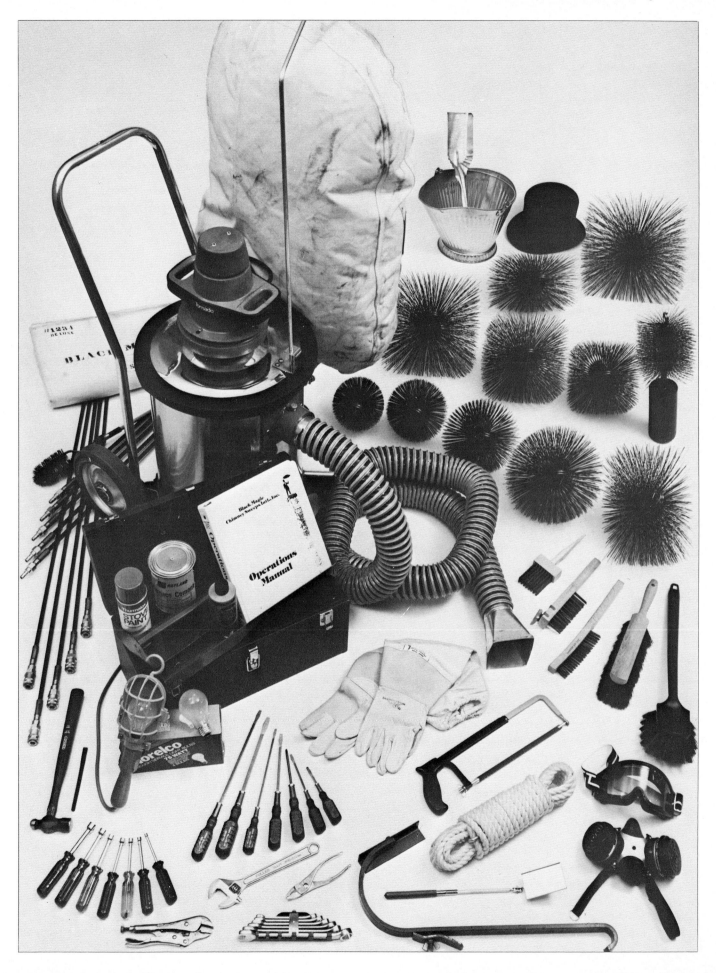

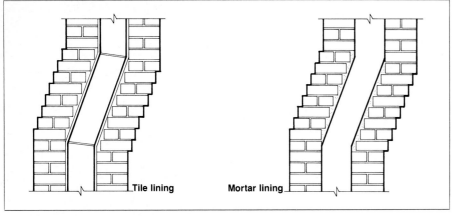

A chimney must be completely smooth on the inside for maximum efficiency of draft and ease of cleaning. Mitre joints are required on flue tile—full mortar jointing for brick.

sional or do the job correctly, using the right tools for the job. Such tools are available from a number of sources, such as Black Magic Chimney Sweeps, Eva's Chimney Brushes, Worcester Brush Company, and Schaefer Brush Manufacturing Co. Inc. The latter two companies make a plastic bristle brush designed to remove heavy soot.

Sealing the Chimney

If your smoke test indicated that there are air leaks in your chimney, those must be sealed before you can use your fireplace or stove. Should the leaking smoke come from major structural cracks, have a mason determine whether the chimney can be repaired or should be rebuilt.

Clean your chimney before repairing it. It is possible, of course, to seal the flue tile joints or to even install a metal flue liner if your chimney currently is only brick masonry—a possibility if your home predates current building codes. Inserting a metal flue liner is the same as installing stove pipe or a prefabricated chimney for a prefabricated fireplace. You will have to include a sealed collar at the base of the chimney flue (the top of the smoke chamber) so that smoke only goes up the pipe flue. These pipe liners often come with prefabricated sealer/collars. Check carefully before buying. Install according to directions. Purchase insulated pipe, which will keep heat inside the pipe and cut down on the buildup of soot and creosote.

If your chimney is lined with flue tile, you can reseal cracks. This is not a one person job; it can be done by two people, but three people will do a better job.

First cover your smoke shelf and firebox floor with disposable drop cloths.

Next, cut a piece of board or ¾ inch plywood so that it will be one inch smaller all around than the smallest part of your flue. This may involve some guess work, but it must be small enough to clear easily. Drill holes in each corner and attach two lengths of sturdy hemp rope, running diagonally from opposite corners. Secure with knots on the underside of the board, leaving enough slack in each piece so that a third piece of rope—long enough to reach all the way from the chimney cap to the hearth—can be attached in the center, where the two pieces cross. Place a flat-bottomed rock or brick on the board under the pieces of crossed rope. Line the bottom of a strong bag made of smooth canvas with straw; lower the board into the bag and surround with straw. Tie the bag securely, around the long rope extending from the bag. Lower the bag until it rests on the smoke shelf; then pull it up to the bottom of the flue. A person kneeling in the firebox can see when the bag closes off all light coming down the flue and can signal—by voice or by pulling a signal cord to the roof (not run through the chimney, of course)—when the bag has reached the base of the flue. If you cannot find a third helper, put a bright utility light in the firebox. When the bag reaches the smoke shelf, light should be visible; when the bag reaches the flue, no light should show.

Mix a batch of fireclay mortar to a consistency of cultured sour cream—it should flow, not run—and pull it or have it carried to the roof by the bucketful. Slowly and carefully pour the mortar down the sides of the flue. Have another person then slowly and carefully pull the weighted, straw-filled canvas bag upward.

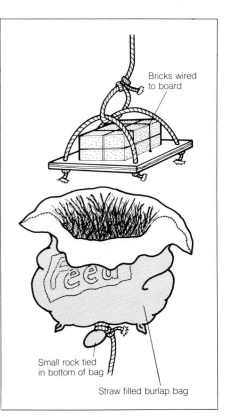

To seal an old chimney with mortar use a "traveler bag" just large enough to fill the flue space and smooth the added mortar.

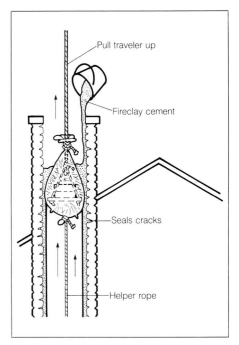

Starting with the traveler bag at the bottom of the flue, pour in mortar; smooth it by pulling the bag up, sealing flue joints.

Repeat the process of pouring and pulling until the chimney flue is lined with a smooth coat of fresh mortar.

If the job goes easily, if your mortar is the right consistency, and if your bag does not get stuck, you should have a lining in your flue in a few hours. Some mortar will probably end up on the smoke shelf or firebox floor, which is why you put down the disposable dropcloths. If your mortar was too liquid, it has probably run off the walls and you will have to repeat the process. If your mortar was too thick, you probably needed a lot of help pulling the bag up. However, you now know how to do the job.

Wait three weeks to be sure the mortar is completely dry before using the fireplace.

TROUBLESHOOTING AND MAINTENANCE

There are other, less hazardous fireplace troubles that, still, are aggravating and should be handled before using the fireplace.

Damper Problems

If your damper does not open or close all the way, and moves stiffly, it could be that soot and ashes have fallen and collected in a pile on the smoke shelf behind the damper. This can be solved by disconnecting the damper's control lever, lifting out the movable plate, and cleaning out the area behind the damper. Clean off any creosote and dirt that may have collected and hardened on the plate's pivot points, and do the same for the areas where these points rest.

Mortar on back of damper. Check the back side of the damper. In many cases the original chimney sealing will have resulted in a layer of mortar adhering to the damper surface. Scrape the coating off for tighter damper closing.

Cleaning the Ashpit

If the ashpit is clogged, and poking down

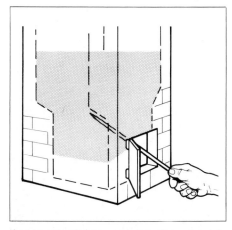

If your ash pit has not been cleaned out in years, it may be clogged. Dig out what you can from the door and then poke ash free.

through the ashdump does not break up the clog, go to the basement or crawlspace and, with a poker, reach inside and poke upwards. Unpack the clogged material. Let it fall so you can clean it out. If this does not work, and the ash is packed tight, you may need to hire a contractor to tear the walls apart and clean it out, righting the problem forever. But this is an extreme, and usually a good jab with the poker or another tool will suffice.

It is important that your ashdump in the hearth have a metal cover and that this cover be kept closed while using the fireplace. The ash in the ashpit is light; if the dump is open and there is a strong, steady draft, the ash may be stirred into the air in the pit. Hot ash and small pieces of burning wood could fall through the open ashdump and cause explosive combustion of the ash-laden air.

Should a chimney fire occur while the ashdump door is open, the resulting draft will almost certainly pull the ash from the pit up and cause an explosive ignition. The ashpit door could be blown off. If this door is in the basement, the fire could easily spread to that area, from which it could spread to the rest of the dwelling.

Chimney Caps

Chimney caps serve several functions and come in many forms. The wind protector and the draft pulling type have been mentioned before, but there are other significant types of caps.

A wire-mesh cap will serve two purposes. The mesh will prevent sparks from leaving the chimney and landing on nearby combustible material. While most codes specify that roofing is supposed to be non-combustible, cedar shakes and wood shingles may not be fully fireproofed. In the autumn, dry leaves may settle in your gutters, and a spark landing there could cause a blaze.

A mesh chimney cap will also prevent instrusions of leaves and windblown debris into the chimney. Probably more important but less often considered is the fact that mesh chimney caps will keep animals out of your chimney and your fireplace and, therefore, your home. If you keep your damper closed except while using the fireplace, you probably will not have animals coming into your home— unless your damper is a model with a pivoting plate. A squirrel, or even a chipmunk could cause a pivoting damper

to tilt, and you could find something living in your sofa stuffing. Larger and more facile animals such as raccoons also have been known to seek shelter in chimneys. A racoon has the capability of lifting a damper plate out of the way and climbing down into a fireplace. Even extremely urban areas offer habitat for a surprising array of wildlife. If small or medium size animals—especially as uninvited guests—make you nervous, a mesh chimney cap will be a good investment.

Prefabricated mesh caps come with mounting instructions. If you make your own, attach with masonry bolts and washers and seal with cement so moisture will not get into the chimney joints.

Another type of chimney cap is designed primarily as a rain cap. Some chimneys seem to catch rain and snow more than others. If your chimney seems to work as a downspout during a rainstorm, and the cement wash at the top slopes toward the outside as it should, you will probably be advised to add a raincap. Discuss this with a local fireplace dealer and install as directed.

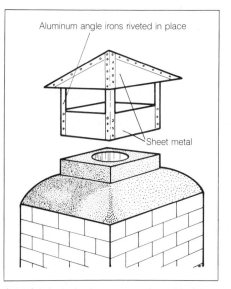

Aluminum angle irons riveted in place

Sheet metal

A prefabricated rain cap may be added to a chimney to cut down on the amount of rain and snow that falls into the fireplace.

Chemical Cleaners

For minor buildup problems of creosote and soot in a chimney, and as a preventive measure, you may want to try a chemical flue cleaner that you sprinkle on a fire. The chemical reaction created tends to carry away the chimney buildup. These should be available at a fireplace dealer or a hardware store. A word of warning, however: do not use any of these if your chimney needs a thorough

Glass doors offer efficiency and safety while burning a fire. These decorator glass doors are used to form a small greenhouse.

cleaning. The only way to clean a dirty chimney properly is with the proper assortment of rods and brushes. However, regular use of the chemical cleaners —following the manufacturer's directions exactly—should lower the frequency of required, full-scale chimney cleaning.

Every chimney should be inspected and cleaned at least once a year. Any problems should be corrected as soon as they are discovered. Fireplaces and stoves offer warmth and comfort to those who maintain and use them correctly, but their potential danger must be respected and all safety precautions must be observed.

Glass Doors

The use of glass doors for fireplaces has increased considerably in recent years. The doors cut down the amount of heated room air pulled into the fireplace for combustion. However, many people find that they are not getting the same amount of heat, even though the doors (or at least some of the doors) are supposed to be designed to reflect heat into the room. If you plan to buy and use glass doors, be sure that you purchase a door unit that has a built-in heat exchanger so that room air will be drawn in, heated, and then returned to the room. This permits you to keep the doors closed. If this feature is not included, buy a unit that has a set of wire mesh screens behind the glass. If you open the doors to allow the heat to radiate into the room, you must have protection against sparks popping out of the firebox. Otherwise, you will have a real fire hazard.

Glass doors can offer considerable benefits; they offer an extra measure of safety if you must leave a banked fire still glowing when you retire. Buy the best possible glass door screen—one that offers both efficiency and safety features; the extra investment is a good one.

A fireplace can be left burning safely behind glass doors. This set has a hammered-metal surface that enhances the stone fireplace.

USING YOUR FIREPLACE IN AN EMERGENCY

One of the tricks played on us by modern life is the occasional failure of convenient services that we all usually take for granted. A breakdown in the delivery of electric power, the interruption of water pressure, or problems with the telephone will create consternation and make us angry. However, these services are usually reliable and are back in order quickly. When they are not, one is faced with having to survive under some difficulty. This takes some wit, calm and presence of mind.

People never expect a natural disaster to interfere with their lives. Each year, however, extremes of weather cause many unexpected and difficult to handle emergency situations. For those who live in areas subject to extremes of weather—especially severe snow, sleet, ice, rain, or wind storms—it is advisable to be prepared for emergencies. Having discussed emergencies in the fireplace, it is time to talk about using your fireplace in emergencies. If you have a fireplace, it is logical to plan to use it as effectively as possible; to do this, you should be prepared. This means, of course having your fireplace in good working order, well maintained, clean, and in good repair. It also means having a good supply of high quality wood stored in an easy-to-reach storage area. You also need a supply of kindling and matches. A sense of humor and adventure will help as well.

Keeping Warm

It is at times like this that the fireplace becomes more than a decorative feature of the home—a pleasant, cheery sight offering a warm glow to a room.

The first purpose of the fireplace was to provide warmth to a room. When modern power sources fail, this historical purpose is again important. A fireplace is not essentially an efficient furnace, but it will function, however, when a modern furnace cannot. When your electric power is out, your thermostat does not work. Oil burners, electrically ignited gas furnaces and heat pumps cannot run. If your area has been struck by a heavy, blowing snow storm or a severe ice storm, you may be without power for a day; in some less accessible areas for several days or a week. You will have to depend on your fireplace to keep you warm.

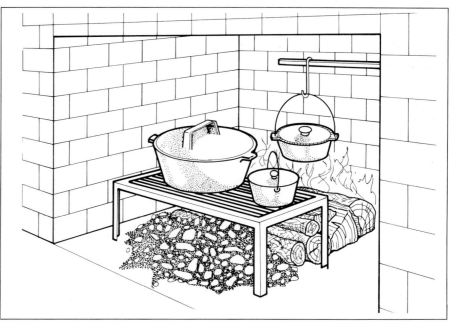

A standard fireplace grate may be used as a cooking surface over wood coals or burning logs. Cast iron pots are the most efficient for cooking over direct heat.

Surrounding a pot with coals will essentially bake what is inside. The coals provide an even, long-lasting heat. Potatoes were baked for centuries among fireplace coals.

Begin by moving into the room—or rooms—with a fireplace. If possible shut off the other rooms. Close doors, close air vents, and pull shades and curtains to keep as much heat as possible in the inside. Shut off and drain as many water lines as you can. Keep those not shut off running in a small trickle. Arrange your furniture to keep heat near the fireplace and settle in this area. Use sleeping bags, blankets and comforters to rest on and in. Plan a schedule so there is always someone awake to watch and to feed the fire. As the fire burns over a long time the masonry will store and radiate more heat.

If you let the fire go out before the end of the emergency, it will seem to become colder than you expect it to be.

If you have a heat circulating fireplace or even a combination glass screen/heat exchanger grate, you will be more comfortable. The important thing, however, is to make the most of what you have. Remember, too, that keeping the family together will help. It improves morale to be close; it also creates a natural warmth—people all generate heat. This is true of animals, too. Do not relegate the family pets to the cold; they will help raise the room temperature. Keep them with you.

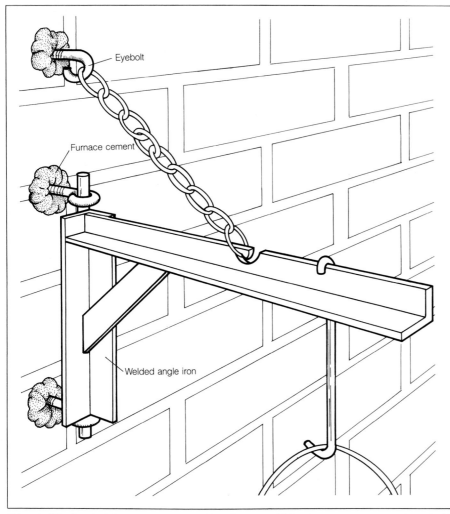

It is not difficult to install a crane to support hanging pots. All fireplaces once were equipped with cranes. Drill into the masonry and secure bolts with fireproof cement.

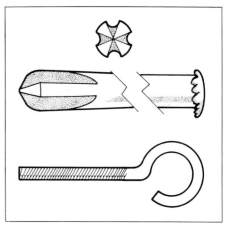

A star-drill or masonry bit will drill the hole needed for the bolt. The hole should be a little larger than the bolt.

Cooking in the Fireplace

If you happen to have a gas stove, hot water heater, and refrigerator, you are more fortunate than many when facing a power emergency. In many homes, however, when the power goes, all means of cooking and cold storing food is interrupted. You can store food out-of-doors unless the neighborhood wildlife is substantial in your area. Cooking is another matter. All electrical appliances are useless for the time being.

It is possible to cook and bake for an entire family in a fireplace. At one time it was the normal method of cooking. It may not permit extensive gourmet meals, but fireplace cooking is both possible and practical. It can be done on a purely emergency basis, and it can be included as a part of overall fireplace plans.

Finding emergency cooking equipment. The simplest emergency cooking utensil is a tea kettle. You can provide a group with warmth, if not sustenance, if you can heat water. You can make tea, instant coffee, instant soup, bouillon, or cocoa, as soon as you have hot water. Use a kettle that is old. You will have trouble getting it clean after it has been used in the fire. To use a tea kettle, just set it in front of the fire. You can set it on a metal trivet on the hearth or forehearth. Watch or listen so that it does not boil dry. The nearer the kettle is to the heat, of course, the faster it will boil. You can maintain a simmering pot for hours once you have established a steady fire and found the right position for the kettle on the hearth.

Other utensils that are appropriate to fireplace use are cast iron pots—particularly dutch ovens with wire, pail-style handles and recessed lids. Pots with plastic handles and lid knobs will be damaged by the heat. Lightweight aluminum will be warped. Aluminum foil, of course, can always be used to wrap potatoes or other vegetables that may be baked in the coals. If you have heavy aluminum or stainless pots, you can cover them with foil to simplify cleanup when you go back to normal after the power is restored.

There are two basic fireplace cooking techniques: Using the coals to bake or roast the food, or using the flames of the fire to sear the food. You may, without any special, added equipment do a lot of cooking in the fireplace. Keep raking coals to the front of the fireplace, or to one side. When you want to cook, put the food into the pot—a roast would work well—add a little water, seasonings and vegetables—and push the pot into the coals. Turn the pot regularly for even cooking. Use fireproof gloves and fireplace tools for doing this. You may prefer to set the pot on coals and then bury it in more coals. An experienced fireplace cook can even bake bread using this basic method.

You may prefer to set your pot(s) over the fire. You can use your fireplace grate to do this. If your grate has long legs, you can build your fire directly on the hearth and place the grate over the burning wood and coals. You can put pots on the grate and cook over the fire. You will probably have to elevate the grate and provide air to the fire for combustion. If you have some bricks, patio blocks, or paver blocks at hand, you can use these to raise the grate; place one or two under each leg. Small pieces of brick, block, or pipe can be laid on the hearth surface to keep logs elevated enough to provide air to the fire for adequate combustion for a good, steady fire. If your grate does not have a level enough surface to hold pots without the danger of spilling, you may be able to lay the grill from your outdoor barbecue or charcoal grill across the fireplace grate and put pots or a kettle securely on that.

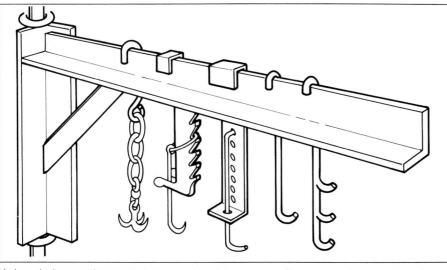

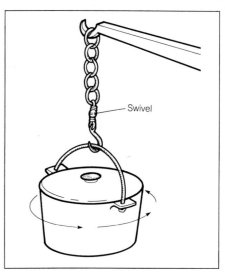

Various devices can be used to hang pots from the crane arm. Some may be fabricated from heavy steel wire or rods. Others are manufactured and available at fireplace shops.

It is best to hang pots on swivel hooks so that the pot can be turned regularly.

An emergency spit. There are few things that taste better than meat cooked over a wood fire. A power emergency may provide you with the chance for a real treat. To roast a chicken, turkey, or piece of beef, you can create a support for each end of the spit with a stack of bricks or concrete blocks. Locate the stacks so the meat will be exposed to the maximum width of the flames and coals. If you have a spit, you can probably adapt it to use in your fireplace. You can create a spit from an old, round, solid curtain rod, securing the meat with wire. Bend one end at an angle so you can brace the spit and turn it as desired to cook the meat evenly. Place a pan under the spit to catch the juices. Use these to baste the meat and to make gravy. You should place a pan to catch juices even if you do not plan to use them. Do this to keep the hearth clean. Not only does this make maintenance easier, it will prevent another problem; insects and rodents are attracted to the greasy spots on the hearth—especially if you cook and leave grease spots over a long period of time. Firebrick is not glazed and is relatively pourous and hard to clean; keep it clean from the start of your cooking process.

You can help in the cooking—and the heating—process by setting up a reflector board to send heat back toward your spit. Setting the board close to the fire will increase cooking speed; setting the board back several feet will reflect heat in your sleeping area. You can create a reflector by covering a large piece of plywood with aluminum foil; attach support legs with bolts so you can adjust the angle of the

A reflector board can be made by covering a piece of plywood with aluminum foil. Attach braces to support the board. Oven thermometer on pot helps gauge temperature for cooking.

reflecting surface. If you have a wood-top card table, you can cover the surface with foil and prop it up with its own legs. You may also create a reflector by turning one or two straight-backed, wood chairs back to the fire and hanging foil from the backs.

Permanent Cooking Adaptations
There are many traditional and contemporary cooking accessories available for permanent installation in the firebox. The traditional accessories include the swing-away crane on which you can hang a pot

directly over the coals or the burning wood. If you have welding experience, you can fabricate a crane; however, large fireplace shops should handle an item like this. You can install a crane with eye-bolts. Drill into the masonry with a star drill or masonry bit. You can fill the holes with masonry anchors or furnace cement and insert the bolts through the holes in the crane and then into the masonry. Be sure the installation is secure; the crane will have to support a great deal of weight. You would not want a meal spoiled by having the crane pull out of the

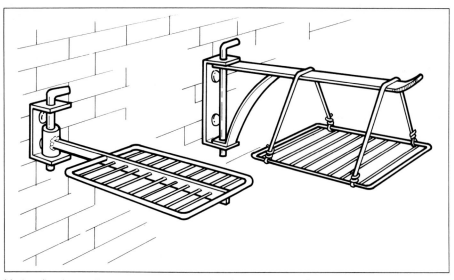

Modern fireplace grilles are generally available at fireplace shops. They are installed with masonry anchors and can be swiveled out of the way when not in use.

Fowl or other meat can be cooked on a spit. Support blocks and a brace hold the spit to cook meat evenly. A pan catches juices to help keep hearth clean and for use in gravy.

Any or all of these cooking techniques can be used in either an emergency or in everyday situations. A fireplace can be a very useful adjunct to your cooking facilities. Beware, however, of using charcoal in your fireplace. Charcoal produces especially toxic fumes and should never be used indoors except in special grills that have been designed specifically for indoor charcoal cooking. Some charcoal grills seem to work when set into a fireplace; however, this is courting danger unless the fireplace is equipped with an electrically powered smoke puller.

PRECAUTIONS TO OBSERVE

Whenever you cook in your fireplace, you increase the danger of fire. Food can be spilled and catch fire and run out onto the forehearth and beyond. This could happen very quickly; you have to be prepared for fire. You should have a fire extinguisher on hand whenever you start a fire in the fireplace. If you use the fireplace over a period of several days, you will be dealing with firebrick that has absorbed and is radiating back the heat of a long-lasting fire. The masonry will grow progressively warmer. Be sure to keep all furniture, carpeting and curtains that might be scorched or burned well away from the fire. For prolonged use, you may want to roll back carpeting—particularly if you are cooking—to protect the surface. Synthetics will melt and can cause severe skin burns. You also should protect wood floors. If you can, put down a temporary, noncombustible covering over any combustible surface.

One of the basic requirements of safe use of a fireplace is that the opening be covered by a screen that will protect the floor and furniture from sparks. When you cook in your fireplace, you will have the screen open a part—or all—of the time. Never leave a cooking fire unattended. If you are cooking in an emergency period, you will probably be on hand all the time, but if you use the fireplace for occasional meals because of the good taste wood smoke gives food, you may find that you will have to have an assistant to keep a close watch on the fireplace.

Always expect anything around the fireplace to be hot. Use fireproof gloves, hot pads and tools to handle pots or equipment. Have a trivet or heatproof pad near the hearth to hold any utensil pulled out of the fire.

wall and dump the pot in the fire. Allow the cement to set several days before using the crane.

The pieces that hang from the crane and support the cooking pots are called trammels. These devices range from simple hooks and chains to adjustable, fabricated hangers. The most important feature of any device you choose or make is that it have a swivel hook. A swivel hook allows you to keep rotating your cooking pot so that it will not cook unevenly because one side is to the heat all the time.

If you feel that a crane would not be appropriate in your fireplace, you may prefer to install one of the more modern cooking grills that can be permanently mounted on the firebox wall. These grills can be used like outdoor grills—food may be cooked directly on them—or to hold cooking pots or pans. Observe good cleaning habits to keep grease off the hearth and the grill after use. These grills are contemporary in style and would fit into a contemporary fireplace without being conspicuous or out of place.

Glossary

Accessory Any item used as an adjunct to or for the operation of a fireplace or stove, including tools, andirons, mantels, screens, grates, etc., as well as factory-produced logs or briquets.

Andirons Free-standing metal supports, usually constructed of cast iron or steel, for firewood on a hearth. Each consists of a horizontal bar supported on short legs. May include decorative fronts.

Ash dump An opening in the hearth through which ashes are dumped.

Ash pit A hollow area in the fireplace foundation where ash collects. Usually has cleanout access door in basement.

Baffles Found in modern wood stoves and in Russian masonry fireplaces. Diverters send smoke and gasses on through circuitous passages from the fire to the chimney. Baffles slow the travel, allowing gasses to be burned in the combustion process, increasing burning efficiency.

Baking soda Bicarbonate of soda, usable as an emergency fire extinguisher. When poured on a blaze, baking soda releases carbon dioxide, which will not support combustion.

Batter boards Guide boards attached to stakes and positioned to provide reference points when determining location of excavations, footings and/or foundations.

Bow saw A hand saw made of a curved frame and a changeable blade. It enables an individual to cut and clean branches from a small tree.

Bridging Extra support pieces added between floor joists. Installed perpendicular to the direction of the joists, pairs of bridging boards usually (1x2 or 1x3) usually are set in an "X" pattern. Bridging increases the stability of floor joists and may be required when a new, heavy load (such as a fireplace) is placed on a floor.

BTU British Thermal Unit. A standard of measure that is used to indicate heat production. Specifically, one BTU equals enough heat to raise the temperature of one pound of water from 60°F to 61°F.

Building Codes A set, or sets, of standards that govern construction in any governmental unit—local, state or national. Codes specifically restrict certain construction, prohibit certain practices, and mandate others.

Building paper A heavy paper that is coated and impregnated with tar or asphaltic material. It may be used on the hearth surface and smoke shelf to protect these areas during fireplace construction.

Burning in/curing firebox A process in which a new fireplace is gradually put into full use. A series of progressively larger fires must be built over a period of several days to adjust the brick, mortar, damper and flue to the stresses of heat and cold. If a large fire is built in a newly constructed fireplace before the masonry has been cured/burned in, the mortar may break down and expansion of metal in the unit may crack the masonry.

Cantilever A construction technique that allows a unit that is unsupported from below to project into an adjacent area. Support is provided by extensions of the framework, so that two-thirds of the frame is attached to load-bearing joists. Forehearth substructures are cantilevered from the fireplace foundation. Support is provided by framework tied into the foundation walls and by a series of reinforcing rods that reach from the back of the fireplace to the front of the forehearth.

Canvas bag traveler A device created by putting a board, weighted with a brick, at the bottom of a heavy canvas bag. A rope is tied to the board and run through the closed top of the bag. When the bag is padded with straw and lowered through the chimney, the bag seals the flue space.

Cap The top of the chimney and any part rising above the masonry. Caps may be a plain and sloped cement wash, a projecting flue tile, a precast chimney pot, a spark arrester, a rain cap, a damper cap, a smoke puller unit, a hood, or a combination of two or more of these termination features.

Cape Cod firelighter A small brass, or other metal, bowl that holds a brass rod with a soapstone knob. When the bowl is filled with kerosene or lamp oil, the soapstone absorbs the liquid. The knob acts as a wick and controls the burning of the absorbed liquid. If used with proper care and precautions, the Cap Cod firelighter will burn long enough with a hot enough flame to ignite most firewood.

Caulk A flexible substance that is forced into cracks and gaps to close these areas. Ideally, caulk remains plastic for years to maintain a tight seal. It comes in waterproof and heat-resistant or fireproof formulas.

Ceramic tile A noncombustible, fired clay material (frequently glazed) in square or rectangular units. With its either plain or decorative surface, ceramic tile is suitable for forehearth, firebox hearth and opening margin.

Chain saw A heavy-duty powered saw (usually gasoline-powered) that is frequently used to cut trees for firewood. The cut is made by a high-speed, motor-driven, notched chain.

Chemical chimney cleaners Any of various commercial products designed to be thrown into a fireplace blaze. The combination of the chemicals and the heat is supposed to clean soot and creosote from the flue walls. Use only as directed, and with care.

Chimney anchors Strong, U-shape straps that loop around flue tile chimney liners and bolt to attic floor joists with lag screws to hold the chimney firm against the dwelling. The straps are hidden by the masonry veneer of the chimney. The holes through which the straps pass into the attic are sealed with caulk.

Chimney breast The area extending from above the opening to the ceiling. It may include a mantel shelf, decorative facing, or be a plain, flat wall surface.

Chimney chase A slightly recessed space on an exterior house wall into which a chimney is set.

Chimney pot The termination of a chimney. The pot may be a section of flue tile that extends above masonry. Other pots may be precast concrete or terra cotta.

Chopper-One ax/maul   A commercially produced ax with a built-in maul. It is used to split wood. The blade cuts into the wood; then spring-loaded wedges drive the wood apart, splitting it.

Circulating fireplace   Either a totally prefabricated unit or an insert designed to draw cool room air from the floor level into a space between inner and outer firebox shells. The air is heated and then released, either by natural convection or forced out by blowers. The circulating fireplace adds heat to the home rather than sending all the heat directly up the chimney.

Circulating stove   A stove that, in addition to radiating heat, includes a heat exchanger.

Class A flue   An insulated double or triple wall pipe approved for use with any fuel.

Cleanout door   An opening in the ash pit through which the pit is cleaned. It has a tightly fitted door. Wherever possible, the door should be located on the exterior of the house.

Clearances   The code mandated distance from a heat-producing surface to nearby combustible construction. Zero clearance refers to no clearance between such surfaces.

Close joints   Masonry joints without mortar.

Cold air ducts   Channels through which cold air is pulled or blown in order to be heated in a firebox shell.

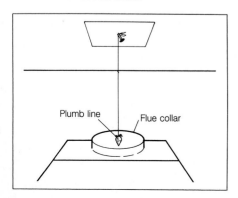

Plumb line   Flue collar

Collar   On any free-standing or zero-clearance fireplace or on any stove, the section to which the chimney sections or stovepipe sections attach.

Combustible materials   Material made of or covered with wood, compressed paper, plant fibers, or other material that will ignite and burn. A wall constructed of noncombustible structural members covered with a combustible material is considered to be a combustible wall, i.e., the entire wall will assume the fire rating of that part with highest combustibility.

Common wall   A shared wall, usually one that separates adjacent apartments or townhouses.

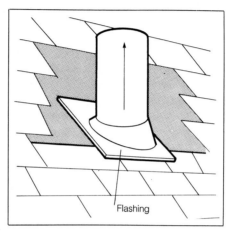

Flashing

Conical-style flashing   A cone-shaped section that fits over prefabricated chimney sections that pass through a steeply pitched roof. The conical flashing fits under upper-level shingles and over lower-level shingles. The cone is adjustable to fit various degrees of pitch. The cone also directs rain away from the chimney and seals the roof opening.

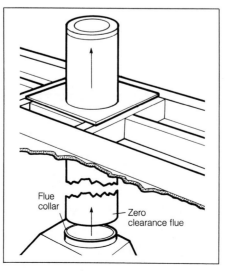

Flue collar   Zero clearance flue

Connector   The pipe connecting the heat-producing appliance to the chimney. Usually, the connector is a single-wall, uninsulated pipe. It may reach very high temperatures and may not be corrosion-resistant. Therefore it is always required to be permanently exposed and usually requires considerable clearance from combustible material. Also called a smoke-pipe, vent connector or chimney connector.

Convection grate   A grate made of hollow, U-shaped tubing. The open ends face the room. The fire is built inside the U section. The air is drawn into the lower tubes by convection and is heated so it rises through the tubes, and out the open upper ends.

Corbel   To lay brick in step fashion, enlarging or decreasing a wall dimension. The foundation of a fireplace is corbeled outward to provide support for the forehearth. The walls of the fireplace firebox are corbeled foreward to create the smoke shelf and throat, and inward to create the smoke chamber and flue support. The chimney top should be corbeled outward to protect the chimney walls from precipitation.

Cord   A measured unit of cut and stacked firewood. It is four feet wide, four feet high and eight feet long. Stacked logs are usually whole and four feet long; they must be cut and split before being used as firewood.

Course   A horizontal row of brick or block, usually set in mortar. One layer in a vertical series.

Creosote   A residue from wood gasses that are released during combustion—especially from a low, slow burning fire. Creosote is a semi-liquid that coats flue tile or stove pipe. It is highly flammable; it is a prime ingredient in chimney fires.

Damper   A steel or cast iron movable plate used to regulate the draft in the flue or to close the flue when the fireplace is not in use, located at the throat above the fireplace opening.

Downdraft   The natural action of cool air sinking down a chimney. The cool air meets rising warmed air and creates a continuous movement that pulls smoke up the chimney.

Draft The pressure available to expel the smoke and other products of combustion through the chimney to the outdoors. Draft is directly related to the height of the chimney, the temperature of the flue gasses, and, to some extent, the cross-sectional area of the flue. Draft may also be affected by wind velocity and air pressure.

Draw A well-designed and functioning fireplace has what is referred to as good draw—the smoke is pulled up into the chimney and air is circulated in the firebox for good combustion. A fireplace with a poor draw sends smoke into the room and provides low efficiency.

Elbow A chimney, gas vent or smoke-pipe fitting, adjustable or nonadjustable, designed to redirect the flow of combustion products. U.L.-listed, factory-built chimney elbows are limited to 30-degree inclinations from the vertical, but smoke-pipe or connector or type B gas vent elbows may incline as much as 90 degrees.

Expanded metal A special wire mesh used as a base to hold plaster. Its appearance resembles chicken wire, but chicken wire cannot be substituted for it.

Eyebolt A piece of hardware threaded at one end to receive a nut and looped back on itself at the other end, creating an "eye" into which something may be hooked or tied.

Face cord A measured unit of cut and stacked firewood that is eight feet long, four feet high and between 16 and 24 inches deep (1/3 to 1/2 a full cord). A common unit used in buying and selling firewood in urban areas.

Faux marbre A decorative painting technqiue used to produce the appearance of marble on another surface. Popular during the late 19th century, it was used to create the appearance of marble when marble could not be used economically.

Fireback A reflective metal sheet attached to or propped against the back wall of a firebox. A fireback reflects heat and light into a room. Decorative, period-style firebacks are available as reproductions.

Firebox The area within the fireplace in which a fire is built. It usually consists of angled side walls, a flat and then sloped back wall, and a hearth. The firebox must be built of firebrick or other material resistant to extremes of temperature.

Firebox grills Contemporary cooking grills that may be permanently installed in a firebox. They are usually deisgned to lift and swivel against a side wall.

Firebrick A heat-resistant clay brick appropriate for areas in contact with high, direct heat such as the walls and hearth of a firebox.

Fireclay (mortar) A compound designed to be used with firebrick. A mortar with resistance to high temperature.

Fireplace crane A device that provides a hanging support for pots. A crane is installed in a side wall, usually near the opening, and swings against the wall when not in use. It is a common installation in fireplaces used for cooking.

Fireplace insert Either a double-shelled fireplace liner or a stove unit designed to fit into an existing fireplace. Usually containing active (blower) heat-circulating features, the units increase the heat efficiency of a fireplace.

Fireproof/heat-resistant gloves Specially designed and constructed gloves that should be worn when adding logs to an established blaze or when handling cooking utensils in a fireplace.

Fire snuffer A box-shaped cover designed so it may be dropped over an established fire to seal off air to extinguish a blaze.

Firestop spacer A barrier of noncombustible material installed in walls or ceilings where prefabricated chimney or stove pipe passes through combustible framing. A section is framed in and a space created to support and insulate the pipe. Spacer material is installed in this space.

Flammable liquid Any liquid that can be ignited. Flammable liquids should not be used in fireplaces as fire starters.

Flashing Material, usually metal, that covers gaps between masonry and framing, where the chimney passes through the roof. Usually it is placed in overlapping units, with part above and part below the shingles.

Flue Interior of the chimney through which smoke, gasses and heated air are expelled.

Flue liner Either clay tile or metal sections set with smooth joints inside a masonry chimney. The liner finish decreases buildup of soot and creosote, acts as an insulating layer, and seals the masonry against leaks.

Flush hearth Base of the firebox and a noncombustible extension to protect the floor surfaces.

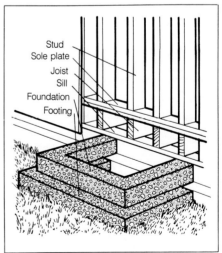

Stud
Sole plate
Joist
Sill
Foundation
Footing

Footing A support section for a foundation. The footing is wider than the foundation wall and is set in the excavation so that the top of the footing is below the frost line to prevent shifting or heaving.

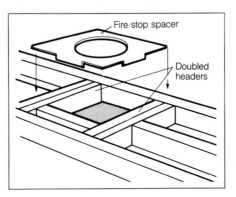

Fire stop spacer

Doubled headers

Forehearth A section of noncombustible material that projects into the room. It should extend 12 inches on either side of the opening and 16 inches in front of the opening to meet minimum standards.

Forms Board framework constructed to contain and shape a material such as concrete. Usually temporary, forms are removed when concrete has cured. In fireplaces, forms will be required for footings and hearth/forehearth construction.

Foundation Concrete or masonry, a wall that supports the upper portions of construction. The foundation extends both below and above ground level.

Framing Pieces of 2x4 or larger stock, which are nailed together to provide basic wall and ceiling support. It also serves as a base for a prefabricated fireplace hearth or face. Framing is usually covered with a finish material.

Franklin stove Fireplace-styled stove. The original design is credited to Benjamin Franklin. The stove was initially intended as a fireplace insert to increase efficiency.

Free-standing fireplace A prefabricated fireplace designed and finished so that all surfaces may be exposed to view. The unit may be positioned at almost any room location.

Frost heave Expansion of soil caused when moisture in the soil freezes or repeatedly freezes and thaws. The expansion of the damp soil is greater than the simple expansion of the frozen water.

Furring strips Strips of board, wood or metal. These attach to a surface to provide a fresh, level nailing surface for wallboard or paneling, or other material.

Galvanized metal Any metal to which another metal has been thinly plated by electric (galvanic) action.

Glass fireplace doors Framed, tempered glass covers for the front of a fireplace. The doors close off the opening to prevent heated room air from being drawn in to support combustion. Glass door units may be combined with mesh screens, and may include air vents or heat exchangers.

Grubka See *Russian fireplace*

Hardwood Wood from deciduous trees (those that lose their leaves in the fall). Harder to ignite and often more difficult to split, hardwoods give off more heat than do softwoods.

Header Any board or pair of boards used to span cut framing members to maintain structural strength. Pairs used in the same location are called double or doubled headers.

Heat chamber (heat exchanger) A space between the inner and outer shell of a prefabricated fireplace or a fireplace insert where circulating air is heated.

Heat exchanger Any unit designed to draw in cool air, heat it and return it to living areas. This includes convection or powered exchangers in the fireplace shell, and hearth grate/door units.

Heat reflector Any sheet metal or foil positioned to reflect heat—either in back of the fire to direct heat into the room or in front of the fire to maintain temperatures for cooking.

Heating area A space that a given heating unit—a fireplace or stove—is expected to heat.

High temperature cement A cement powder formulated for use in high-temperature areas such as fireplaces.

Hinge When cutting a tree, a notch is cut on the heavy or leaning side of the tree, with a straight cut on the opposite side to create a hinge. The tree will bend on the hinge as it falls. A correctly cut hinge will help control the direction of the fall.

Hood A decorative and sometimes functional metal canopy installed over the opening of a fireplace. May be installed to prevent some smoking problems or radiate additional heat.

Hooded chimney A chimney on which two opposite masonry sides rise above the flue and support a flat cover. Chimneys are hooded to control the flow of wind over the flue to maintain even draw or to prevent one chimney from drawing smoke from another.

Insulation Any noncombustible material that will not transmit heat. Required in fireplace construction at any place where metal contacts masonry in order to accommodate the metal's expansion.

I.C.B.O. International Conference of Building Owners. A group that sets certain building construction and fire safety standards.

Jambs The facing or surround area on either side of the fireplace opening. Jambs are usually brick or other masonry.

Jointer A tool used to smooth and shape the surface of mortar joints. Jointers are designed to give flush, raked or rounded joints.

Joists Floor and/or ceiling framing made of 2x10s or 2x12s, usually mandated by building codes to be set on 12, 14, 16, 18, or 24 inch centers, perpendicular to wall stud framing.

Lag screw A large, threaded screw with an oversize, multi-sided head.

Level A builder's tool that uses a centered bubble in a tube to indicate when a surface is level—can be either horizontal or vertical.

Liner The steel interior of a firebox, or a portion thereof, such as a rear or side panel, sometimes replaceable.

Lintel A steel angle iron, large stone or precast concrete slab that spans a masonry opening to support masonry above the opening.

Load-bearing members Any part of framing that carries the weight of other sections of the building.

Mantel A decorative shelf projecting above the firebox opening.

Masonry anchors Bolts or rods inserted into masonry construction in order to ensure permanent union with later construction.

Maul A wedge unit that drives a split in a log, creating enough pressure to complete the cut.

Molly bolts A two-section bolt designed to permit installation of heavy units on a hollow wall, such as drywall over stud framing.

Mortar A combination of cement, sand, water and a small amount of hydrated lime. Used to permanently unite brick, block or stone.

Mortar board A device, usually a board with a handle, that allows a worker to conveniently carry around small amounts of mortar while laying brick, stone or block.

Mud box A wooden box with angled ends, used in mixing batches of mortar or cement.

Multi-face fireplace A fireplace that has two or more openings. It is possible to have two adjacent, two opposite, three adjacent, or four open faces. The four-faced version is essentially a firepit with a suspended, four-sided hood.

Nails *Cement,* for use in masonry.
Ring shank, a nail with raised rings on the shank; gives more secure connection than a smooth-shanked nail.

National Fire Protection Agency An organization that publishes information and standards for fireplace construction, prefabricated fireplace or stove installation. Its purpose is to prevent unsafe or potentially dangerous construction or appliance installation.

Non-Com A pressure-treated lumber that will not ignite. Non-Com will char but not burn. Although not generally available, it is the first and best choice for interior fireplace framing.

Notch A wedge shape cut out of the leaning, or heavy, side of a tree being felled.

Opening The "hole" in the wall that gives access to the firebox.

Parge To coat a masonry surface with mortar for a completely smooth surface.

Peavey rod A pointed rod with a movable hook; used to turn and position large logs or cut trees for trimming.

Penned logs A method of cutting and stacking to promote faster drying of the wood.

Plaster/decorative Molded plaster rosettes, scrolls and moldings. Used extensively in 18th century architectural detailing.

Plumb, plumb bob, plumb line A straight vertical line. All walls should be plumb. Plumb can be determined through use of a plumb line and plumb bob. The bob is tied to the end of the line and the line is suspended.

Pointing trowel A trowel used in tuckpointing mortar. Tuckpointing is a repair method in which mortar is dug out of joints and replaced.

Portland cement Basic cement used in formulation of structural concrete.

Prefabricated fireplace Any fireplace unit that is purchased and then installed in the home. The term covers free-standing fireplaces, fireplace inserts and units to be framed in and covered.

Rafter/ridgepole Roof components. The ridge pole runs along the peak of the roof. Rafters run between the ridgepole and side wall top plates.

Rain cap Usually of galvanized metal, a rain cap is a peaked, protective cover for the chimney flue.

Reinforcing rods Metal rods, ranging from relatively fine wire to heavy steel rods, installed in concrete to add strength and stability.

Returns The sections of the jambs between the opening and the interior side walls.

Rubble Waterworn or rough broken stone or brick used in masonry construction. As fill, it is combined with mortar.

Rumford fireplace An energy efficient design for a masonry fireplace. The designer was Count Rumford (nee Benja-

min Thompson of Massachusetts). The small, shallow fireplace burns a good fire and reflects heat into the room.

Running bond A frequently used brick pattern. Joints of alternate rows are centered on bricks of the courses directly above and below.

Russian fireplace A large, hollow masonry wall with many interior flue baffles to ensure a long and complete burn. The masonry absorbs almost all the heat and radiates it into the house.

Safety harness Either a manufactured leather strap vest and rope unit, or a looped and tied rope vest and safety line.

Simulated brick/stone Noncombustible materials manufactured to look like natural brick or stone. Frequently used as facing material for new prefabricated installations or to renovate older fireplaces. May range in thickness from units of the same thickness and size as natural material (as in precast concrete "stones") to very thin facing units.

Single-face fireplace The traditional fireplace is a single face construction with facing and firebox areas visible from only one direction.

Smoke chamber A roughly pyramid-shaped space from the level of the smoke shelf to the base of the flue. It tapers to direct smoke from the firebox to the flue opening.

Smoke puller An electrically powered fan installed at the top of the chimney as part of a cap unit. May be required to draw smoke up the chimney in areas where topography or weather conditions create problems of uneven or insufficient natural chimney draw.

Smoke shelf The smooth-finished, curved shelf at the base of the smoke chamber. It is designed to create a swirling upward- and forward-moving air current, so that cool downdraft air is directed back up the chimney with rising smoke.

Soapstone An extremely porous stone found in North America. Soapstone is absorbant. It will absorb a liquid like kerosene and serve as a wick as in a firelighter. It is used in the manufacture of some wood stoves because of its capacity to absorb and radiate heat over a long period of time. It can be carved and polished for decorative finishes. A polished slab is often used as a griddle.

Softwood Wood from coniferous trees—pines, firs, spruces. The wood contains highly flammable sap and has highly compacted fibers. As firewood, softwood ignites easily and generally splits easily; however, it tends to burn quickly and does not give off high levels of heat.

Soldier (course) A row of brick or stone set vertically (on end) with the narrow face forward. Soldier courses may be used decoratively or to create openings for air ducts—particularly for warm air vents in circulating fireplace facings.

Spark arrester A wire mesh covering for a chimney cap to prevent release of sparks or burning debris. Required for chimneys passing through wood-shingled roofs. Also advisable wherever there are nearby combustible materials, such as eaves, trees or older dwellings.

Square Either a carpenter's square, which is a measuring device with two legs set at a 90° angle, or a function of construction to achieve and maintain a 90° relationship—as in 90° corners at wall junctures.

Storm collar A flashing unit for prefabricated chimney pipe. The collar is designed to direct heavy precipitation away from the chimney roof joint.

Stove board A fireproof sheet that can be used as a protective cover for combustible walls near a stove. A stove board also is used to seal a fireplace opening so a stove may be vented out the chimney.

Stove pad A prefabricated, fireproof stove hearth. To protect the floor, a stove pad should be placed under any stove installation and extend beyond the stove 12 to 18 inches (see local codes). May also be used under prefabricated fireplaces.

Subfloor A layer of roughly finished material that is laid on floor joists to provide a level surface for finished flooring.

Subhearth A level, poured concrete base that extends from the exterior chimney/foundation wall to the front edge of the forehearth. The concrete must be reinforced with rods that reach from the back to the front and from side to side. The rods are tied together wherever they cross.

Tarbuck knot A safety knot designed for use by mountain climbers. The Tarbuck knot is used in creating a rope safety harness.

Tees Stove pipe connector sections used to join horizontal runs to vertical runs.

Termination cap A finished top to a prefabricated chimney pipe flue. Usually comes complete with spark arrester and rain cap.

Therms A unit by which natural gas is sold. A therm is equal to 100,000 BTUs.

Thermostatic controls A temperature-sensitive device used to control furnaces, dampers, or air vents so they will operate when a preset temperature is reached.

Thimble A noncombustible seal that protects any wall or ceiling material at the point where a stove pipe passes through. Usually of metal or terra cotta, thimbles sometimes have decorated surfaces.

Throat The fireplace region between the top of the opening and the edge of the smoke shelf. This space narrows from front to back because at this point, the back firebox wall slopes forward.

Trammel A metal strap or chain, hooked at either end, used to suspend cooking pots from a fireplace crane.

Traveler See Canvas bag traveler

TSP Trisodium phosphate, a strong detergent that can be used to clean smoke stains from brick.

Underwriters Laboratories, Inc. A testing laboratory that tests electrical equipment, stoves and other manufactured goods for safety and flammability.

A UL label/listing indicates that the material has passed the tests.

Wall anchors A device for securing a screw or bolt to a wall surface that will not accept or hold an ordinary nail or screw. These are designed for hollow walls or solid masonry walls.

Wall ties Various styles of wire, rods or crimped metal strips used to provide security and bonding strength between two adjoining surfaces—such as two-wythe brick walls, concrete block and brick or stone veneer, or frame walls and brick or stone veneer.

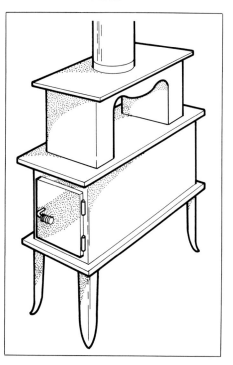

Warming shelf A shelf at the back of a stove or attached to a stove pipe so food may be kept warm. The original purpose of a mantel was to serve as a warming shelf.

Wood gasses Gasses released during combustion of wood. These gasses may also be ignited, if the fire is hot enough, to increase fuel efficiency. If they are not ignited, they condense on the chimney or stove pipe walls. The resulting residue may be ignited by a later fire, thus creating a chimney fire.

Zero-clearance fireplace A prefabricated fireplace that is so well insulated that it may be placed against a combustible wall; therefore, it requires no, or zero, clearance.

Metric Conversion Charts

LUMBER

Sizes: Metric cross-sections are so close to their nearest Imperial sizes, as noted below, that for most purposes they may be considered equivalents.

Lengths: Metric lengths are based on a 300mm module which is slightly shorter in length than an Imperial foot. It will therefore be important to check your requirements accurately to the nearest inch and consult the table below to find the metric length required.

Areas: The metric area is a square metre. Use the following conversion factors when converting from Imperial data: 100 sq. feet = 9.290 sq. metres.

METRIC SIZES SHOWN BESIDE NEAREST IMPERIAL EQUIVALENT

mm	Inches	mm	Inches
16 x 75	⅝ x 3	44 x 150	1¾ x 6
16 x 100	⅝ x 4	44 x 175	1¾ x 7
16 x 125	⅝ x 5	44 x 200	1¾ x 8
16 x 150	⅝ x 6	44 x 225	1¾ x 9
19 x 75	¾ x 3	44 x 250	1¾ x 10
19 x 100	¾ x 4	44 x 300	1¾ x 12
19 x 125	¾ x 5	50 x 75	2 x 3
19 x 150	¾ x 6	50 x 100	2 x 4
22 x 75	⅞ x 3	50 x 125	2 x 5
22 x 100	⅞ x 4	50 x 150	2 x 6
22 x 125	⅞ x 5	50 x 175	2 x 7
22 x 150	⅞ x 6	50 x 200	2 x 8
25 x 75	1 x 3	50 x 225	2 x 9
25 x 100	1 x 4	50 x 250	2 x 10
25 x 125	1 x 5	50 x 300	2 x 12
25 x 150	1 x 6	63 x 100	2½ x 4
25 x 175	1 x 7	63 x 125	2½ x 5
25 x 200	1 x 8	63 x 150	2½ x 6
25 x 225	1 x 9	63 x 175	2½ x 7
25 x 250	1 x 10	63 x 200	2½ x 8
25 x 300	1 x 12	63 x 225	2½ x 9
32 x 75	1¼ x 3	75 x 100	3 x 4
32 x 100	1¼ x 4	75 x 125	3 x 5
32 x 125	1¼ x 5	75 x 150	3 x 6
32 x 150	1¼ x 6	75 x 175	3 x 7
32 x 175	1¼ x 7	75 x 200	3 x 8
32 x 200	1¼ x 8	75 x 225	3 x 9
32 x 225	1¼ x 9	75 x 250	3 x 10
32 x 250	1¼ x 10	75 x 300	3 x 12
32 x 300	1¼ x 12	100 x 100	4 x 4
38 x 75	1½ x 3	100 x 150	4 x 6
38 x 100	1½ x 4	100 x 200	4 x 8
38 x 125	1½ x 5	100 x 250	4 x 10
38 x 150	1½ x 6	100 x 300	4 x 12
38 x 175	1½ x 7	150 x 150	6 x 6
38 x 200	1½ x 8	150 x 200	6 x 8
38 x 225	1½ x 9	150 x 300	6 x 12
44 x 75	1¾ x 3	200 x 200	8 x 8
44 x 100	1¾ x 4	250 x 250	10 x 10
44 x 125	1¾ x 5	300 x 300	12 x 12

METRIC LENGTHS

Lengths Metres	Equiv. Ft. & Inches
1.8m	5' 10⅞"
2.1m	6' 10⅝"
2.4m	7' 10½"
2.7m	8' 10¼"
3.0m	9' 10⅛"
3.3m	10' 9⅞"
3.6m	11' 9¾"
3.9m	12' 9½"
4.2m	13' 9⅜"
4.5m	14' 9⅓"
4.8m	15' 9"
5.1m	16' 8¾"
5.4m	17' 8⅝"
5.7m	18' 8⅜"
6.0m	19' 8¼"
6.3m	20' 8"
6.6m	21' 7⅞"
6.9m	22' 7⅝"
7.2m	23' 7½"
7.5m	24' 7¼"
7.8m	25' 7⅛"

All the dimensions are based on 1 inch = 25 mm.

NOMINAL SIZE (This is what you order.)	ACTUAL SIZE (This is what you get.)
Inches	Inches
1 x 1	¾ x ¾
1 x 2	¾ x 1½
1 x 3	¾ x 2¹∕₂
1 x 4	¾ x 3½
1 x 6	¾ x 5½
1 x 8	¾ x 7¼
1 x 10	¾ x 9¼
1 x 12	¾ x 11¼
2 x 2	1¾ x 1¾
2 x 3	1½ x 2½
2 x 4	1½ x 3½
2 x 6	1½ x 5½
2 x 8	1½ x 7¼
2 x 10	1½ x 9¼
2 x 12	1½ x 11¼

PIPE FITTINGS

Only fittings for use with copper pipe are affected by metrication: metric compression fittings are interchangeable with Imperial in some sizes, but require adaptors in others.

INTERCHANGEABLE SIZES		SIZES REQUIRING ADAPTORS	
mm	Inches	mm	Inches
12	⅜	22	¾
15	½	35	1¼
28	1	42	1½
54	2		

Metric capillary (soldered) fittings are not directly interchangeable with imperial sizes but adaptors are available. Pipe fittings which use screwed threads to make the joint remain unchanged. The British Standard Pipe (BSP) thread form has now been accepted internationally and its dimensions will not physically change. These screwed fittings are commonly used for joining iron or steel pipes, for connections on taps, basin and bath waste outlets and on boilers, radiators, pumps etc. Fittings for use with lead pipe are joined by soldering and for this purpose the metric and inch sizes are interchangeable.

(Information courtesy Metrication Board, Millbank Tower, Millbank, London SW1P 4QU)

WOOD SCREWS

SCREW GAUGE NO.	NOMINAL DIAMETER		LENGTH	
	Inch	mm	Inch	mm
0	0.060	1.52	3/16	4.8
1	0.070	1.78	1/4	6.4
2	0.082	2.08	5/16	7.9
3	0.094	2.39	3/8	9.5
4	0.0108	2.74	7/16	11.1
5	0.122	3.10	1/2	12.7
6	0.136	3.45	5/8	15.9
7	0.150	3.81	3/4	19.1
8	0.164	4.17	7/8	22.2
9	0.178	4.52	1	25.4
10	0.192	4.88	1 1/4	31.8
12	0.220	5.59	1 1/2	38.1
14	0.248	6.30	1 3/4	44.5
16	0.276	7.01	2	50.8
18	0.304	7.72	2 1/4	57.2
20	0.332	8.43	2 1/2	63.5
24	0.388	9.86	2 3/4	69.9
28	0.444	11.28	3	76.2
32	0.5	12.7	3 1/4	82.6
			3 1/2	88.9
			4	101.6
			4 1/2	114.3
			5	127.0
			6	152.4

Dimensions taken from BS1210; metric conversions are approximate.

BRICKS AND BLOCKS

Bricks
Standard metric brick measures 215 mm x 65 mm x 112.5. Metric brick can be used with older, standard brick by increasing the mortaring in the joints. The sizes are substantially the same, the metric brick being slightly smaller (3.6 mm less in length, 1.8 mm in width, and 1.2 mm in depth).

Concrete Block

Standard sizes

390 x 90 mm
390 x 190 mm
440 x 190 mm
440 x 215 mm
440 x 290 mm

Repair block for replacement of block in old installations is available in these sizes:
448 x 219 (including mortar joints)
397 x 194 (including mortar joints)

NAILS

NUMBER PER POUND OR KILO

Size	Weight Unit	Common	Casing	Box	Finishing
2d	Pound	876	1010	1010	1351
	Kilo	1927	2222	2222	2972
3d	Pound	586	635	635	807
	Kilo	1289	1397	1397	1775
4d	Pound	316	473	473	548
	Kilo	695	1041	1041	1206
5d	Pound	271	406	406	500
	Kilo	596	893	893	1100
6d	Pound	181	236	236	309
	Kilo	398	591	519	680
7d	Pound	161	210	210	238
	Kilo	354	462	462	524
8d	Pound	106	145	145	189
	Kilo	233	319	319	416
9d	Pound	96	132	132	172
	Kilo	211	290	290	398
10d	Pound	69	94	94	121
	Kilo	152	207	207	266
12d	Pound	64	88	88	113
	Kilo	141	194	194	249
16d	Pound	49	71	71	90
	Kilo	108	156	156	198
20d	Pound	31	52	52	62
	Kilo	68	114	114	136
30d	Pound	24	46	46	
	Kilo	53	101	101	
40d	Pound	18	35	35	
	Kilo	37	77	77	
50d	Pound	14			
	Kilo	31			
60d	Pound	11			
	Kilo	24			

LENGTH AND DIAMETER IN INCHES AND CENTIMETERS

Size	Inches	Length Centimeters	Inches	Diameter Centimeters*
2d	1	2.5	.068	.17
3d	1/2	3.2	.102	.26
4d	1/4	3.8	.102	.26
5d	1/6	4.4	.102	.26
6d	2	5.1	.115	.29
7d	2/2	5.7	.115	.29
8d	2/4	6.4	.131	.33
9d	2/6	7.0	.131	.33
10d	3	7.6	.148	.38
12d	3/2	8.3	.148	.38
16d	3/4	8.9	.148	.38
20d	4	10.2	.203	.51
30d	4/4	11.4	.220	.58
40d	5	12.7	.238	.60
50d	5/4	14.0	.257	.66
60d	6	15.2	.277	.70

*Exact conversion

Contributors, Sources, Picture Credits

We wish to extend our thanks to the individuals, associations, and manufacturers who graciously provided information and photographs for this book. Specific credit for individual photos is given below, with the names and addresses of the contributors.

Allmilmo Corporation c/o Hynes-Williams Incorporated 261 Madison Avenue, New York, New York 10016 (*kitchen cabinets*) 16 lower left

All Nighter Stove Works 80 Commerce Street, Glastonbury, Connecticut 06033 (*wood stoves*) 87, 93, upper center and upper right

American Olean 2583 Cannon Avenue, Lansdale, Pennsylvania 19446 (*ceramic tile*) 21, 98

Bennett Ireland, Inc. 23 State Street, Norwich, New York 13815 (*fireplace accessories*)

Adele Bishop, Inc. Box 577, Manchester, Vermont 05254 (*stenciling kits*) 12 lower

Black Magic Box 977, Stowe, Vermont 05672 (*chimney cleaning equipment*) 108, 109

Brick Institute of America 1750 Old Meadow Road, McLean, Virginia 22101 12 lower right, 26 upper left, 27 upper right, 73, 74

Craig Buchanan photographer, 490 2nd Street, San Francisco, California 94107 14, 15 lower left, 17 upper, 23 upper

Buck Stove Center 138 South Street, Waukesha, Wisconsin 53186 (*wood stoves*)

Childcrest Distributing Inc. 6045 North 55th Street, Milwaukee, Wisconsin 53218 (*ceramic tile*) 10 upper center

Chopper Industries Easton Pennsylvania 18042 (*ax-splitter*) 103 upper right

Cumberland Valley Metals, Inc. Box 15666, Nashville, Tennessee 37215 (*fireplace equipment*) 86 lower right

Duravent c/o Falcon Marketing, Redwood City, California 94064 (*chimney liner*) 88

Frahm Fireplace Grate, Inc. 256 South Pine Street, Burlington, Wisconsin 53105 (*fireplace equipment*) 85 lower left

Frontier J & J Enterprises 4065 W 11th Ave., Eugene, Oregon 97402 (*wood stoves*) 93 upper left, 97 center

GAF 140 West 51st, New York, New York 10020 (*flooring*) 35 upper

General Electric Company, Lamp Division, Nela Park, Cleveland, Ohio 44112 (*lighting equipment*) 11 right

Glowmaster Fireplaces c/o Wilt & Company, Des Moines, Iowa 50309 (*wood stoves, fireplace inserts*) 12 center, 90 upper left

Gorman, Inc. 429-A Merchandise Mart, Chicago, Illinois 60654 (*antique reproduction mantels*) 15 lower right, 35 lower, 39 lower

Hearthmate, C & D Distributors P.O. Box 766, Old Saybrook, Connecticut 06475 (*woodstoves*) 88 upper right, 93 lower, 95 lower right, 97 lower right, 106 lower left

Hearthstone Corporation Northgate Plaza, Morrisville, Vermont 05661 (*soapstone stoves*) 91 upper center

Heatilator Fireplaces Mount Pleasant, Iowa 52641 (*prefabricated fireplaces*) 25 upper and lower right, 26 lower right

Heat-N-Glow Fireplaces 1100 Riverwood Drive, Burnsville, Minnesota 55337 (*free-standing fireplaces*) 76 right, 81

Robert E. Jones Newport Beach, California 92663 103 left

Jotul U.S.A., Inc. P.O. Box 1157, Portland, Maine 04104 (*wood stoves*) 90 lower center, 91 upper left, 92 top

Kronos Products, Corp. Louisville, Kentucky 40223 (*firebacks*) 86 upper left

LaFont Corporation 1319 Town Street, Prentice, Wisconsin 54555 (*convention grates*) 85 center

Lemee's Fireplace Equipment 815 Bedford Street, Bridgewater, Massachusetts 02324 (*fireplace equipment*)

Malm Fireplaces 368 Yolanda, Santa Rosa, California 95404 (*prefabricated fireplaces*) 91 upper left

William Manly Interior Design 6062 North Port Washington Road, Milwaukee, Wisconsin 53217 17 lower

Marome Coating Inc. Ashville, New York 14710 (*stove pads and boards*)

Milwaukee Marble Company P.O. Box 741, Milwaukee Wisconsin 53201 (*marble mantels, facings, hearths-custom work*) 27 lower

Pacific Fireplace Furnishings Box 160, Tualitin, Oregon 97062 (*fireplace equipment*) 9, 12 upper right, 23 lower

Pennsylvania Firebacks Ambler, Pennsylvania 19002 (*firebacks*)

Preway Wisconsin Rapids, Wisconsin 54494 (*prefabricated fireplaces*) 81, 84 lower right

Pyrosolar Industries P.O. Box 858 Hwy CC, Rolla, Missouri 65401 (*prefabricated fireplaces*) 77

Ready-Built Products P.O. Box 4306, Baltimore, Maryland 21223 (*mantels and facings*) 37, 53 right

Refab Industries, Inc. Box 212, Sherrodsville, Ohio 44575 (*custom replacement fireboxes*)

Rustic Crafts 65 West Sheffield Avenue, Englewood, New Jersey 07631 (*mantels, facings and electric fireplaces*) 39 right, 41, 80, 84 upper left, 104

S & S Construction Co. Suite 700, 8383 Wilshire Boulevard, Beverly Hills, California 90211 10 lower center

Schaefer Brush Manufacturing Co., Inc. 117 West Walker, Milwaukee, Wisconsin 53204 (*chimney cleaning equipment*)

Sternkopf's Inc. 779 North Water, Milwaukee Wisconsin 53202 (*fireplace equipment*)

Superior Fireplace Co. 4325 Artesia Avenue, Fullerton, California 92633 (*prefabricated fireplaces*) 31, 34, 75, 76 lower, 79

Texas Fireframe Co. P.O. Box 3435, Austin, Texas 78764 (*grate*) 86 lower left

Lis King/Tile Council of America Box 503 Mahwah, New Jersey 07430 (*ceramic tile*) 82

Waterford Stoves c/o Capitol Export Corporation 8825 Page Boulevard, St. Louis, Missouri 63114 (*wood stoves*) 89, 90 lower left

James Eaton Weeks Interior Designs, Inc. 223 East Silver Spring, Milwaukee, Wisconsin 53217 16 lower right

Western Red Cedar Lumber Association Yeon Building, Portland Oregon 97204 19, 24

Wilkening Manufacturing Co. Rt. #1, Walker, Minnesota 56484 (*prefabricated fireplaces*)

Wonderbrix Brick Master/SK Sales P.O. Box 2849, Livonia, Michigan 48151 (*artificial brick*) 22

Woodstock Soapstone Co., Inc. Box 223, Woodstock, Vermont 05091 (*soapstone stoves and griddles*)

Worcester Brush P.O. Box 658 Worcester, Massachusetts 01601 (*chimney cleaning equipment*)

Z-Brick Woodinville, Washington 98072 (*synthetic brick*) 27 lower right, 28, 36, 92 lower

Index